America in the World Economy: A Strategy for the 1990s

C. FRED BERGSTEN

America in the World Economy: A Strategy for the 1990s

INSTITUTE FOR INTERNATIONAL ECONOMICS

Washington, DC
November 1988

C. Fred Bergsten has been Director of the Institute for International Economics since its creation in 1981. He was formerly Assistant Secretary of the Treasury for International Affairs (1977–81), Assistant for International Economic Affairs to the National Security Council (1969–71) and a Senior Fellow at the Brookings Institution, Carnegie Endowment for International Peace, and Council on Foreign Relations. Dr. Bergsten is the author, co-author or editor of seventeen previous books on international economic issues including The United States–Japan Economic Problem (1987), Bank Lending to Developing Countries (1985), Trade Policy in the 1980s (1982), American Multinationals and American Interests (1978), The Dilemmas of the Dollar (1975), World Politics and International Economics (1975), *and five volumes of selected articles. Dr. Bergsten has received the Exceptional Service Award from the Treasury Department and the Meritorious Honor Award from the Department of State.*

INSTITUTE FOR INTERNATIONAL ECONOMICS
11 Dupont Circle, NW
Washington, DC 20036
(202) 328–9000 Telex: 261271 IIE UR
FAX: (202) 328–5432

The Institute for International Economics was created by, and receives substantial support from, the German Marshall Fund of the United States.

Printed in the United States of America
92 91 90 89 88 5 4 3 2 1

Library of Congress Cataloging-in-Publication Data

Bergsten, C. Fred. 1941–

America in the world economy: a strategy for the 1990s/C. Fred Bergsten.
p. cm.
Bibliography: p. 201.
Includes index.
1. United States—Economic policy—1981–
2. United States—Economic conditions—1981–
3. United States—Foreign economic relations.
4. Competition, International. I. Title.
HC106.8.B465 1988 88–39852
337.73—dc19 CIP
ISBN 0–88132–082–X

Contents

Tables

Figures

To my colleagues at the

Institute for International Economics,

whose superb scholarship and enormous assistance

made this volume possible.

INSTITUTE FOR INTERNATIONAL ECONOMICS

11 Dupont Circle, NW, Washington, DC 20036
(202) 328-9000 Telex: 261271 IIEUR FAX: (202) 328-5432

Preface

The international economic and financial position of the United States has undergone dramatic change in the 1980s with the onset of huge external deficits and the corresponding shift from being the world's largest creditor country to the world's largest debtor. The United States has become increasingly dependent on international trade and financial flows, and external economic events in the next few years may have a decisive impact on America's prosperity and even on the success of its foreign policy.

This book proposes a comprehensive international economic strategy for the United States to respond to the unprecedented challenges it will face in the world economy of the 1990s. In the first instance, the book is addressed to the new administration and Congress that will take office in Washington in January 1989. But it places the proposed policy of "competitive interdependence" in the economic and global contexts that the United States will face well into the next decade, and thus adopts a medium-term as well as immediate perspective.

The book addresses all major aspects of international economic policy: America's trade and current account deficits, the corresponding surpluses in Japan and elsewhere, "domestic" economic policies in the United States and the other major countries, exchange rates, the international monetary system, trade policy and related microeconomic concerns, Third World debt, allied burden sharing and the role of the international financial institutions. It links the issues together within a cohesive strategic framework, and suggests how the proposed policy changes could be implemented in practice.

This book is different from most publications of the Institute in two regards. First, it does not include extensive original research. The objective is rather to develop a comprehensive policy strategy, within which the individual issues are logically related to each other and to the fundamental goals of the United States and the world economy. I refer extensively to earlier and forthcoming Institute studies, and the book—the fiftieth publication by the Institute since its creation seven years ago—thus represents the first effort to draw our work together in a systematic manner.

Second, this volume is addressed specifically to the policies of the United States. Considerable attention is of course devoted to interactions between America and other countries, as is essential in any international economic analysis. But the advent of a new administration offers a rare opportunity for fresh thinking and the adoption of new policies by the United States, whose actions will be of enormous importance to the entire world. Hence I address the analysis, in the first instance, to those who will be managing and influencing the international economic policy of the United States from January 1989 until well into the next decade.

This book would not have been possible without the assistance and support of my colleagues at the Institute for International Economics, to whom it is dedicated. As noted, their past and current research provided much of the analysis and many of the ideas that are incorporated here. Several members of the senior staff, particularly Stephen Marris and William Cline, offered extensive advice throughout the process. Kimberly Ann Elliott provided invaluable assistance in the preparation of the manuscript. David Weiner's editing made a major contribution to clarifying the presentation. Alda Seubert, with assistance from Capathia Adams, processed the text over many long hours with great efficiency and good humor. I deeply appreciate their help.

The Institute for International Economics is a private nonprofit institution for the study and discussion of international economic policy. Its purpose is to analyze important issues in that area, and to develop and communicate practical new approaches for dealing with them. The Institute is completely nonpartisan.

The Institute was created by a generous commitment of funds from the German Marshall Fund of the United States in 1981 and now receives about twenty percent of its support from that source. In addition, major institutional grants are being received from the Ford Foundation, the William and Flora Hewlett Foundation, and the Alfred P. Sloan Foundation. A number of other foundations and private corporations are contributing to the increasing diversification of the Institute's resources. A generous grant from William M. Keck, II supported this study.

The Board of Directors bears overall responsibility for the Institute and gives general guidance and approval to the research program of the Institute—including identification of topics that are likely to become important to international economic policymakers over the medium run (generally, one to three years), and which thus should be addressed by the Institute. The Director, working closely with the staff and outside Advisory Committee, is responsible for the development of particular projects and makes the final decision to publish an individual study.

The Institute hopes that its studies and other activities will contribute to building a strong foundation for international economic policy around the world. We invite readers of these publications to let us know how they think we can best accomplish this objective.

C. Fred Bergsten
Director
October 1988

1

A Strategy of "Competitive Interdependence": Overview and Recommendations

THE ISSUES

The new administration and Congress that take office in early 1989 will immediately face a series of major international economic challenges. They will confront a current account deficit that remains well over $100 billion, and that will probably never fall much below $100 billion on the basis of present policies and exchange rates. They will have to attract several hundred billion dollars of additional foreign financing for these deficits during the next presidential term even if a transition to a sustainable external position is successfully launched. They will be the first administration and Congress in almost eighty years to govern a United States that is a net debtor country—indeed, a United States that is for the first time in modern history the world's largest debtor, with a net foreign debt that could rise to $1 trillion in the early 1990s in the absence of corrective action. They will face growing concerns, both at home and abroad, that the United States can no longer compete effectively in the world economy and is losing its leadership role and ability.

The new administration will have to decide whether to continue, abandon, or accelerate the efforts of the world's major economies during the past three years to achieve more active management of exchange rates and better coordination of national policies, as exemplified by the Plaza Agreement of September 1985 and the Louvre Accord of February 1987. It will have to avoid a precipitous fall in the dollar, as in 1987 (and 1978), which would push up inflation and interest rates. But it will also have to avoid a premature strengthening of the dollar, as in 1988, which would produce a renewed deterioration in the current account and heighten the risk of a future crash of both the currency and the economy.

The new government will also confront a number of important trade policy questions. Should it try to speed the reduction of the trade deficit and protect American industries and jobs by restricting imports, at least those from countries with "unfair" trading practices? Should it provide direct federal assistance to boost exports? How can it strengthen America's competitive position, especially in high-technology sectors?

The Congress and the key domestic constituency groups—notably agriculture, business, and labor—will look for early signs of whether the new administration "can be trusted to defend American interests." They will watch closely its responses to the numerous stipulations in the Omnibus Trade and Competitiveness Act of 1988 (henceforth referred to as the Omnibus Trade Act), which was signed into law in August 1988. Early decisions will have to be taken on a wide range of sectoral problems, including agriculture, aircraft, semiconductors, steel, and textiles.

A third set of issues relates to specific international financial questions. Third World debt now exceeds $1.2 trillion and continues to hamper world growth, to threaten financial disruption, and to jeopardize political stability in a number of countries in Latin America and elsewhere. There is growing pressure on some of America's chief allies to assume larger shares of the costs of maintaining global peace and prosperity. In light of these and related questions, important decisions must be made concerning the roles of the World Bank, the International Monetary Fund (IMF), and the Inter-American Development Bank (IDB), and the size of future US financial contributions to these institutions.

Underlying these pressing issues are fundamental questions concerning the role of the United States in the world economy of the 1990s. America has become increasingly dependent on events occurring outside its borders. Its earlier ability to dominate global economic outcomes has eroded with the rising capabilities of other countries. Yet the United States remains by far the most powerful individual nation, with substantial leverage to pursue its international economic interests and a central role in determining the course of the world economy. America can neither dominate nor abdicate, but must find a new leadership role that is consistent with its current needs and relative power position.[1]

The rest of the world will be watching closely US decisions on all of these issues, knowing that every newly elected administration of the past 20 years (Nixon, Carter, Reagan) has begun its tenure with sharp departures from the course set by its predecessor. Will the United States maintain a basically cooperative approach, or will it veer toward unilateralism—of either a "benign neglect" or aggressively mercantilist nature? Will the United States pursue an open trade policy, turn inward toward protection, or fall somewhere in between? Will it push for a successful Uruguay Round of multilateral trade negotiations and try to halt the erosion of the General Agreement on Tariffs and Trade (GATT) system, follow a primarily bilateral route, or try to do both? How will it respond to the charge that "foreigners are buying up America" and need to be stopped?

This array of international economic challenges presents an extraordinarily difficult agenda for the new administration and Congress. Reducing the domestic budget deficit, which lies at the heart of an effective program to reduce the external deficit, seems to have become an intractable domestic political problem. Maintaining economic growth and cutting the trade gap have seemed to demand incompatible policies. Coordinating national policies to achieve satisfactory international outcomes raises delicate issues of sovereignty in each country. Japan, Germany, and other key countries abroad are far less anxious to reduce their surpluses than they were to build them up. There are sharp differences of view, both within the United States and around the world, on how economies respond to particular policy changes, and there is disagreement on some of the key economic variables, such as the correct level of exchange rates.

The apparent absence of immediate threats to the current pros-

1. The global setting for American international economic policy is elaborated in Chapter 3.

perity, both in the United States and in most of the other industrial countries, may make it difficult to muster the political determination to implement substantial policy changes. The American economy indeed appeared to be in good shape as 1989 approached. The longest peacetime expansion was continuing. Unemployment was near its lowest level in 15 years. Inflation remained relatively subdued, and oil prices were falling again. Exports were booming. The trade deficit had started to come down. The dollar, far from collapsing, had risen through much of 1988.

THE URGENCY OF POLICY ACTION

The current prosperity, however, has a precarious foundation.[2] It is based to a very large extent on borrowing—both from America's own future and from the rest of the world. In particular, the external financial position of the United States represents an enormous threat to future prosperity, both in the short run and over time.

No respectable analysis shows the current account deficit, given present policies and exchange rates, ever falling much below $100 billion. It could begin rising again by 1990, or even sometime during 1989. Without a significant shift in policy, the United States would thus have to continue indefinitely to attract about $10 billion of net capital inflow each month from the rest of the world. Its net foreign debt would continue to rise at breathtaking speed.

If foreign investors and central banks finally stop lending such quantities to the United States, recognizing the unsustainability of the situation, the dollar will plunge and interest rates will soar. The result could be a revival of both double-digit inflation and sharp recession. There would be enormous disruption to a financial system that is already quite fragile. US income distribution would be skewed further because the poorest groups are hit hardest by inflation and are the first to lose their jobs in a recession. Neither fiscal nor monetary policy would be available to respond to the crisis. The outcome would be even worse if foreigners were to withdraw some

2. The short-run and underlying US economic positions are analyzed in Chapter 2. The macroeconomic policy changes recommended for the United States are developed in Chapter 5.

of the $1.5 trillion in liquid assets that they already hold in the United States. Capital flight by Americans, in the wake of such foreign outflows or even in anticipation thereof, would add to the turmoil.

These risks are not theoretical: the first steps of this scenario, and related international developments, triggered the sharp falls in the bond market in early 1987 and in the stock market later that year. Rapid and massive intervention was required by the world's monetary authorities to avoid a "hard landing" for the economy. The United States was able to attract the capital needed in 1988 with little difficulty, but this may have been due largely to the market's recognition that the major central banks would do whatever was necessary to support the dollar during an American election year, when serious adjustment measures could not be expected.

The risks are greater now than in any recent period. Foreigners have lent $700 billion to the United States over the past six years, and their appetite for additional dollar assets could wane at any moment—especially if the US trade deficit stops improving. With the US economy near full employment and domestic demand growing rapidly, however, continued improvement of the trade balance at anything like the recent pace would generate heavy pressure on resources and ignite a sharp rise in inflation, which could also trigger a loss of confidence. So a sharp fall of the dollar is now quite possible whether or not the trade deficit continues to fall, unless the growth of domestic demand drops simultaneously.

With concerns about inflation already emerging, such a fall of the dollar could trigger rapid price rises and a quick move by the markets to higher interest rates. The Federal Reserve (Fed) would have to tighten monetary policy to counter the inflationary pressure, producing increases in real interest rates that could turn the economy downward. Such a combination of higher interest rates and economic turndown would trigger more bankruptcies within the country and threaten defaults abroad.

Alternatively, rather than exploding over a short period, the loss of foreign confidence could build up over time, as large trade deficits persisted and the ratio of US foreign debt to exports and GNP continued to rise. In this case, interest rates would have to remain high to attract the required foreign funds and avoid withdrawals. Growth would slow. Investment would be discouraged. Productivity would suffer. Periodic market disruptions, like those in 1987, could be expected. An increasing share of national output would have to be diverted away from domestic uses to service the growing external debt.

But the crisis could not be averted forever. Indeed, it could erupt when the condition of the economy was much less favorable. If growth had already slowed, a sharp rise in interest rates would be far more painful. The need to tighten fiscal policy would come at a much worse moment. The time for strong remedial action could arrive long after the new administration's "honeymoon" period is over, making it far more difficult to forge an effective political response.

In political terms as well, it would seem far better for the President to move preemptively early in his new term to deal with the chief problems he inherits, rather than being forced to react to a crisis later. President Reagan accepted the deep recession of 1982 to quell the rapid inflation that he inherited, and both economic growth and his political popularity were booming again at reelection time in 1984. By contrast, President Carter tried to prolong an expansion, in the face of rising inflation and external deficits, and had to seek adjustment at the worst possible time—just prior to the next election.

On both economic and political grounds, it would be extremely risky for the new administration to try to skate through four more years of massive borrowing from the rest of the world. One of the central goals of its economic policy should therefore be to eliminate the current account deficit during its new term, reducing it at an average annual pace of about $35 billion from the expected 1988 level of $130 billion to $140 billion.[3] Early adoption of a credible program to achieve this ambitious goal is essential to avoid a crisis (sooner or later); to ensure market confidence in the dollar; to attract the sizable financing that will be needed during the extended adjustment period; and to provide a solid foundation for a sensible trade policy, an adequate response to Third World debt, and other key US policy objectives.

A credible program to eliminate the external deficit, while maintaining economic growth and financial stability, must include three components. Significant changes in macroeconomic policy in

3. The current account situation and outlook are analyzed in detail in Chapter 4.

the United States and complementary macroeconomic measures in the major surplus countries (mainly Japan and Germany, but also several smaller European countries and Taiwan and Korea) to keep their markets growing, along with further changes in exchange rates, lie at the heart of the effort. An aggressive trade policy is essential to promote American exports and open markets abroad, and to counter the powerful domestic pressures for more import protection, which would undermine the effort to boost American competitiveness. More effective strategies are needed to resolve the debt crisis in the Third World in order to restore growth and expand markets in those countries, mainly by using the international financial institutions in more ambitious and innovative ways.

ELIMINATING THE TWIN DEFICITS

To eliminate its external deficit over the next four years, the United States must reorient its economy toward exports and private investment (to boost export capacity and overall productivity), and away from consumption and government spending. Exports have been rising at annual rates of 20 to 30 percent since the middle of 1987, primarily because of the sharp fall in the exchange rate of the dollar since early 1985. This indicates an impressive restoration of American competitiveness in world markets. The United States should thus be capable of achieving export-led growth into the early 1990s, as it did in the late 1970s. The annual expansion of total domestic demand must be held 1 to 1.5 percentage points below the growth of potential output (about 2.5 percent annually) to permit a transfer of resources of the requisite magnitude into the improvement in the trade balance.

The only assured and constructive means to achieve these results is for the United States to eliminate the federal government's structural budget deficit (about $150 billion) during the four-year term of the new President. The Gramm-Rudman-Hollings schedule already sets such a course, mandating cumulative annual reductions in the deficit of about $36 billion, which would bring it to zero in FY 1993 (ending September 1993). The new President and Congress should follow this prescription by promptly adopting a balanced package of cuts in government programs and tax increases, designed to slow the rise of public spending and private consumption, that will phase in irrevocably during the adjustment period.

Such a program would increase national saving by eliminating the drain of government dissaving through the budget deficit. It would dampen inflation and calm fears of a new spiral. It would reduce interest rates, perhaps considerably, in both nominal and real terms. One result should be an increase in private investment, while simultaneously reducing and in time halting the buildup of foreign debt. Such a program would build a firm foundation for eliminating the external deficit and reinforcing market confidence because it would free resources for export (from domestic consumption by individuals or the government) and spur investment in new capacity to produce the needed goods and services.

Growth would be sustained by steady improvement in the trade balance, by increases in private investment induced by the fall in interest rates, and by the continued expansion of interest-sensitive components of consumption. The main threat to the economy in the short run, a collapse of the dollar and a return of inflationary recession, would be preempted. Fiscal policy would again become a flexible policy instrument, available to respond to future slowdowns. The prospects for higher levels of national saving, private investment, and productivity, and hence improved living standards over the long run, would be greatly enhanced. The main cost of such a program would be a slowdown in the growth of consumption to very modest rates during the adjustment period, after it had risen by about 3 to 3.5 percent per year during the initial phase of the expansion.

Purely domestic considerations call for similar policies. The economy neared full employment in 1988 following the creation of over 17 million jobs since the deep recession of 1982. Renewed inflation and higher interest rates have become the primary domestic concerns in the short run. There is no economic theory that justifies budget deficits near 3 percent of GNP when the economy is so close to full employment. As they address economic policy in 1989, the new administration and Congress should face no contradiction between the country's domestic and international priorities.

The longer term goals of the US economy point in the same direction. The American standard of living has grown very modestly over the past fifteen years. Other countries, especially Japan and the newly industrialized countries (NICs) of East Asia, are catching (or passing) the United States in global competition. The underlying source of both problems is the modest rate of American productivity growth, which is caused in large part by the low and declining rate of national saving to support productive investment. The economy's expansion during the past six years was made possible only by the importation of $700 billion of capital from abroad, which turned the United States into the world's largest debtor nation and mortgaged its future increasingly to the actions of foreign creditors.

It is thus essential that the United States, for long-term structural as well as for immediate reasons, sharply raise its levels of domestic saving and investment. There is no conflict between the short and long runs. The international dimension plays a central role in both, because trade deficits and a continued dependence on foreign capital could jeopardize the country's ability to achieve its fundamental objectives over both time horizons.

The need to avoid a protectionist relapse, and further severe erosion of the trading system, adds strongly to the case for the adoption of the program proposed here to eliminate the current account deficit. If the decline in the external deficit were to stall at or above $100 billion, and especially if it were to start rising again, the political message would be that the effort to solve the problem primarily through macroeconomic measures had failed. The proponents of this approach—former Treasury Secretary James A. Baker III, who launched the strategy in 1985 in large part to head off the threat of rampant protectionism; Federal Reserve Chairmen Paul Volcker and Alan Greenspan; officials in the other key countries; and virtually all economists around the world—would be discredited. Even if the real problem were a failure to implement the macroeconomic approach effectively, because of inadequate US budget deficit cuts or insufficient growth abroad, the entire strategy could be jettisoned.

Given the absence of feasible alternatives, a major swing to protectionism might ensue. An American import surcharge would become a distinct possibility, as in the similar—but far less extreme—circumstances of 1971. Widespread foreign retaliation and emulation would be certain. The entire trading system could be shattered. Both the United States and its major partners abroad have compelling reasons, arising from considerations of trade policy as well as from those of growth and financial stability, to take the necessary steps to complete the adjustment of the current imbalances.

AN ACTIVIST TRADE POLICY

The proposed macroeconomic steps by the United States will have to be supported by macroeconomic steps abroad, which are described below, to achieve the full international adjustment. The United States itself, however, should also adopt a series of microeconomic measures to exploit its restored price competitiveness, transfer resources into the external sector, and bolster its international competitive position over the long run.

Active export promotion is particularly critical to overcome the marketing reentry problem faced by many firms that were priced out of global competition in the early 1980s by the overvalued dollar.[4] A new "Export Expansion and Removal of Disincentives Act" could sharply expand the direct lending and guarantee programs of the Export-Import Bank and eliminate or reduce many of the self-imposed constraints on American sales abroad.

Trade policy must also ensure that foreign markets remain open to US exports and exert continuing pressure on other countries to reduce existing import restraints. Successful negotiation of multilateral cuts in barriers in the Uruguay Round will be the most effective way to rebuild global momentum for trade liberalization, opening markets for the American export drive. To help achieve maximum liberalization in the industrial countries, the new administration should propose that they eliminate all tariffs on their trade in industrial products by the year 2000. To obtain maximum concessions from both industrialized and developing countries, the United States should offer to reduce its own key barriers (including those for agriculture and textiles) on a fully reciprocal basis.

With exports booming and American price competitiveness restored, and with macroeconomic policy geared to export-led growth for several years, it would be folly for the United States to take protectionist steps that would lead to emulation abroad. As other countries' trade balances shrink to accommodate the American improvement, any new US controls—against direct investment as well as imports—would encourage and justify reciprocal actions by other countries at the worst possible time for the United States.

Developments in Europe add a particular urgency to this component

4. The full package of trade policy proposals is in Chapter 6.

of the proposed strategy. The member countries of the European Community (EC) have made a firm commitment to "complete the internal market" by 1992, and are already moving in that direction. This intra-European integration could have major positive effects for the United States and the rest of the world economy, by increasing growth in the world's largest market and providing a stronger European partner to help share international responsibilities.

There is considerable concern outside the Community, however, that the adjustment costs of internal liberalization will be passed on to outside countries in the form of new external barriers and discrimination (including measures against firms based in non-EC countries). Pressures in this direction could be significant since Europe, especially Germany, must simultaneously accept a considerable reduction in its external surplus as part of the global adjustment. If the world economy were to turn down, as a result of a collapse of the dollar or for any other reason, these pressures would be even more acute.

The United States thus has a major interest in pursuing initiatives that engage Europe externally while it is uniting further internally. The most important is the Uruguay Round, which aims to reduce trade barriers on a global basis and to write new rules to govern trade in agriculture and other areas of US–European contention. It might in fact be desirable to aim for a two-stage outcome for the Round: an initial package in 1990 could center on short-term measures and a framework agreement for agriculture that would influence the US farm legislation scheduled for 1990; the final deal in 1992 would coincide with Europe's target date and would maintain external pressure on the Community throughout its internal process. Conversely, the erection of new barriers by the United States would be extremely risky because it would add to protectionist pressures in Europe that may already be formidable. New American efforts to negotiate bilateral or regional free trade areas, modeled after the agreement with Canada, could also induce Europe to concentrate on deepening its "bloc" rather than cooperating on a global basis.

The United States should adopt several other trade policy changes. It should reject any future use of so-called "voluntary" restraint agreements (VRAs) to limit imports, largely because they enable the foreign competitors of American companies to reap billions of dollars of windfall profits that ultimately enhance their competitive positions, and offer to convert existing VRAs to less noxious forms of restraint (tariffs or auction quotas). The United States should substantially improve the adjustment assistance program, especially for workers in industries hurt by foreign competition. It should require all industries seeking import relief to apply through designated legal channels, and to offer a comprehensive plan for fundamental adjustment. These changes would promote the competitiveness of the US economy and should be adopted primarily for domestic reasons. However, they could also strengthen the country's international negotiating position and enhance the prospects for a successful Uruguay Round.

The United States will also need to adopt a number of microeconomic measures ranging beyond trade policy to support its international economic position. Private investment might be stimulated through a revival of a modified investment tax credit and permanent status for the research and development credit (as well as by the lower interest rates resulting from budget correction). A refurbishing of the entire educational system, which is responsible for developing the nation's human capital, is clearly required. The country should designate a new institution, perhaps the Council on Competitiveness created by the Omnibus Trade Act, to develop projections for the future of key American industries and to assess the impact on them of the policies of foreign governments. These analyses would provide baselines against which to judge industry requests for import relief or other governmental assistance and the need for US responses to other countries' trade and industrial policies.

On all these issues, it is essential that future US policy take full account of the need to support the country's international economic and financial position. Historically, most American economic (and other) policies have been determined on strictly domestic grounds. The external dimension was ignored or the country tried to export its internal preferences to the rest of the world. With the increase in America's dependence on world markets and the decline in its ability to dictate global outcomes, that approach is no longer viable. From this point forward, both macroeconomic policy and microeconomic measures will have to be adopted with full cognizance of their implications for the country's external position—the "competitive" component of the strategy of competitive interdependence suggested in this volume.

THE FOREIGN DIMENSION

The United States cannot do all this alone. The necessary improvement of about $150 billion in America's current account[5] will require an equivalent reduction in the aggregate current account position of other countries. Management of the dollar and trade liberalization require cooperation from many countries. More effective responses to Third World debt and a range of other financial issues must be developed multilaterally. Market perceptions of schisms in international cooperation shock confidence and bring instantaneous instability. Any comprehensive American strategy must contain an "interdependence" component as well.

Fortunately, the rest of the world has a major incentive to cooperate with the United States in this effort. A hard landing of the American economy would have enormous effects on other countries, most of which are far more dependent on international trade and international financial stability than is the United States. Their major market would shrink abruptly. Their own interest rates would be driven up by the rise in American interest rates. Renewed global inflation would threaten, as in the early and late 1970s. Protectionist pressures would accelerate and Third World debt could erupt, choking their markets further.

Many countries are experiencing their own external deficit or debt problems, however, and thus cannot bear much, if any, current account decline. Canada and some of the European nations (including France, Italy, and the United Kingdom) are in this position. The bulk of the American adjustment must therefore be targeted on the small number of countries that are running surpluses: Japan, Germany and a few smaller European countries, and the Asian NICs (notably Taiwan and Korea).

One group of countries that can paradoxically contribute to the global adjustment because of its current weakness is the Third World debtors. The most troubled debtors (the "Baker 15"[6]) are now paying

5. A cut of $150 billion in the US current account deficit in nominal dollars will require a cut of about $200 billion in the merchandise trade deficit in volume terms. The arithmetic is developed in Chapter 4.

6. The "Baker 15," so-called because they are the objects of the "Baker Plan" to respond to the Third World debt problem, are: Argentina, Bolivia, Brazil, Chile, Colombia, Ecuador, Ivory Coast, Mexico, Morocco, Nigeria, Peru, Philippines, Uruguay, Venezuela, and Yugoslavia.

about $30 billion more in annual debt service than they are receiving in new loans. This "negative financial transfer" requires them to run sizable trade surpluses, in contrast to the deficits that they have traditionally run, which are far more appropriate for countries at their stage of development. The shift in these countries' trade balances made a significant contribution (perhaps $15 billion to $20 billion) to the deterioration of the US trade balance in the early 1980s.

These countries would clearly like to grow faster and stop running such large trade surpluses, but they must experience a sustained reduction—or reversal—of their net financial outflow to be able to do so. A four-part response to their problems, which would also reduce the risk of financial instability triggered by further interruptions of debt servicing, could eliminate or begin to reverse the "negative financial transfer" over the proposed four-year adjustment period and enable these countries to increase their imports by a like amount (see table 1.1).[7]

The first component of the effort would be the reduction in dollar (and probably world) interest rates and the other beneficial results of the US budget correction and the reduction of imbalances among the industrial countries. Each one percentage point decline in interest rates reduces the annual debt service of the debtor countries by about $5 billion. The macroeconomic policy changes proposed in this volume would cut interest rates by at least one to two percentage points, and therefore reduce the annual debt service costs of the poorer countries by $5 billion to $10 billion. Continued world growth and renewed trade liberalization would also boost debtor export growth, providing a further improvement in their external positions (though no additional decline in their debt service payments); further dollar depreciation would reduce the real value of their debt.

This part of the proposed package for the debtors would have no net impact on the global current account imbalances, even if fully offset by a reduction in their trade surpluses, because of the reduction in interest earnings and increase in imports of the industrial countries. However, the remaining $25–40 billion of the package would contribute to the foreign counterpart of the American external adjustment. Moreover, by reducing the "negative financial transfer,"

7. Details of this program are in Chapter 7.

this element of the package would help limit the financial risks emanating from Third World debt, and thus further support the case for the industrial countries to adopt the proposed economic adjustment program.

Second, the key international financial institutions should be prepared to increase significantly their lending to the debtor countries in support of more effective growth and adjustment policies. The World Bank should as rapidly as possible raise its available commitments from the present annual level of about $15 billion to about $25 billion, instead of the $21 billion now planned, and it should speed its disbursements by placing greater emphasis on structural adjustment loans. The Inter-American Development Bank should double its annual lending capability from the current level of about $3 billion and speed its disbursements. The IMF should start lending considerably larger amounts to countries with effective stabilization programs, by utilizing the full "enlarged access" limits that permit it to transfer up to 90 percent of a country's quota annually rather than the considerably smaller amounts applied in most cases now. It should subsequently double the quotas of all members to permit even larger transfers.

Each of these three institutions is now contributing to the "negative financial transfer" by withdrawing funds from the large debtors rather than providing them with net inflows. The United States should support these proposals because they further its interest in faster growth in the developing countries (and thus political stability in Latin America, the Philippines, and elsewhere) and would ease global financial risks, as well as contribute directly to the US external adjustment. This will require the United States and other donor countries to follow the recent British example and provide their full subscriptions to the new capital increase in the World Bank immediately, rather than staging the payments over six years as now planned, to provide the capital base for the acceleration in lending (and for a new guarantee program described below); to agree on a capital increase for the IDB; and to support a doubling of quotas at the IMF. The budget costs of these measures are minuscule: because only a small portion of capital in the development banks is paid in and no outlays at all are required for the IMF, the United States can support an increase of about $200 billion in the combined resources of the three institutions with budget outlays of only $645 million

TABLE 1.1 **Proposed Program for Eliminating the "Negative Financial Transfer" from the "Baker 15" Heavily Indebted Countries[a] by 1992** *(billions of dollars)*

Instrument	Impact by 1992	Comment
Reduced interest payments resulting from elimination of US budget deficit and correction of imbalances among industrial countries.[b]	5–10	Each 1 percent decline in US interest rates reduces interest payments by about $5 billion.
Increase in World Bank lending and speedup of disbursements.	5–10	Contingent on adoption of effective adjustment program by borrowers. Facilitated by greater emphasis on structural adjustment loans. Supported by General Capital Increase (GCI).
Increase in Inter–American Development Bank lending and speedup of disbursements.	5	Same as above. Requires new capital increase of about $25 billion (with US share of about $9 billion).
Increase in IMF lending.	5	Same as above. Facilitated by using "enlarged access" limits fully and doubling country quotas.

(of which $50 million for the World Bank was already appropriated in 1988).

The third element of the strategy for Third World debtors is a broadening of the mechanisms available for the voluntary extension of debt relief by commercial banks. Comprehensive debt relief plans

TABLE 1.1 *(continued)*

Instrument	Impact by 1992	Comment
Voluntary debt relief.	5–10	Facilitated by World Bank guarantees of exit bonds for countries with effective adjustment programs. Includes buybacks, debt-equity swaps, and other devices.
Additional flows of private capital and officially supported export credits.	5–10	Especially direct investment and purchases of equities, but perhaps including modest amounts of new bank lending.
Total	30–50	

a. The countries included are Argentina, Bolivia, Brazil, Chile, Colombia, Ecuador, Ivory Coast, Mexico, Morocco, Nigeria, Peru, Philippines, Uruguay, Venezuela, and Yugoslavia.

b. This would reduce the interest earnings of industrial countries (including the United States) and thus does not contribute to the global current account adjustment addressed in the text and summarized in table 1.2.

are impractical because there is no way to force banks to participate, no way to limit the relief to countries with effective adjustment programs, and no prospect of providing large amounts of public funds to support them. But schemes in which banks voluntarily write off part of their claims have already been worked out for Bolivia, Chile, and Mexico. Further innovation in relief techniques will add to the menu of possibilities, and a major expansion of this approach would be possible with the issuance of World Bank guarantees for exit bonds sold by debtor countries with approved adjustment programs to banks that wished to drop out of future lending programs. Depending on their maturity and the magnitude of the discounts involved, such bonds could substantially reduce the level of outstanding debt over time and provide at least modest cash-flow relief in the short run.

Finally, every effort should be made to increase the flows of direct investment, equity capital, and other forms of private capital to the debtor countries. The capital-exporting countries and, in particular, the debtor countries themselves will need to make a number of policy changes to induce these flows. It will probably be some time before the flows become sizable, given the adverse environment created by the debt crisis itself. But the potential for significant increases is clearly demonstrated by the record of less debt-burdened developing countries. More immediately, the export credit agencies of the industrial countries (including the Export-Import Bank of the United States, as discussed in Chapter 6) should restore and expand their programs in debtor countries with effective adjustment programs.

With this program, about $10 billion of the external adjustment of the United States could derive directly from its trade with the Baker 15. The marginal propensity of these countries to import from the United States is about one-third, and the induced increase in American exports would be offset only slightly by the decline in earnings stemming from lower US interest rates. In addition, the remainder of the pickup in Third World imports would reduce the extent of trade balance deterioration in the rest of the world needed to accommodate the American correction.

The rest of the correction must come primarily from changes in the small number of countries with large surpluses.[8] Japan is the world's largest surplus country, by far, and it will need to accept an adjustment of about $60 billion. Germany is the key to Western Europe, the world's largest market and largest trading entity, and it is running a surplus that is second largest in absolute terms and

8. One other group of countries that might "contribute" to the global adjustment is OPEC, if the oil price were to fall substantially and it were able to borrow enough externally to avoid a corresponding cutback in imports. The magnitude of any such effort would depend on the extent of the price decline and the countries' creditworthiness. The group's current account deteriorated from rough balance in 1984–85 to a deficit of about $30 billion when the price of oil plunged in 1986, and leveled off by 1988 at a deficit of about $15 billion.

larger than Japan's relative to the size of its economy; Germany needs a correction of about $40 billion, and the three smaller surplus countries in Europe (Belgium, the Netherlands, and Switzerland) should add another $10 billion. The Asian NICs, mainly Taiwan and Korea, have by far the largest external surpluses relative to GNP—about 13 percent and 8 percent, respectively, compared with 3 to 4 percent for Germany and Japan—and should adjust by about $20 billion (see table 1.2).[9]

Some of the reduction in these countries' surpluses will derive from the proposed policy changes in the United States. But they will need to contribute actively in three areas: achieving and maintaining sufficient growth of domestic demand in their own economies; keeping their markets open and reducing their trade barriers; and cooperating to reach and sustain equilibrium exchange rates among the dollar and the other key currencies. Fortunately, such steps would meet the most pressing internal needs of the countries themselves: a sharp cut in Europe's still high unemployment and growing intraregional imbalances, and a steady rise in living standards and welfare in Japan and the Asian NICs.

There is considerable debate among economists about the benefits to the American trade effort of faster growth abroad (see Chapter 5) and the liberalization of foreign trade barriers (see Chapter 6). Some analyses show very modest gains from one or the other, while others show substantial payoffs. The importance of achieving the full correction is so great and the required magnitude is so large, however, that the message for policy is straightforward: maximize the effort on all fronts, as already outlined with respect to reducing trade barriers.

Domestic demand is already expanding vigorously in Japan, rising by more than 7 percent in 1988, and needs to grow at about 6 percent per year throughout the adjustment period. The large

---

9. Such an allocation among the surplus countries (with higher absolute numbers, because there was no quantification of the reduction in the trade surpluses of the Third World debtors) was recommended by a group of 33 leading international economists, including representatives of each of the key surplus countries, who met to assess the global economic and financial situation in late 1987. The decline in the merchandise trade surpluses of these countries would be greater than the fall in their current accounts, because all of them are experiencing steady increases in earnings on their foreign investment positions. See *Resolving the Global Economic Crisis*, 3.

TABLE 1.2 Proposed Allocation of the Adjustment of Current Account Positions, 1987 to 1992 *(billions of dollars)*

Country	1980–81 average	1987	Proposed[a] 1992	Proposed[a] Change from 1987
United States	5	−155	−5	150
Japan	0	90	30	−60
Germany	−10	45	5	−40
Smaller European[b]	−5	15	5	−10
15 Heavily Indebted Countries[c]	−30	−10	−40	−30
Taiwan and Korea	−5	30	10	−20

a. A significant fall in the world price of oil, if sustained through this period, could produce a further increase in the current account deficit of OPEC countries and reduce the needed adjustment in countries other than the United States. On the other hand, some allowance is made for reductions in the deficits of countries other than the United States (such as the United Kingdom).

b. Belgium, the Netherlands, Switzerland.

c. The Baker 15. See table 1.1.

European countries other than Germany are all running deficits and cannot expand on a sustained basis alone, but Europe as a whole (and Canada) can and should expand domestic demand by about 4 percent annually through 1992. Since the external surpluses of Japan and Europe would be declining (in real terms) at about 1 percent of GNP annually through the four-year adjustment period to achieve the international adjustment, the resulting growth of GNP would be about 5 percent in Japan and 3 percent in Europe. The models used in this volume suggest that such growth rates could expand US exports by about $50 billion annually after they had worked their way through fully to the trade flows.[10]

Another key international consideration, beyond these macroeconomic policy changes and the trade negotiations addressed earlier,

10. The models are described in the Annex.

is burden sharing among the allies. The security arrangements that were developed in the early postwar period have worked exceedingly well, as has the compartmentalization of security and economic relations among the allies that has prevailed for most of the period. With the rise of General Secretary Gorbachev in the Soviet Union and the possibility of new progress on security issues, it will be especially crucial to maintain (and even strengthen) alliance solidarity into the 1990s and avoid any destabilizing interaction between these two sets of issues.

Alliance security arrangements were developed, however, at a time when the relative economic capabilities of the allies were considerably different than they are today. In the United States, there is rising domestic political pressure for a change in distribution of the costs of maintaining global security, including its economic components, such as foreign assistance and debt relief. The stability of the security system can be assured only if there is a substantial reallocation of responsibilities according to economic capacity—carrying with it, of course, a corresponding reallocation of economic rights.

It is noteworthy that some of the major surplus countries—especially Japan, Germany, and Korea—are also among America's most important allies and are in fact linchpins of its most important collective security systems. When they respond to US adjustment needs—whether this involves growth rates, exchange rates, trade liberalization, or financial contributions to the relief of Third World debt and poverty—these countries need to have these broader considerations very much in mind. The most promising venue for changes in burden sharing is the international financial institutions. Japan and the others should sharply increase their funding for these organizations through such measures as an early Selective Capital Increase (SCI) in the World Bank and perhaps similar steps in the regional development banks; a possible new facility at the World Bank to back exit bond guarantees; and further adjustment of quotas in the IMF. The United States and the allies, particularly Japan, should discuss these issues explicitly and reach an early agreement on the methods by which better burden sharing will be achieved, and on the concomitant shifts in leadership roles within the institutions.

THE DOLLAR AND THE MONETARY SYSTEM

The final component of the adjustment package is exchange rate policy. The decline of the dollar has restored a good deal of America's price competitiveness. By late 1987, the dollar had roughly reversed the appreciation of 1980–85. However, this was not enough to restore balance in the current account, even if macroeconomic policies both at home and abroad were altered, because the United States had shifted to debtor status in the interim and because other structural changes had occurred. Moreover, the renewed rise of the dollar in 1988 "gave back" some of the adjustment that had been anticipated earlier.[11]

Several steps will therefore be needed in this area. First, the dollar must reverse the appreciation of 1988. At the time of this writing in October 1988, with the dollar worth about 128 yen and 1.82 deutsche marks (DM), the appreciation amounted to about 5 percent from the average of the fourth quarter of 1987 (but about 12 percent from the trough at the end of the year). Second, if the other macroeconomic policies proposed here for the United States and the other key countries are put into place, a further depreciation in 1989 averaging about 15 percent in real terms from the level of the fourth quarter of 1987 should be sufficient to eliminate the current account deficit by 1992. (If the surplus countries abroad failed to maintain the growth rates proposed above, the additional dollar depreciation would have to be over 20 percent. These countries thus have a choice, to a degree, between faster economic growth and greater currency appreciation.)

Third, these further currency movements will have to fall primarily on the surplus countries. As noted above, a substantial portion of across-the-board changes would affect weaker countries that could not accept them and would therefore take offsetting measures, aborting the adjustment and prompting a series of iterations until the bulk of the impact ultimately fell on the stronger countries in any event. Above-average appreciations will thus be required for the surplus countries, taking their currencies to perhaps 100:1 for the

11. These issues are developed in Chapter 5.

yen, 1.25:1 for the DM, 23:1 for the New Taiwan dollar and 675:1 for the Korean won. Such a DM appreciation implies a realignment of about 20 percent within the European Monetary System (EMS), which will clearly be needed in light of the growing trade imbalances between Germany and its European partners.

Fourth, it will be essential to avoid any premature renewed appreciation of the dollar. The necessary expansion of US exports will take place only if American firms substantially increase their export capacity, and many are reluctant to do so because they fear being priced out of foreign markets by a rising dollar again before their new plants could come on stream. The dollar might fall on its own if the United States enacts the budget policies proposed here and interest rates decline in response. But it could also surge, given an improved trade outlook and the sense that America was finally "fixing the only thing that is broke." The authorities will have to resist any such appreciation until full correction of the external deficit is achieved and maintained for some time. To this end, they might announce an agreed ceiling for the exchange rate of the dollar and defend it vigorously.[12]

Fifth, the major countries should work out the details of a system of target zones for their currencies and install it as soon as the required adjustment policies are in place and the currencies have reached levels that are likely to be sustainable. This would help avoid any premature rise of the dollar. Over time, it should promote the orderly achievement of required currency changes as needed (such as a steady appreciation of the yen in response to Japan's lower inflation, its higher productivity, and its rapidly rising investment income as the world's largest creditor country). Target zones should also provide a strong foundation for improving international coordination of national economic policies (and thereby helping to maintain a global orientation for the European countries even if they

12. An alternative scenario would be for the dollar to depreciate by the needed amount, either due to spontaneous market developments or with some encouragement from the authorities (including the newly elected US authorities), prior to the launching of the proposed budget policies. Announcement of those policies should then arrest the dollar's slide and provide the internal transfer of resources needed to translate the further depreciation into sustained improvement in the trade balance. The authorities would still have to agree to resist any resulting upside pressures on the dollar, but under this scenario might have better prospects for maintaining an equilibrium level.

deepen their internal arrangements through the EMS). Again, short-run and longer-term considerations point to the same policy approach.

The nonsystem of floating exchange rates that has been in place since 1973 has permitted (or even fostered) huge currency misalignments, generating major economic distortions and protectionist trade pressures. The governments of the world's leading economies, the so-called Group of Five (G-5) and Group of Seven (G-7), have been groping toward a new system since the Plaza Agreement of September 1985.[13] They installed "reference ranges" for most of their currencies in February 1987. Completing the process with a full target zone system should provide greater monetary stability and an effective mechanism for forging closer policy coordination. The IMF, supported by a doubling of its quotas, should ultimately manage the system and again assume a central role in global financial affairs.

We noted at the outset that a precipitous fall of the dollar could have devastating effects on the US and world economies. Indeed, a central goal of the entire strategy proposed here is to avoid such an event. But we have just suggested that the dollar must come down by another 15 to 20 percent to achieve the needed adjustment, even if the major countries abroad maintain domestic demand growth at the recommended rates. How are these two views to be reconciled?

The critical distinction is whether the dollar falls because of the absence of a comprehensive adjustment program or in the context of such a program. In the former case, with the United States near full employment and domestic demand rising rapidly, the main effect of a sizable and rapid dollar decline would be faster US inflation (and thus little depreciation of the exchange rate in real terms). Interest rates would rise and the "hard landing" scenario set forth above could ensue. The trade deficit might decline, but it would do so mainly because of a US recession (unless other countries experienced recessions of similar magnitudes in which case there would be little or no improvement in the US trade balance but an even sharper fall in world growth). The size of the dollar decline could also turn out to be far greater than the average of 15 to 20 percent (in real terms) that is needed, because it would be caused by a lack of confidence in the dollar, or even by flight from it, that was in turn the

13. The G-5 consists of the United States, France, Germany, Japan, and the United Kingdom. The G-7 includes Canada and Italy.

consequence of a widespread belief that the United States was never going to "get its house in order" by dealing with the twin deficits.

In contrast, a depreciation of the dollar in tandem with the proposed macroeconomic changes in the United States and abroad would achieve effective adjustment and thereby enhance the prospects for an orderly completion of the currency realignment. Such a package would simultaneously expand the supply of American goods available for export, at more competitive prices, and increase demand for those products around the world (see summary in table 1.3). The US fiscal program and companion steps abroad should ensure confidence in the underlying strength and stability of the dollar. Further dollar depreciation as part of the package proposed here should enhance stability, whereas a depreciation of similar magnitude in the absence of such a program could be destabilizing and counterproductive.

IMPLEMENTING THE STRATEGY

The United States can best pursue its international economic interests through a strategy of "competitive interdependence" in the context of an essentially cooperative, but vigorously competitive, world economy. The "competitive" component of the proposed strategy would be implemented largely through three new legislative packages, worked out by the new administration in full consultation with Congress: one aimed at reducing the budget deficit, another to promote export expansion (including related microeconomic measures), and a third intended to strengthen the ability of the international financial institutions to help resolve the problems of Third World debt and alliance burden sharing. The "interdependence" component would encompass a series of major international negotiations: to coordinate national economic policies among the industrial countries and reduce the impact of Third World debt, in order to eliminate the present imbalances and ensure continued growth; to achieve equilibrium among the key currencies and maintain it with a reformed international monetary system; to renew the process of trade liberalization through a successful Uruguay Round of negotiations under the GATT, and bilateral talks where necessary; to improve and expand substantially the programs of the international financial

TABLE 1.3 Proposed Program for Adjustment of the US Current Account Deficit by 1992 *(billions of dollars)*

Instrument	Impact by 1992	Comment
Elimination of US budget deficit and 15 percent decline of trade-weighted dollar from average level of fourth quarter 1987.	90[a]	Depreciation targeted largely against currencies of surplus countries (yen, DM, Swiss franc, Dutch guilder, Belgian franc, NT$, won). Also requires reversal of dollar rise in 1988 (5 percent from fourth quarter 1987, as of 13 October 1988).[b]
Increase of about 1 percent above expected baseline in annual growth of domestic demand in other industrial countries during 1989–92.	50	Requires GNP growth of about 5 percent in Japan and 3.5 percent in Germany, 2.5 percent to 3 percent in rest of Europe and Canada.
Increased capital transfers (including through voluntary debt relief) to 15 heavily indebted countries of Third World (see table 1.1).	10	Enables Third World debtors to reduce debt constraint, grow faster, and import more.
Total	150	

a. This impact would be greater ($15 billion per percentage point per year) if the US budget correction produced a slowdown in US economic growth. The analysis in the text suggests, however, that GNP growth would be maintained because the induced improvements in the trade balance and, because of lower interest rates, in private investment and other interest-sensitive expenditures would offset the cutbacks in government spending and other private consumption.

b. Based on the trade-weighted exchange rate used in the model described in the Annex, adapted from the Federal Reserve's Helkie-Hooper model.

institutions; and to redistribute the allies' contributions to the maintenance of a stable world economy in closer accord with their ability to pay.

The United States would gain significantly from the proposed strategy, most crucially by eliminating its external deficit and thus the constant financial threat to its prosperity and stability. The risks of financial instability would also be reduced, over both the short run and the long run, by the improved response to Third World debt and by the new system of target zones. The United States would also benefit from the relative increase in the contributions of other countries to shared international economic goals, and from the renewed liberalization of world trade. The United States would contribute substantially to this world adjustment by bringing its budget deficit under control, agreeing to stabilize the dollar once equilibrium levels were reached, liberalizing its own trade barriers (including those in sensitive sectors), and providing more financial resources to the international financial institutions (with very modest budget outlays).

Japan, Germany and the smaller European surplus countries, and the Asian NICs (notably Taiwan and Korea) would need to ensure continuing rapid growth of domestic demand throughout the adjustment period, further liberalize their import restraints, accept additional appreciation of their currencies, and increase their shares of funding for the international financial institutions. In return, these countries could resolve their most pressing internal economic problems: unemployment and regional imbalances (which could impede further economic integration) in Europe, low standards of living (including poor housing and inadequate social infrastructure) in Japan and the Asian NICs.

These countries would gain from the enhanced prosperity and stability that would result from an orderly correction of the global imbalances, the creation of a more effective monetary regime, renewed liberalization of trade, and a resolution of the Third World debt problem. Particularly for Japan, larger contributions to the system of economic management would mean greater influence. A cooperative response to the economic problems would strengthen these countries' security ties with the United States and improve the prospects for successful negotiations with the Soviet Union. Most importantly, as open economies heavily dependent on international trade and financial stability, these nations would benefit enormously by avoiding the hard landing of the American economy that could push the world into inflationary recession and disrupt the global economic order.

At this point in time, there are no fundamental contradictions between the internal and external policy objectives of the major countries that could impede the implementation of this program. Nor are there conflicts between the countries' immediate and longer-term goals. The United States must become much more outward-oriented, both because of its permanently increased dependence on the world economy and to correct its current imbalances. The surplus countries must rely much more heavily on expanding domestic demand, rather than exports, both for their own long-term growth and to correct the present imbalances. Both the domestic and international political dimensions of the situation suggest that the proposed program is necessary and quite feasible.

The new package could be unveiled at a special international summit meeting in the spring of 1989, or even at the regular summit in France on Bastille Day. Such a launching would have a dramatic positive effect on market confidence around the world. It would provide the strongest possible start for the new administration and Congress. It would greatly strengthen the credibility of the process of international policy coordination. Targeting such an agreement for an international summit, with full contributions by all the major countries, could help galvanize political support for the needed policy changes within each of them.

It will be vitally important for the new administration and Congress to adopt, launch, and begin to implement such a strategy within their first few months in office. Their action on the US budget is the centerpiece of the program; without it, little else may be possible. The markets and foreign officials may not wait long before rendering a judgment, via their attitudes toward the dollar, on the new administration. The Third World debt crisis could erupt at any time. The Omnibus Trade Act requires early action on a number of components of trade policy. The economic summit is already scheduled for July 1989.

It is also true that there are only a few windows of opportunity within which American governments can adopt major policy initiatives. The checks and balances of the constitutional system, particularly those between the executive branch and Congress, usually preclude dramatic change except in response to crises. The greatest opportunity tends to come in the initial stages, or "honeymoon period," of a new administration. The popular mandate from the election enables it to launch new initiatives, and the Congress will tend to give it the benefit of the doubt. Rapid action is thus necessary for both substantive and political reasons.

AMERICA IN THE WORLD ECONOMY OF THE 1990s

The proposed strategy of competitive interdependence rests on two central premises: American prosperity has become inextricably linked to the health of the world economy and to the maintenance of a strong American position in that world economy, and the United States retains the ability to pursue its interests effectively on the global scene, albeit in different ways than in the past. The strategy attempts to provide a cohesive framework for decisions by the US government on specific international economic issues.

Internally, the proposed strategy calls for a reorientation of America's economic policies, especially at the macroeconomic level but also in some microeconomic areas, much more heavily in the direction of achieving and sustaining a strong international economic and financial position. In this era of heightened dependence on the external environment and reduced (though still substantial) unilateral clout, the United States must tailor its "domestic" policies increasingly to the realities of the world economy. This is the "competitive" component of the proposed strategy. Internationally, this strategy advocates negotiating actively to promote immediate US interests and to improve the global systems of trade and finance—the "interdependence" element of the approach.

The strategy of competitive interdependence thus views any return to the "benign neglect" of the first Reagan administration (and the early years of the first Nixon administration) as extremely dangerous. It holds that a substantial expansion of the policy coordination efforts of the second Reagan administration offers considerable advantages to the United States, and thus rejects the suggestion that "the United States should now explicitly but amicably abandon the policy of international coordination of macroeconomic policy" (Feldstein 1988, 12). It rejects protectionism or more subtle versions of "managed trade" (Choate and Linger 1988), which would undermine America's central needs for a more competitive economy at home and more effective policy cooperation abroad.

The United States must be prepared to deploy its considerable leverage—arising from the appeal of its market, the role of the dollar, and its security guarantees—to pursue its goals, as all countries do. It can probably use these sources of leverage more successfully as inducements than as threats, given the specific nature of each. It can clearly do so with the greatest prospect of success within an essentially cooperative international framework, rather than in an institutional vacuum or in an environment of hostility triggered by unilateral steps of its own. The United States can also achieve its goals far more effectively if it puts its own house in order and keeps it that way by bringing its budget deficit under control, avoiding protectionist steps that close its own markets, and making its fair contributions to the financial institutions.

Explicit adoption of this strategy, and widespread communication of its premises and policy implications, are needed to produce an American foreign economic policy that is consistent across issues and over time. It is also essential to provide clear guidance to the numerous domestic actors involved—including the business community, labor, farm groups, the bureaucracy, and the media—and to other countries. If the new administration and Congress fail consciously and publicly to adopt a coherent strategic approach and stick to it, the different constellations of political actors that revolve around individual issues will inevitably produce an incoherent pattern of outcomes—some protectionist, some ignoring the external dimension, some lashing out internationally in a counterproductive manner. At a minimum, the result would be a further erosion of both US interests and US influence in the world economy. At worst, the fundamental American objectives of prosperity and stability would go unrealized and America's economy and foreign policy would both be at risk.

THE PLAN OF THE BOOK

Having summarized the proposed strategy for the new administration and Congress in this first chapter, we now turn to the underlying analyses and more detailed recommendations. They begin with the domestic economic setting (Chapter 2) and international framework (Chapter 3) that will usher in the 1990s. These chapters highlight the problems American officials will have to address, the constraints they will face, and the levers that they can deploy in response. The proposed strategy is then described in depth, beginning with the central goal of eliminating the current account deficit (Chapter 4). The strategy embraces a three-part program of macroeconomic steps by the United States and other countries, accompanied by changes in exchange rates and the international monetary system (Chapter 5); trade policy (Chapter 6); and an expanded role for the international financial institutions, particularly to address the problems of Third World debt and alliance burden sharing (Chapter 7). Chapter 8 recapitulates the key steps needed to implement the strategy, and provides a short summary of the recommendations.

2

The Economic Setting

THE RECORD OF THE 1980s

The United States has experienced six consecutive years of expansion with the creation of 17 million jobs. The economy approached full employment in 1988, with the unemployment rate declining to about 5.5 percent. Inflation has remained at relatively modest rates of about 4 percent through most of this period. Productivity growth in manufacturing has picked up considerably, rising at an average annual pace of 4 percent since 1981. Since the middle of 1987, exports have been growing at an annual rate of 20–30 percent. The trade and current account deficits declined significantly in 1988. The budget deficit fell by about $70 billion, almost 2 percent of GNP, in FY 1987.

Inflation has begun to accelerate, however. Real interest rates remain very high by historical standards. The bond and stock markets suffered big hits in 1987. The federal budget deficit and the external deficit remain extremely large. Overall productivity has only been growing by about 1 percent annually. National saving remains very low both by international and US historical standards, and private saving has dropped further in the 1980s. Average real wages, according to some measures, are lower today than in the 1970s. Income distribution became more uneven over the past decade.[1]

---

1. Real wages for production and nonsupervisory workers in 1987 were 7 percent below the average for the 1970s (Council of Economic Advisers 1988, 298). Between 1969 and 1986, each of the lowest three quintiles of the population received declining shares

Fundamental questions must be raised about the outlook for the American economy and how its international dimension relates to the overall situation.

Since the deep recession of 1982, the United States has enjoyed the longest peacetime expansion in its history. The economy boomed in 1983 and the first half of 1984, and has grown at an average rate of about 3 percent annually since then. The outlook is for continued growth into 1989 and perhaps beyond.

The expansion has been particularly noteworthy for its relatively modest rate of inflation. After reaching double digits in 1979–81, consumer price increases have averaged about 4 percent (except for a sharp fall in 1986 due to the collapse of world oil prices). Wages, which account for two-thirds of business costs, have lagged behind overall inflation. Until quite recently, capacity utilization has remained well short of the levels that have traditionally triggered an acceleration of price increases. Commodity prices, despite sporadic jumps, have generally remained depressed (with adverse effects on particular sectors, such as energy and agriculture). Oil prices have remained well below their levels of the early 1980s.

Another unique feature of this expansion is that domestic spending in the United States has far exceeded domestic production. During its six-year duration to date, Americans have consumed and invested about $700 billion more than was made available from their internal resources. This has been possible because the rest of the world has been willing and able to provide a large portion of the goods that were sought by American consumers, industrial firms, and governments (federal, state and local) and was also prepared to lend Americans the money to pay for them. This "excess" demand produced the large and growing trade deficits and the rapid buildup of foreign debt.[2]

---

of total income, while the highest quintile increased its share from 40.6 percent to 43.7 percent (*Wall Street Journal,* 21 March 1988, 1).

2. Although real wages have dropped and more people are in poverty today than in the 1970s, total consumption has risen steadily for several reasons. First, the fraction of the population that is working has risen as the baby boom has matured. Second, the fraction of working-age Americans who actually work has risen more rapidly than before. Third, government transfer payments have augmented earned income to a greater extent, while personal taxes have been reduced. Finally, the personal saving rate has fallen considerably (Friedman 1988, 154–156).

This combination of sustained growth, relatively stable prices, and external imbalances was caused by a number of developments. The sharp increase in federal budget deficits beginning in 1982 prompted a traditional Keynesian recovery from the recession.[3] A substantial relaxation of monetary policy by the Federal Reserve from the middle of 1982, despite episodes of subsequent tightening, accommodated the increase in demand (even though real interest rates remained high by both historical US and contemporary international standards). Competitive pressures triggered by deregulation in several key sectors helped loosen the traditionally close relationship between high growth and rising inflation. Excess supply in most world commodity markets, especially for oil and farm products, held prices down and sustained the expansion.

In addition, a number of factors instilled in business and labor a sense of caution that helped prevent excessive inventory buildups, wage pressures, and other potential impediments to stable recovery. Fresh memories of the sharp recession of the early 1980s and recent double-digit inflation were extremely important in this context. So was an unemployment level that remained well above the "natural" or noninflationary rate until quite recently.

International factors also played a major role. The enormous rise in the exchange rate of the dollar through 1984, by sharply cutting foreign demand for US products and directing a good deal of American demand to foreign goods, exported part of the inflationary pressure generated by the recovery.[4] Reduced import prices maintained competitive pressure on domestic prices and wages in the tradeable goods sector. The capital inflow associated with the external deficits held interest rates down by at least five percentage points (Marris 1987, 44), which supported continuing growth and avoided

3. Some analysts believe that the tax cuts in 1981 had a separate, independent effect in promoting and sustaining the recovery. See Friedman (1988) for a compelling response to this argument and for detailed analysis of many of the domestic economic issues discussed in this chapter.

4. Most estimates suggest that every 10 percent appreciation of the trade-weighted value of the dollar dampens the US price level by about 1.5 percentage points (Hooper and Lowrey 1979). The rise of 40 percent to 60 percent in the dollar from mid-1980 to early 1985, depending on the precise time period and weights chosen, thus may have limited inflation by 1 to 2 percent annually during this period (Sachs 1985, 146).

the crowding out of private investment that many had expected to result from the budget deficits. These external deficits and capital inflows permitted domestic consumption and investment to rise much faster than would have been possible given actual levels of domestic output.[5]

The policies of the other major countries reinforced these developments in the United States well into the mid-1980s. Japan and Germany, in particular, sought sharp reductions in their budget deficits, which had ballooned in the 1970s. Their domestic demand thus grew more slowly than their domestic output, and they relied on improvements in their trade balances for a considerable portion of their total economic growth. The result was huge surpluses in their external positions: Japan moved from a deficit of $10 billion in 1980 to a surplus of almost $90 billion in 1987, Germany from a deficit of $14 billion to a surplus of $45 billion. This was the reverse of the American experience, and it freed up foreign goods for Americans (see table 2.1 and figure 2.1).

Sharp cuts in government dissaving in the other major industrial countries, and the modest economic growth that ensued, also generated large pools of investable funds that were attracted by the high interest rates, political stability, and rapid growth of the United States. The resulting capital inflow satisfied the American desire to invest more than could be funded domestically and financed the huge current account deficits. The exchange rate was the primary mechanism through which these real and financial transfers took place. The dollar soared in value against the yen, the DM, and a number of other currencies as a result of the inflow of foreign funds, thereby pricing much of American industry and agriculture out of world markets and even the domestic market. Deficit America lived symbiotically with surplus Japan and Germany for several years, each reaping immediate benefits but setting the stage for major difficulties in the future.

The onset of the Third World debt crisis had similar effects. The sharp fall in foreign lending to the heavily indebted countries after 1982 required them to achieve an aggregate increase of almost $50

5. A different policy mix, with smaller budget deficits and lower interest rates, would presumably have produced a recovery from the recession of 1982 with far less deterioration in the external position of the United States.

TABLE 2.1 Changes in Real GNP and Domestic Demand, 1980–1989 *(in percent)*

	1980	1981	1982	1983	1984	1985	1986	1987	1988[e]	1989[e]
United States										
Domestic demand	−1.8	2.2	−1.9	5.1	8.7	3.8	3.7	3.0	3.0	2.7
Foreign balance	1.7	−0.2	−0.7	−1.5	−2.0	−0.6	−0.9	0.2	0.9	—
GNP	−0.2	1.9	−2.5	3.6	6.8	3.4	2.8	3.4	4.0	2.8
Japan										
Domestic demand	0.8	2.2	2.8	1.8	3.8	3.9	4.0	5.1	7.4	4.9
Foreign balance	3.4	1.5	0.3	1.5	1.3	1.1	−1.4	−0.7	−1.4	−0.7
GNP	4.3	3.7	3.1	3.3	5.0	4.8	2.5	4.2	5.8	4.2
Germany										
Domestic demand	1.1	−2.6	−2.0	2.3	2.0	0.8	3.5	3.1	3.2	2.0
Foreign balance	0.4	2.7	1.0	−0.3	1.3	1.1	−1.1	−1.2	−0.2	—
GNP	1.5	—	−1.0	1.9	3.3	1.9	2.3	1.8	2.9	1.9

e = Estimate based on current policies and exchange rates; — = negligible.

Source: IMF (1988, tables A2 and A3).

FIGURE 2.1 Current Account Balances

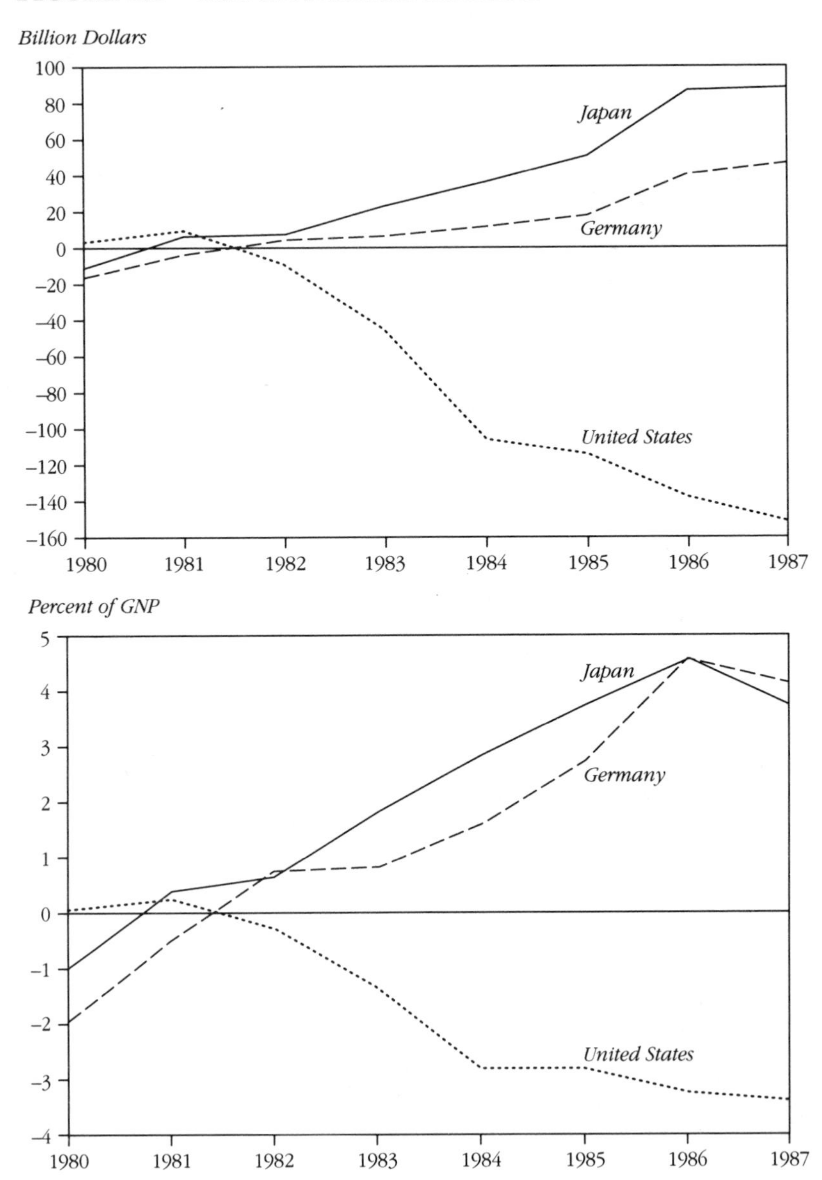

Source: IMF, *International Financial Statistics,* various issues.

billion in their trade surpluses between 1981 and 1984–85 to continue servicing their external obligations. This made still more foreign goods available for American consumers, and induced US capital that had previously been exported to remain at home.

As the expansion continued into the late 1980s, clouds began to appear on the horizon. The underlying concerns of most significance were, of course, the twin deficits (see table 2.2). The federal budget deficit grew from less than 2 percent of GNP in 1979 to more than 6 percent at its peak in 1983; it remained near that level before dropping sharply in 1987 and then planing off at about 3 percent in 1988 and 1989. These fiscal imbalances have caused a number of problems. They drain American savings, which are low in any event, away from more productive deployment in the private sector; this reduces productivity, growth, and living standards over the long run. The deficits place upward pressure on real interest rates, discouraging private investment and other interest-sensitive sectors of the economy. They levy a substantial burden of debt service on future generations, shifting consumption from the future to the present.

Perhaps most importantly, at least in the short run, the budget deficits could contribute to a significant acceleration of inflation by continuing to stimulate demand even though the economy has approached full employment and full capacity utilization. The sharp increase in net government spending was justified, on either traditional Keynesian or "supply side" grounds, to help speed the recovery from the recession of 1982. But there is no rationale for maintaining the budget deficit at or above 3 percent of GNP, or even much less, when private spending has risen to a level that approaches full utilization of domestic resources. Indeed, the budget is now further from balance than in any postwar expansion (Minarik and Penner 1988). The President and Congress have accepted this logic by agreeing on the Gramm-Rudman-Hollings timetable to eliminate the budget imbalance by FY 1993, but they have only begun to implement the policy changes required to meet that objective.

Most of these problems have been mitigated to date by the second imbalance—the current account deficit and the associated net inflow of foreign capital, which reached a peak of more than $150 billion in 1987 and whose cumulative total from 1983 through 1988 approximated $700 billion. As noted above, the growth of the fiscal

TABLE 2.2 The Twin Deficits, 1980–1992

	Budget balance				Current account balance			
	CBO baseline[a]		GRH targets[b]		Cline baseline[c]		Proposed targets[d]	
	billion dollars	percent of GNP	billion dollars	percent of GNP	billion dollars	percent of GNP	billion dollars	percent of GNP
Actual								
1980	−74	2.7			2	0.1		
1981	−79	2.6			7	0.2		
1982	−128	4.0			−9	0.3		
1983	−208	6.1			−46	1.4		
1984	−185	4.9			−107	2.8		
1985	−212	5.3			−115	2.9		
1986	−221	5.2			−139	3.3		
1987	−150	3.3			−154	3.4		
1988[e]	−155	3.2			−136	2.8		

Projected								
1989	−148	2.9	−136	2.7	−105	2.1	−105	2.1
1990	−136	2.5	−100	1.8	−115	2.1	−70	1.3
1991	−131	2.3	−64	1.1	−137	2.4	−35	0.6
1992	−126	2.0	−28	0.5	−155	2.5	0	0.0
1993	−121	1.8	0	0	n.a.	n.a.	0	0.0

n.a. = Not available.

Source: Council of Economic Advisers (1988); Congressional Budget Office (1988); International Monetary Fund (1988); Cline (forthcoming).

a. Budget deficit, on a fiscal year basis, projected by Congressional Budget Office assuming no additional policy action. For reasons noted in the text, these projections are very optimistic.

b. Budget targets established originally by the Balanced Budget and Emergency Deficit Control Act of 1985, and amended in the Balanced Budget Emergency Deficit Control Reaffirmation Act of 1987. The targets are popularly known as Gramm-Rudman-Hollings and are endorsed in this study.

c. Current account deficit projected by Cline model (forthcoming, Chapter 2) with no additional policy action and exchange rates at their fourth quarter 1987 average (with the dollar about 5 percent lower than on 13 October 1988).

d. Current account targets proposed in Chapter 4.

e. Estimated.

and current account deficits played a major role in both the initiation and the continuation of the expansion with reasonable price stability. The deficits permitted domestic demand to outpace domestic output without triggering severe inflation and have held real interest rates to lower (if historically high) levels. An assessment of the economic results and policies of the 1980s must therefore rest largely on a judgment of the wisdom of permitting these external imbalances to develop and the extent to which they can be reversed without heavy costs.

THE RISKS AHEAD

In making such an assessment, the central consideration should be the vulnerability of the American economy that results from its continued reliance on large inflows of foreign capital to finance the current account deficit. At present and foreseeable levels of the deficit, the United States will require net capital inflows of about $10 billion per month for the indefinite future. Since American investors and lenders will clearly continue to export sizable amounts of capital, the gross foreign inflow must be far greater.

If foreign private investors and monetary authorities became unwilling to invest in these magnitudes in the United States at existing interest rates and exchange rates, two things would have to occur to induce them to continue doing so. First, the dollar would have to fall, perhaps considerably. Second, interest rates in the United States would have to rise further, perhaps by as much as 3 to 5 percentage points (Marris 1987, 44, 141). The situation would be much worse if foreign investors withdrew some of the $1 trillion in liquid assets that they already hold in the United States, in addition to avoiding new commitments in the dollar. Capital flight by Americans, which could readily follow (or anticipate) withdrawals from abroad, could add significantly to the problem.[6]

The result in this scenario would be renewed inflation and possibly a sharp recession. Each 10 percent decline of the dollar tends to push

6. In technical economic terms, the *ex post* net inflow of capital must equal the current account deficit. The issue is whether foreign demand for the dollar will provide the needed inflows on an *ex ante* basis. If it does not, the key prices—the exchange rate and interest rate—must change.

prices in the United States up by about 1.5 percentage points through its direct effects on imports and import-competing domestic products; these effects could be even stronger now with the proximity of the economy to full employment and full capacity utilization (Hooper and Lowrey 1979; Sachs 1985). A fall of 20–30 percent in the dollar, in the absence of corresponding measures to limit the growth of domestic demand, could push inflation near, or even back into, double digits.

Such a rise in inflation would drive nominal interest rates up by at least as much, and perhaps even more because of the induced jump in inflationary expectations. In addition, with the economy near full employment, and inflation fears accelerating as it continues to expand faster than the growth of productive capacity, the Fed would almost certainly feel compelled to boost real interest rates to brake the dollar's fall, to contain the resulting inflation, and to reduce the risk of capital flight. Long-term rates could approach 15 percent (from about 9.5 percent now) and short-term rates could climb well into double digits (from about 7 percent now). The stock market, witnessing a renewal of inflation and higher interest rates, could dive again. The economy could slide quickly into recession with the induced drop in investment and interest-sensitive spending.

Another important consideration is that the US government would not have access to the policy tools that have traditionally enabled it to extricate the economy from recession. The large budget deficit, which would rise further due to the recession itself, would preclude any major fiscal stimulus. Monetary policy would be constrained by the runup in inflation, and possibly by continued uncertainty over the dollar. The trade stimulus that would result from the further currency depreciation would occur only with a lag, and the downturn could last for some time.

The first stages of this scenario actually played out on two occasions in 1987. In the spring, a drying up of the private capital inflow—sparked to a large extent by leaked statements by high US officials that they sought a further fall in the dollar—pushed long-term interest rates up by 3 percentage points. In the fall, fears of yet another dollar decline—reinforced on this occasion by public disputes between top American and German officials over the international adjustment effort—raised the specter of an additional rise in interest rates and led to the dramatic fall in the stock market.

To be sure, other elements were involved in these events. In the case of "Black Monday," a correction of the previous market runup was probably in order, and technical factors internal to the markets added to the severity of the decline. Moreover, both markets subsequently stabilized and even recovered to a degree; fears that their behavior presaged an early end to the expansion proved to be premature. But these events took considerable quantities of wealth out of the economy and were clearly initiated by the precarious external position of the United States. They should be interpreted as "warning shots across the bow."

In both instances, central banks intervened—spending about $120 billion to support the dollar during the course of 1987—in time to avoid lasting damage to the real economy (Bank for International Settlements 1988, 188–189). In 1988, the authorities resolved to support the dollar sufficiently to avoid renewed crises because they knew that the United States would not take the required internal adjustment actions in an election year in any event. The markets became aware of this tacit commitment, and private investors and speculators, realizing that they faced a one-way bet, bought dollars and precluded the need for much official action.

The external imbalance and dollar problems thus remained in suspended animation in 1988. Reinforced by a series of declines in the monthly US trade deficits and higher US interest rates, the dollar actually rose during much of the year, compelling the central banks to support the DM and other currencies. If the higher dollar that resulted remains in place for very long, it will of course bring an earlier end to the improvement in the US current account deficit and a further increase in the US reliance on foreign capital in the future. While relieving pressures in 1988, the dollar's rise creates future difficulties.[7]

The greatest risks to the US economy for the foreseeable future thus derive directly from the external deficit and its financial consequences. A new fall of the dollar could occur for any number of reasons: a renewed deterioration in the monthly trade numbers (which, given present policies, will probably occur in 1989); market

7. Our models suggest that, on the basis of exchange rates as of 15 August 1988 and unchanged policies, the US current account deficit would rise to almost $200 billion by 1992.

recognition of the continuing need for large amounts of foreign financing even with somewhat lower current account deficits; higher interest rates abroad; fears that the Fed would not tighten monetary policy to counter a further pickup in US inflation; internal financial instability caused by the continuing crisis of the savings and loan industry and banks in some regions of the country, particularly if another slump in oil prices causes further damage to the energy sector; or, perhaps most critically, as discussed below, expectations that the new US administration and Congress will fail to reduce the budget deficit decisively and that the external deficit will thus remain large (above $100 billion) and even start growing again. Foreign (and American) investors can easily find alternatives to dollar investments in their domestic markets or in other currencies, at least over any short- to medium-term period.

A dollar slide could now occur even more suddenly, and proceed much further than previously, because of the runup of its value in 1988. With inflation already picking up, and interest rates rising to head it off, the consequences of a fall could be even more damaging than envisaged when the risk of a "hard landing" was first contemplated.[8] The advent of higher prices and interest rates also suggests that the central cure for the external problem, a sharp cut in the budget deficit, is necessary for purely domestic reasons as well.

The alternative is to try to skate through four more years of large deficits, hoping for continuing inflows of foreign financing at exchange-rate and interest-rate levels that will not disturb the economy. It is conceivable this could work. Sustained US growth could attract investment, especially if expansion faltered in the other major countries and Third World debt continues. American interest rates might offset the costs to foreign investors of expected future declines in the dollar. The central banks could fear a hard landing by the dollar so much that, whatever their stern words, they would try to provide enough financing to head it off.

But such a course of inaction would be an enormous gamble. Each of the events cited above could cause the dollar to plunge at almost any time. The continuing buildup of foreign debt by the United

8. Stephen Marris originally outlined the hard landing scenario in "Crisis Ahead for the Dollar," *Fortune,* 26 December 1983. The view was elaborated in *Deficits and the Dollar,* 1985 and updated in 1987. See also Shultz (1985) and Volcker (1988).

States will reduce the willingness of its creditors to supply additional loans.[9] The market hits of 1987 demonstrated the potential costs of policy passivity. The risk of falling into an inflationary recession is very real.

It would also be imprudent to assume that foreign central banks will always rush to the rescue when private demand for dollars dries up. It is true that these institutions were able to run down their dollar holdings to a degree during the appreciation of 1988, offsetting some of their purchases of about $150 billion between 1986 and early 1988. It is also true that they want to avoid the results of a free fall of the dollar: financial instability, higher dollar interest rates, an American recession, capital losses on their existing dollar holdings, and renewed deterioration of their countries' price competitiveness.

Three considerations could deter the central banks from supporting the dollar, however. First, dollar purchases add to their domestic money supplies and thus tend to promote inflation (and especially inflationary expectations, as money supply targets are exceeded). Techniques for sterilizing the monetary impact of intervention are available, and they are usually effective in countering moderate levels of intervention. But the increased concerns over a possible rise in global inflation will add to the authorities' caution, particularly given their vivid memories of the two great inflations of the early and late 1970s, which were associated with massive intervention efforts to avoid a collapse of the dollar (McKinnon 1984, 47–48).

Second, the central banks are not anxious to add to their holdings of a currency that is likely to fall further. The Bundesbank was subjected to considerable domestic criticism for the losses it recorded in 1987 as a result of the dollar's fall, for example, and the resulting decline in the profits that it could transfer to the federal budget was

9. Simple portfolio theory suggests that the volume of dollar assets already acquired by many of these investors reduces their demand for more. In particular, there is evidence that some of the large Japanese institutional investors have now reached the desired level of dollar diversification and may even cut back in the future if the dollar appears headed for further depreciation. For example, Yasuhiko Ueyama, President of Sumitomo Life Insurance Company, estimates that the share of total external investment by Japanese institutional investors coming to the United States dropped from 55.3 percent to 50.5 percent in 1987 and says that the ratio is likely to shrink even more (1988, 64).

a major factor prompting the German government to enact subsequent tax increases.

Third, the foreign authorities may at some point decide it is simply imprudent to continue financing "excess" American spending and budget deficits. To be sure, they have financed large American deficits on numerous occasions during the past three decades—frequently complaining along the way and threatening to halt the process, but revealing little desire actually to do so. Nevertheless, their actions or threats were sufficiently persuasive to induce the United States to launch major adjustment initiatives in 1971 (to devalue the dollar preemptively) and in 1978 (to stabilize the dollar after a precipitous fall). At a minimum, they will certainly require—as the price of continued dollar support—evidence of a credible effort by the United States to bring its imbalances under control, and perhaps much more extensive sharing of the exchange risks by the United States itself.

The policies adopted by the new American government will have a major influence on the attitudes of both private investors and officials abroad. Adequate financing could be sustained if there were an early indication of serious action to cut the external deficit and foreign borrowing requirements, mainly by cutting the domestic budget deficit. But inaction that implied four more years of large imbalances could bring an early attack on the dollar. A hard landing would be virtually certain at some point during the four-year term of the new administration. It will thus have a large stake in the rapid development and implementation of a policy package that offers a credible prospect of correcting the external imbalance and steadily reducing the need for foreign funds.

A failure to address the international imbalances effectively could also trigger a breakdown of the international trading system, with further severe costs to the US economy (and the world economy as a whole). The emergence of these imbalances, and especially the huge currency misalignments that accompanied them, were a major cause of the erosion of the global trading regime in the 1980s (see Chapter 3). Indeed, the potential for major protectionist initiatives in the Congress in the fall of 1985 was the proximate cause of the reversal of the Reagan administration's basic approach toward the dollar, international policy coordination, and trade (Funabashi 1988).

Since that time, the United States has basically pursued a macroeconomic strategy to correct its external deficit, encompassing budget reduction in the United States, faster growth abroad, and a significant decline in the value of the dollar. The fall of the dollar and the resulting reduction of the US trade deficit checked at least the most extreme protectionist pressures.[10] However, if the deficits were to fail to come down substantially, and stay down, during the next few years, the political message would be that the macroeconomic strategy had failed—whatever the actual reason for the result, such as a continuing US failure to deal with the budget deficit or continuing dollar overvaluation. Those who have advocated the macroeconomic course—former Treasury Secretary Baker, Federal Reserve Chairmen Volcker and Greenspan, nearly all the world's governments and most private economists—would be discredited.

It is virtually axiomatic that protectionism would escalate again, at least in the United States. Few alternatives are available that would appear to offer any prospect of substantially reducing the trade and current account deficits, and the financial risks that they entail, within a reasonable period of time. It is thus likely that Congress, perhaps encouraged both by the business community and by labor, would again seize the initiative in trade policy (as it did with the Omnibus Trade Act) and push the United States in a sharply protectionist direction. An import surcharge, or similar across-the-board measures, would be possible in such an environment (as they were in much less critical conditions in 1971).[11]

Such measures would almost certainly fail to provide any lasting reduction in the trade deficit. Their implementation would of course impose heavy costs on the world economy and on the United States itself, and might even trigger a hard landing of the dollar because of their adverse impact on market confidence. The inevitable emu-

10. The decline in the trade deficit in volume terms, at an annual rate of $70 billion from the second quarter of 1986 through the second quarter of 1988, is probably more important in this context than the much smaller reduction in the current account deficit in dollar terms (an annual rate of $36 billion from the third quarter of 1987 through the second quarter of 1988). The volume numbers more accurately reflect levels of output, market shares and jobs—and thus political pressure for protection. (The current account deficit in dollar terms defines the external financing requirement.) The volume decline in the deficit was probably a major factor in permitting the Omnibus Trade Act to be stripped of its most protectionist features.

11. The costs of an import surcharge are discussed in Chapter 6, 130–131.

lation and retaliation of other countries could destroy much of the open international trading system that has been so crucial to postwar prosperity. The stakes involved in resolving the US deficit promptly and constructively thus include the future of the world trading system, as well as the financial stability and economic prospects of the United States itself.

THE LONG-TERM OUTLOOK

The long-term economic objectives of the United States include a steady improvement in living standards and an equitable distribution of income. There are disquieting signs on both fronts. According to some measures, as already noted, average real wages and the distribution of income have worsened over the past two decades. Productivity growth is the key to increasing real income, and its lag is of particular concern. The most important single component of productivity growth is technological change, much of which is embodied in new investment, which in turn rests heavily on the availability of savings to finance additional and more efficient output.

It is here that some of the deepest concerns about the long-term strength of the economy emerge. America's saving rate is already the lowest of the major industrial countries (see table 2.3). The level of US investment was actually lower in 1987 than in 1979. The current expansion was made possible only by the importation of $700 billion in savings from abroad. But this heavy borrowing has deeply exacerbated the long-run problem by shifting the United States from being the world's largest creditor country, as recently as 1983, to the world's largest debtor country by 1986. The net debtor position will be about $500 billion at the end of 1988 and rise to at least $750 billion in the early 1990s before there is any possibility that it could level off. Net foreign debt on the order of $1 trillion is likely in the absence of an adjustment effort as proposed in this volume.[12]

The United States is not like Brazil, Mexico, or other debtor countries of the Third World (or even like Australia, Canada, and

12. There are serious shortcomings in the official data on both the asset and liability sides of the international balance sheet of the United States, but the balance is probably about right and the rapid trend deterioration is unambiguous. See Islam (1988, 8–11).

TABLE 2.3 Saving Rates in the United States and Its Major Competitors *(domestic savings as a percent of GDP)*

	United States	Japan	Germany	United Kingdom	France	Korea	Taiwan
1973	20.4	38.1	28.2	19.7	26.8	23.3	34.6
1974	19.3	36.6	26.5	17.0	25.2	20.6	31.7
1975	17.8	32.8	22.6	16.9	23.7	18.1	27.3
1976	18.4	32.6	23.8	18.8	23.3	23.2	33.0
1977	18.9	32.5	23.4	20.3	24.6	26.5	33.3
1978	20.2	32.6	23.6	20.7	24.5	28.2	35.1
1979	19.9	31.6	24.0	20.1	24.3	27.6	34.5
1980	18.4	31.3	23.0	19.2	23.0	23.4	33.1
1981	19.0	32.0	21.7	18.1	20.9	23.7	32.4
1982	16.0	30.9	22.1	17.5	20.0	24.2	30.4
1983	15.2	30.1	22.4	17.4	19.7	27.8	32.0
1984	16.9	31.1	22.9	17.0	19.8	30.5	33.0
1985	16.1	31.9	23.1	18.3	19.4	31.1	32.3
1986	15.4	32.5	24.7	16.6	20.1	34.9	36.3
1987	15.0	32.8	24.7	16.3	20.1	37.0	n.a.

n.a. = Not available.
Note: Domestic saving rates are derived by subtracting domestic consumption (private and government) from GDP and dividing by GDP.

Source: International Monetary Fund, *International Financial Statistics,* various issues.

other industrial country debtors). The United States borrows primarily in its own currency, so it could never "run out of foreign exchange" and be forced to declare a moratorium on debt service payments. Precisely because its foreign creditors carry the exchange rate risk, however, key prices in the US economy—notably the exchange rate and the interest rate—have become acutely vulnerable to decisions made abroad, and thus so have growth and price stability. A withdrawal of foreign funds, or even a cessation of new lending while the current account is in deficit, could trigger a sharp rise in inflation and a recession at almost any time. The mechanisms are different, but the consequences are ultimately the same for any debtor country when its credit runs out.

Even if such runs on the dollar could be permanently avoided, the debtor status of the United States will make it much harder to achieve the country's fundamental economic goals. To deter capital withdrawals and attract new funding, interest rates will have to remain higher—perhaps much higher—than would otherwise be warranted by domestic considerations (A. Solomon 1987). Satisfactory levels of investment will thus be even harder to achieve. Foreign savings, even if available at the higher price, will add further to the debt itself and thus the risk of external shocks. The United States may have fallen into a vicious cycle from which extrication will be quite difficult.

In addition, a higher portion of national output will have to be permanently transferred abroad to service the debt owed to foreigners. If the net external debt were to level off at $750 billion, the shift from net investment earnings of over $30 billion in 1981 to net payments of about $30 billion by 1992 would represent an annual loss of about 1 percent of GNP at that time.[13] This will reduce, on a permanent basis, the availability of resources either to support additional investment or to satisfy consumer demand.

America's future standard of living will thus be reduced by three external effects: the need to bring spending back within the bounds of domestic production, the permanent cost of servicing the foreign debt, and the decline in the purchasing power of the dollar that will be needed to achieve both (Lawrence 1988, 23). The inflationary recession that could be triggered by a collapse of the dollar would have damaging effects on the distribution of national income, because the poorest groups in any society are least able to defend themselves against inflation and are usually the first to lose their jobs. Long-run as well as immediate considerations highlight the urgency of limiting these costs by shoring up America's international economic and financial position as quickly as possible to reverse the trade and financial deterioration that accelerated so sharply in the 1980s.

Moreover, the United States was experiencing a sharp increase in its structural dependence on the world economy even before the advent of huge current account deficits. Exports and imports of goods and services rose from 10 percent of GNP in 1963 to over 22 percent in 1988. Until the sharp fall of farm exports in the early 1980s, almost one-half of American agricultural production was sold abroad.

---

13. Islam (1988, 14). The costs to the United States of net debtor status are analyzed comprehensively in Bergsten and Islam (forthcoming).

The extensive international exposure of US manufacturing heightens the importance of correcting the external imbalances, in structural terms, because of the central role of manufacturing in the economy. Almost one-quarter of all manufactured goods are now exported. It has been estimated that 70 percent of all US industrial output is directly or indirectly subject to foreign competition (Choate and Linger 1988, 89). About 90 percent of the increase of $132 billion in the trade deficit from 1981 to 1987 was accounted for by manufactured products, and most of the corresponding improvement needed over the next few years will have to come from that sector as well.

According to one study, manufacturing was responsible for more than 95 percent of private research and development expenditures in 1984, a crucial element in maintaining and improving productivity and the standard of living (Dornbusch, Poterba, and Summers 1988, 8). Labor productivity in manufacturing has been growing at an annual rate of about 4 percent in the 1980s, compared with less than 1 percent for the rest of the economy. Manufacturing wages are about 10 percent higher than in other sectors. Manufacturing is an important customer for the services sector.[14] A successful export-led manufacturing boom could increase the sector's share of GNP by a full percentage point by 1995 (Lawrence 1988, 32), and thereby strengthen the American economy in a number of ways.

THE POLICY AGENDA

Longer-term considerations thus reinforce the short-term need for the new administration and Congress to devote the highest priority to improving the country's international economic and financial position. The future of American living standards, as well as the more immediate stability and continued expansion of the economy, has become inextricably tied to America's global performance. This reality has significant implications for the basic philosophy with

14. A recent Office of Technology Assessment (OTA) study estimated that 6.5 million services jobs in 1984 were "tightly linked" to manufacturing and that a total of 27.7 million jobs (including 1.8 million involved in natural resources production), nearly one-third of the nonagricultural total, were directly or indirectly involved in manufacturing (OTA 1988, 53–54).

which the country must approach its role in the world, as well as for a host of specific policy decisions.

History clearly reveals that there is no permanent escape from such international imbalances. The rest of the world will simply not finance any country on acceptable terms forever, as the United Kingdom can attest from its experience from the 1920s through the 1960s, and as the United States itself should have learned in the early and late 1970s. The only issue is how and when the adjustments will take place; whether the country and its partners abroad will act to address the imbalances preemptively, or whether they will wait for market hits (like those in 1987, but probably much more severe) and accept long-term economic erosion. A failure to take preemptive steps usually makes it necessary to adopt stronger reactive measures later, when the situation has worsened, and when the costs to incumbent governments are much greater.

America's economic successes in the 1980s were made possible by borrowing against the future from the rest of the world. The growth of domestic spending substantially exceeded the growth of domestic output, a relationship that will have to be reversed for some time to correct the external imbalance. It will be necessary to close the gap between the country's low saving rate and the levels of private investment required to boost productivity growth and the standard of living without going further into debt to foreigners. American industry will have to orient itself increasingly toward export markets to enable the country to continue growing while stopping the build-up of foreign debt. The shift of the United States to net debtor status may in fact turn out to be the most enduring legacy of the 1980s.

Fortunately, there is no longer any contradiction between the policies that are needed to pursue the country's domestic and international economic objectives. With the advent of full employment and the related revival of inflation fears, restraint in domestic spending—primarily through large and steady cuts in the federal budget deficit—are called for by both sets of goals. Furthermore, both the long-term and more immediate needs of the economy demand a similar approach.

A number of structural elements in the economy must also be reassessed in light of the overwhelming need to ensure productivity growth and an internationally competitive economy in the 1990s and beyond. The educational system is the key to the human resource base of the nation. The flexibility and efficiency of the labor markets are crucial. As noted above, there is doubt over the adequacy of present incentives to save. Private investment must be spurred to create new productive capacity and innovation in commercially competitive products and processes. Industry itself must take a longer-run view, stress the product quality and servicing that have become the hallmarks of other countries, and make much more aggressive efforts to export.

The payoff from changes in these areas will only come over an extended period of time, and these topics range far beyond the scope of this book. But the salience of the problems posed here suggests that they deserve priority attention. All of them will affect the potential level of the American standard of living during the coming decades. Internationally, these structural elements will significantly determine the extent to which the United States achieves and maintains a sustainable position without relying on a steady decline in the value of the dollar.

There are a number of other longer-term issues that are of great significance to the US economy and have important international dimensions but are less urgent and thus not addressed in this volume. Energy policy is perhaps the most important. Environmental policy is another. Assistance for the poorest countries is a central concern both for humanitarian and economic reasons. It may be necessary to work out new international arrangements to deal with microeconomic issues such as taxes and antitrust.[15] We do not mean to slight these issues, but we have chosen to focus on the more immediate agenda for the new administration and Congress.

CAN AMERICA COMPETE?

Before addressing the policy changes that are needed soon, it is essential to answer a fundamental question that is frequently raised

15. Building perhaps on the agreement reached by several of the major financial centers in 1988 to adopt uniform capital requirements for their financial institutions. A specific proposal to begin negotiating a "GATT for Investment," which would address a number of such issues within the context of foreign direct investment and multinational enterprises, is included in Chapter 6.

in both the United States and abroad: Can America compete? Do the structural concerns just cited suggest that American industry and labor will be unable to restore balance in the country's international position even with the adoption of appropriate macroeconomic policies and much greater attention to underlying sectoral needs? A negative answer suggests steady and inexorable future decline, while a positive answer offers hope that constructive policies can in fact ensure American strength in the world economy during the 1990s.

Despite the economy's problems, there are compelling reasons to believe that American industry will be able to achieve the needed adjustment if macroeconomic policies in the United States and abroad are set right and supported by the specific steps included in our proposed program.[16] As recently as the late 1970s, before the dollar soared and priced many American goods out of world markets, the United States in fact enjoyed export-led growth. During that period, American exports grew twice as fast as world trade. Market shares were regained in every manufactured goods sector and in every geographic region, in some cases returning to the level of the 1960s. This occurred despite the rapid trade progress of Japan and the emergence of the NICs. The US current account improved by over $20 billion between 1977–78 and 1980–81, moving into surplus, despite an increase of almost $40 billion in the cost of energy imports during the second oil shock. American industry was competing quite well less than a decade ago, just prior to the macroeconomic disturbances that triggered the large reversal of America's position in the world economy.

In the intervening period, which included deep recession and dollar overvaluation, the productivity of the manufacturing sector in the United States grew at an average annual rate of 4 percent. This is considerably higher than the rate of previous decades (see table 2.4). It is higher than the rate of major competitors such as Canada, Germany, and France and represents a much smaller gap vis-à-vis Japan than in previous decades. Manufacturing will have to provide the great bulk of the needed improvement in the US trade balance, as noted above, so its performance is encouraging. Aggregate measures showing that total US productivity has been growing at only 1

16. See also Lawrence (1984).

TABLE 2.4 **Changes in Manufacturing Productivity in the United States and Its Major Competitors**
(average annual percentage change)

	United States	Japan	Canada	France	Germany	United Kingdom
1981	2.2	3.7	4.8	3.1	2.2	5.1
1982	2.2	6.1	−4.5	7.0	1.4	6.1
1983	5.8	5.4	7.2	2.6	5.9	8.5
1984	5.4	7.2	10.8	3.0	3.8	5.5
1985	5.2	5.6	2.5	3.1	3.9	3.6
1986	3.7	1.7	−0.3	2.4	1.7	2.8
1987	2.8	4.1	1.8	3.7	1.3	6.9
Average, 1961–70	3.0	17.9	4.9	9.1	7.7	4.4
Average, 1971–75	3.0	7.1	3.4	5.4	5.3	3.6
Average, 1976–80	1.8	7.1	2.2	4.6	3.9	1.4
Average, 1981–87	3.9	4.8	3.2	3.6	2.9	5.5

Source: Bureau of Labor Statistics, "Current Labor Statistics," *Monthly Labor Review*, August 1988.

percent annually, due to the slow progress in services, are misleading, because most service products are not traded and have no direct bearing on the country's international competitiveness.

Perhaps the most compelling evidence of the potential strength of American industry, however, comes from the actual performance of American exports once the decline of the dollar had time to affect product prices. Since the middle of 1987, these exports have been growing at annual rates of 20–30 percent (depending on the precise time period one considers and whether volume or value figures are used). World trade has been rising at about 5–7 percent in volume terms, so the recovery of market share by US exporters is extremely impressive. This has occurred despite substantial growth of domestic demand in the United States and, especially in the earlier part of the period, modest growth in many of its major markets (both industrial and developing) abroad. It has occurred despite the less-than-expected pass-through of currency appreciation into higher goods prices, at least in the case of Japan, and despite the strong efforts of many foreign companies to hold their market shares.

There is obviously no room for complacency, but the underlying competitive position of the US economy seems strong, and has improved in recent years.[17] The prospects are thus good for restoring a solid international economic and financial position for the United States if it can adopt appropriate policies of its own and win sufficient cooperation from abroad. We will turn to an assessment of those policies after considering the global framework within which they will be pursued.

17. Nye (1988, 129) makes the same point regarding the international security position of the United States: "It is important not to mistake the short-term problems arising from the Reagan period's borrowed prosperity for a symptom of long-term American decline."

3

The Global Framework

The global framework within which the United States will address these issues adds further to their complexity. Four related changes of great significance have occurred over the past generation: the globalization of markets; the rise to world-class competitive status of a substantial number of countries; the related decline of America's relative international economic power (though not its absolute strength); and the erosion of the postwar international economic system. Some of these developments have important implications for the overall foreign policy of the United States, as well as for its economic prospects.

THE GLOBALIZATION OF MARKETS

Over the past quarter century, markets have become truly global for most goods, many services, and especially for financial instruments of all types. World product trade quadrupled while world output "only" tripled. According to this measure, international economic integration rose by one-third. The international openness of the United States has grown even more rapidly, as noted in Chapter 2, doubling over the same period.

The most dramatic increase in globalization has occurred in financial markets. It is estimated that an average $420 billion crossed the world's foreign exchanges each day in 1987, of which more than 90 percent represented financial transactions unrelated to trade or investment.[1] Much of this activity takes place in the so-called "Euromarkets," markets outside the country whose currency is used.

This pervasive growth in market interpenetration makes it increasingly difficult for any country to avoid substantial external impacts on its economy. In particular, massive capital flows can push exchange rates away from levels that accurately reflect competitive relationships among nations if national economic policies or performances diverge in the short run. The rapid dissemination rate of new technologies speeds the pace at which countries must adjust to external events. Smaller, more open countries (such as the Netherlands and Switzerland) long ago gave up the illusion of domestic policy autonomy. But even the largest and most apparently self-contained economies, including the United States, are now significantly affected by the international economy.

To be sure, virtually all countries on occasion attempt to resist these external pressures. Indeed, increases in economic interdependence intensify national efforts to escape the world economy's reach and retain freedom of action (Geiger 1988). Countries can even succeed in doing so for a time, particularly if their dependence is less pronounced. The United States, as noted in Chapter 2, was able to export part of the inflationary pressure emanating from its rapid recovery in 1983–84 through the sharp appreciation of the dollar. It has also negotiated export restraints with major foreign suppliers to try to limit the decline of domestic industries such as textiles and apparel, steel, automobiles, and, more recently, semiconductors.

These examples reveal, however, that efforts to resist the forces of market globalization can succeed only partially and for limited periods of time. The dollar overvaluation, which exported inflationary pressures and enabled American spending to exceed domestic production for a time, also produced the massive trade deficits that turned the United States into the world's largest debtor country and rendered its economy dependent on attracting $10–15 billion of foreign capital each month. Import controls increased the competitiveness of the main foreign rivals of the protected American industries by enabling those rivals to raise their prices and capture large windfall profits.[2] In some cases, the controls also caused the domestic industries

1. Estimate by Morgan Stanley cited in *Forbes*, 22 August 1988, 69–72.

2. Virtually all recent US trade controls for major industries have been administered

to permit a sharp decline in their own competitiveness (as with steel in 1969–74) and hurt other American industries by driving up the prices of imported inputs (as with the auto industry, which was hurt by the steel quotas, and the computer industry, which has suffered from the recent semiconductor restraints).

The overwhelming message of market globalization is that living standards of countries that seek to resist the tide will decline relative to others, and perhaps even in absolute terms. The benefits of global markets are simply too great to forgo, especially when one's neighbors and competitors take advantage of them. Countries that have traditionally relied heavily on government intervention in their economies, ranging from France and Japan to key developing countries (such as Brazil and Mexico), and even to the communist giants, now embrace internationalization to an increasing extent. Those few that have held out, including the USSR until quite recently, are in economic shambles. Even when international economic engagement levies sharp blows, as it has in Latin America throughout this decade, the response has typically been to initiate domestic reforms to expand that engagement rather than retreat from it.

Market globalization of course correlates highly with increased reliance on the price mechanism. History demonstrates that it is extremely difficult for a national economy to function effectively without a heavy reliance on markets; the great complexity of the world economy entirely rules out any alternative. Economic internationalization has thus been both an important driving force and a consequence of the increased orientation toward market forces throughout the world. The Reagan administration effectively promoted and expanded these trends, and they clearly produce a global environment that is congenial to American philosophy.

These developments have several important implications for the United States. One is that the United States cannot for long escape the internal consequences of external instability, whether the latter

---

by the exporting country in the form of "voluntary" restraint arrangements (VRAs). These market-sharing agreements enable the foreign firms to set the price of the product and thereby capture the scarcity rents created by the quantitative trade restrictions, which have totaled billions of dollars annually for some of the major industries involved (autos, steel, textiles and apparel). See Bergsten, et al. (1987) and the further discussion in Chapter 6.

is triggered by events largely outside its control (such as the oil shocks in the 1970s) or by actions of its own (such as the budget deficits of the 1980s). This highlights the need for taking full account of external factors, and the domestic repercussions of the international impact of internal actions, in setting US economic policy. At the microeconomic level, it requires effective governmental programs to ease the adjustment of firms and workers that are adversely affected by rapid changes in trade flows. It also means that direct controls over international capital flows are no longer a viable policy option for insulating a country from outside influences. The Bretton Woods charter explicitly envisaged capital controls, and the United States employed them to defend the dollar in the 1960s.[3] But the globalization of financial markets, especially in conjunction with the key currency role of the dollar, renders such efforts virtually inconceivable today.

THE RISE OF OTHER COUNTRIES

The second key change in the global setting facing the United States is the increased economic capability of a large number of other countries. World economic power has become more widely diffused and American hegemony is gone forever. At the same time, the pluralization of the new structure precludes the rise of a new hegemon. This leaves the United States as the strongest single country, with enough "veto power" to block the initiatives of others. But collective action, by at least a small group of the most important actors, is now required to achieve positive changes in international economic policies and arrangements.

Europe led the revival of multipolarity with its postwar recovery in the 1950s and the development of the Common Market in the 1960s. It has become the world's largest trading unit. After a period of so-called "Europessimism" in the late 1970s and early 1980s, European leaders have resolved to "complete the internal market" by 1992. An integrated European market would encompass more

3. The Interest Equalization Tax and Voluntary Credit Restraints (on capital exports by banks and companies) were the core of the Kennedy-Johnson balance-of-payments programs in 1963, 1965, and 1968.

than 320 million people and would have a larger economic output than the United States. Successful achievement of this goal could trigger a renewed burst of European economic vitality and self-confidence, further enhancing its international economic clout.[4] Germany alone is the world's largest exporting country.

The creation of a European central bank and common currency, now widely discussed in Europe, could enable Europe to extend its current co-leadership role with the United States and Japan from trade policy into other arenas. This could especially be the case in the financial area, since the combined monetary reserves of the EC countries swamp those of all other regions (even when the large US gold stock is valued at market prices).

Japan rose dramatically into global economic prominence with double-digit growth rates in the 1960s and the development of world-class industries by the early 1970s. Despite its enormous dependence on energy imports, Japan adjusted much more quickly and effectively than any other major country to the two oil shocks of the 1970s. It largely avoided the world recession of 1982. Since 1986, in perhaps its most impressive performance to date, Japan has adjusted to a near doubling in the dollar value of the yen by shifting with remarkable speed from the export-led growth of the early 1980s to a domestic-led expansion that has produced a burst of rapid growth despite the steady decline of its trade balance in real terms (Balassa and Noland 1988).

Japan has become the world's largest creditor country, with projected net assets abroad of over $300 billion at the end of 1988—a larger creditor position, even in real terms, than ever enjoyed by the United States. At present exchange rates, Japan enjoys a higher per capita income than the United States. Its technology, manufacturing firms, and financial institutions are world leaders in many sectors.

A number of OPEC countries, particularly in the Persian Gulf region, came to prominence in the 1970s and early 1980s with the

4. An internal study of the potential effects of completing the internal market, the Cecchini report, estimated that removal of remaining barriers could increase GDP by 4.5 to 7 percent over 6 years and add 2–5 millon new jobs, depending upon whether a passive or an accommodative macroeconomic policy was followed. See the March 1988 issue of *European Economy*, which summarizes the results of the multivolume study.

two sharp rises in the price of oil and the resulting large increases in their financial capabilities. Several newly industrialized countries, primarily in East Asia but also in Latin America, before the onset of the debt crisis, became significant global actors in the late 1970s and early 1980s.

The United States must therefore take a growing number of countries into consideration in its international economic dealings, and it must increasingly share power with them. At the same time, however, each of these new economic powers has significant limitations that preclude it, at least for the foreseeable future, from replacing the United States as the leader of the system.

Europe is still a collection of very different countries that operate externally as a single unit only on most trade issues. Germany, its largest individual component, has an economy only one-fourth as large as the United States; depends on exports for about one-third of its total output and is thus incapable of fully independent action; and, as former Chancellor Helmut Schmidt never tired of recalling, "is the size of Oregon."[5] The United Kingdom, despite the global leadership aspirations of Prime Minister Margaret Thatcher, an economic renaissance during the 1980s, and strong financial markets, remains a middle-income country with high unemployment, deep structural problems, and a weak underlying current account position.

Japan is the most plausible successor to the United States, and will certainly play a growing leadership role in some areas. For all its strengths, however, Japan has several fundamental weaknesses. It remains almost wholly dependent on imports for energy, other raw materials, and most of its food. Its modest geographical size and its remoteness from major trading partners, even in an age of rapid communication and transportation, are relative disadvantages. Its domestic emphasis on painstaking consensus-building, its penchant for pragmatism rather than ideology, and its lack of interest in exporting its own ideas and institutions have made it a follower rather than a leader in international affairs throughout the postwar period. Japan's lack of extensive military power also weakens its global influence.[6] Like Germany, its security dependence on the

5. See Bergsten (1975, 185–191) for an analysis of the importance of "aloofness" in gauging a country's international economic power.

United States and memories of World War Two decrease the likelihood that it will play a dominant role.

OPEC and the NICs are too small, too dependent on external markets, and too weak in noneconomic terms to assume positions of global leadership. The OPEC countries, in addition, remain dependent on a single product whose price fluctuates widely. Similarly, the vulnerability to global growth trends and financial conditions of even the largest Latin American countries has been starkly displayed in the 1980s. A widespread outbreak of protectionism could substantially weaken the Asian NICs.

THE RELATIVE ECONOMIC DECLINE OF THE UNITED STATES

The United States is therefore not in the position of past hegemons, vulnerable to being overtaken and pushed into second-class status by a new global leader. Its dependence on external events, while growing rapidly, is much less than was the case for its predecessors—most recently the United Kingdom, early this century.[7] There is no plausible successor waiting in the wings, as was the United States itself during the closing decades of the British Empire. The United States need anticipate neither the anguish nor the comfort of giving way to another dominant country. Indeed, as noted earlier, the United States retains the power to block virtually any conceivable international economic initiative undertaken by others.[8]

---

6. As the military weakness of the United States prior to World War One limited its global role despite rapidly rising economic strength (Kennedy 1987). Nye (1988, 118–119) notes that "Japan has chosen the strategy of a trading state rather than of a military power."

7. At its peak in the 1920s, British exports of goods and services reached 30 percent of total output whereas the US ratio is about one-third as high. Britain's net creditor position peaked in 1913 at 180 percent of GNP and produced 7–8 percent of total national income, whereas the maximum US ratios were 15 percent and 1 percent, respectively. See Matthews, Feinstein, and Odling-Smee (1982, 433); Council of Economic Advisers (1988, 248–249); and Bergsten and Islam (forthcoming).

8. Nye (1988) rejects the historical analogies of "imperial overstretch," drawn by Kennedy (1987) between the United States and earlier world leaders, on other grounds as well: that the share of the US economy devoted to military spending is much smaller and has changed little since the 1950s, and that it is unclear whether such spending is a drag on a country's economy.

It is also critical to distinguish between *absolute* and *relative* economic positions. In absolute terms, the American standard of living has continued to rise throughout the postwar period (although, as noted in Chapter 2, a recent slowdown in its expansion has raised important questions about productivity growth and other fundamental elements of the economy). The rapid growth of other countries has contributed to the American improvement. Since the growth of others was a major policy objective of the United States throughout the postwar period, there is considerable irony in the dismay now expressed by some over the results.

It is the relative decline of the United States that is more important in terms of the country's ability to work its will in international encounters.[9] However, the United States can still exert considerable influence on other countries through its own economic actions (Nau 1984–85). The fact that world interest rates tend to rise when interest rates go up in the United States indicates the continued dominance of the dollar in international financial transactions. Reflecting America's continued weight in the world economy, several countries felt compelled to cut their marginal tax rates on personal income, to head off the risk of a "brain drain," after the United States cut its rates in 1981 and again in 1986.

It is equally clear, however, that the United States cannot dictate global outcomes. Its "positive power" is no longer sufficient to compel most countries to accept its views on many issues, or to induce them to do so with financial and other rewards. One indication of the relative decline of American power is the inability of the United States to achieve agreement on some of the major international economic initiatives that it has launched during the past few years. The US failure was nearly total in the effort to start a new round of multilateral trade negotiations at the GATT Ministerial meeting in November 1982. US proposals that the G-7 countries commit themselves to "automatic" policy adjustments triggered by "objective" economic indicators were rejected at the Tokyo Summit in 1986, and the actual results of the policy coordination process pursued fervently by the United States since late 1985 have been meager.

9. Even in relative terms, most of the decline in America's global position occurred before the 1980s. During this decade, GDP has grown as rapidly in the United States as in the rest of the world and the US share of GDP among the G-7 countries has risen (Bosworth and Lawrence forthcoming).

Even in the IDB, traditionally a US preserve, recent efforts to secure veto power over individual loan decisions have produced stalemate rather than victory. The sweeping US proposal for the elimination of all government supports for agriculture by 2000 seems destined to fail, at least in this extreme form.

Pluralistic management of international economic affairs has become necessary. It has already been essential to the American successes in international economic negotiations during the past few years: the Bonn Summit package of 1978; the dollar support program of the same year; the Plaza Agreement to bring down the dollar in 1985; the 1987 Louvre Accord to set "reference ranges" for the major currencies; and the "Baker Plan" for Third World debt. While the United States remains the largest single power, with considerable ability to influence world events and the policies of other countries, it now must rely on cooperation with others for most major initiatives and for a good deal of the day-to-day management of the system. The United States must provide active leadership to achieve international outcomes that promote its interests, but it cannot dictate.

America's Levers

Within this framework, the United States will have to pursue its goals by using both carrots and sticks with great skill. There are three main avenues through which the United States can exercise leverage: its market for imports (and perhaps for foreign investment); its central financial position due to the key currency role of the dollar; and its status as military defender of its main economic partners.

The first lever derives from America's continuing position as the world's largest market—with imports of over $400 billion in 1987, far more than any other country or region (when intra-European trade is excluded from the EC total, as it should be for these purposes). On the positive side, offers of greater access to the American market can be extremely useful in international negotiations, as revealed most recently in the US–Canada Free Trade Agreement (FTA). To be meaningful in the future, such offers would have to promise either preferred access (as with Canada and Israel) or reductions in long-standing barriers in sensitive sectors (such as agriculture and textiles).

On the negative side, threats of market closure can also have considerable impact. This is especially true for countries that depend heavily on the American market, such as Japan and the Asian NICs. Some leverage may be obtained by offering commitments to avoid future restrictions, either on a global basis (by pledging not to impose an import surcharge) or for specific countries (as in the FTA with Canada).

The second major US lever is provided by the dollar. As demonstrated in recent years, American threats to drive the dollar down are almost always credible because of the sensitivity of the markets to a few words from the Secretary of the Treasury, let alone publicized dollar sales by the Fed. These threats can induce other countries to pursue alternative adjustment policies, such as faster growth in their own economies.

Correspondingly, an American willingness to stabilize the dollar is usually valued highly by other countries, who want to halt the appreciation of their own currencies, and can be used to elicit concessions. In April 1987, Japan explicitly committed itself to expand its fiscal stimulus program in exchange for a US stabilization pledge (Funabashi 1988, 189). Foreign proposals to "reform the international monetary system" are sometimes aimed primarily at preventing further falls in the dollar, so commitments by the United States may provide it with substantial leverage. Agreements to share the foreign exchange risks of defending the dollar in the currency markets can also supply leverage, as was the case with Roosa bonds in the early 1960s and with Carter bonds in 1978–79.[10]

Third, the global security position of the United States also provides leverage on economic issues. The United States can help defend countries in return for economic favors. Some of the implicit commitments made to Saudi Arabia, Kuwait, and other countries in the Persian Gulf region in both the 1970s and 1980s undoubtedly helped persuade those countries to maintain adequate flows of oil and to avoid disruptive financial maneuvers. Conversely, the United States can threaten to withdraw at least part of its defense umbrella

10. These were US Treasury securities denominated in foreign currencies. They are discussed further in Chapter 5.

in the absence of economic cooperation. This kind of threat, buttressed by congressional pressure, helped induce Germany to conclude military offset agreements with the United States in the 1960s.

More subtly, countries that rely on the United States for their security but seem to benefit economically at its expense can anticipate the rise of domestic political pressures in the United States to limit the US defense commitment to them. Administrations have on occasion linked security and economic issues directly, in part to head off congressional pressure, as with the offset agreements with Germany and the reversion of Okinawa to Japan in the early 1970s.[11]

When considering the negative use of all three of these levers, the United States must recognize that each represents a double-edged sword. New trade barriers increase domestic inflationary and anti-competitive pressures, invite foreign retaliation, and contribute to the systemic erosion described in the next section. Deliberate depreciation of the dollar can go too far too fast, triggering higher inflation and interest rates—the hard landing described in Chapter 2. Troop withdrawals or other reductions in security ties, or even widespread anticipation of these, could weaken US defense, destabilize particular regions of the world, and encourage the Soviet Union to resume a more adventurous course. They could also cost the United States more money both in the short run, if the troops were redeployed domestically, and in the long run, if security conditions deteriorated as a result and led to a subsequent military buildup. Thus, the use of any of these three levers could weaken, rather than strengthen the international economic position and bargaining clout of the United States.

On the other hand, the carrots that the United States can offer in international economic negotiations frequently promote American as well as foreign interests. While it may levy adjustment costs on particular firms and workers, trade liberalization is demonstrably beneficial for the economy as a whole. Currency stabilization, once equilibrium levels are achieved, is highly desirable. Closer security relationships that promoted economic objectives would presumably be considered only if they made sense in security terms as well.

---

11. On the German offset program, see Treverton (1978). On the linkage of textile export restraints to the reversion of Okinawa, see Destler, Fukui, and Sato (1979), especially Chapter 5.

The most effective deployment of American leverage in the pluralistic world economy of the 1990s is thus probably two-pronged: maximum use of the carrots of enhanced access to the American market and dollar stabilization, and judicious use of threats in cases in which the desired outcome would be worth the price of their actual execution. The Omnibus Trade Act follows such an approach (except for the military dimension): it authorizes further reductions in US trade barriers and directs the President to conclude more extensive international monetary arrangements, while calling for more aggressive threats of market closure to pry other countries open to US exports. In launching the program proposed here, the new administration should candidly state its intention to use these levers as necessary.

America's strongest lever is probably leadership by example, as has been recently reaffirmed by its successes in accelerating the global trend toward reliance on market-oriented policies.[12] For such leadership to continue, however, it is critical for the United States to put its own house in order through the necessary adjustments in its own economic policies, instead of financing domestic spending and a huge debt buildup with savings from the rest of the world. It will mean American support for a reformed international monetary system that will stabilize the dollar, once equilibrium exchange rates have been established. It will mean avoiding new trade and investment restrictions and eliminating protectionist measures that were instituted during the 1980s, while the United States was urging other countries to liberalize. It will mean pulling America's full weight in the international economic institutions instead of retarding the needed expansion of resources at the World Bank, the IDB, and the IMF (and failing to pay dues to the GATT). The international negotiating position of the United States will be strengthened significantly when it takes these steps, which will render the use of individual carrots (and sticks) both more effective and less necessary.

The United States will also have to be willing to address the concerns of other countries. For example, it will need to reform its own unfair trade practices. It should provide financial support for initiatives agreed upon and funded by others, such as the Enhanced

12. Some analysts, however, believe that American power is no longer adequate to provide leadership "by precept and example" (Geiger 1988, especially Chapter 7). Gilpin (1987, 365–381) makes a similar argument.

Structural Adjustment Facility at the IMF and debt relief for the poorest African countries.

The blending of these carrots and sticks in pursuit of US international economic objectives during the next five to ten years will require one of the most delicate and sophisticated balancing acts of American policy during the postwar period. It will require full consistency of priorities and tactics within the administration. It will require cohesion between the administration and the Congress, based on full consultation in the formulation and implementation of the new program. A major effort to educate the public on the wisdom of the chosen course will be needed to obtain the political support required for responsible fiscal policies, trade concessions, and the modest appropriations needed to support American initiatives.[13]

THE EROSION OF THE SYSTEM

The fourth key component of the global setting that will face the new administration and Congress, in large part a product of the first three, is the erosion of the international economic order that had provided a relatively stable underpinning for the world economy during the first postwar generation. The globalization of markets has outrun the ability of governments to cope in some circumstances. The advent of additional economic powers has greatly complicated systemic management. The decline of America's economic power relative to other countries has deprived the system of some of its leadership.

This erosion is clearest in trade. On the other hand, there has been a continuing decline in tariffs during the 1970s and 1980s in the wake of the Kennedy and Tokyo Rounds of multilateral trade negotiations. There has been some liberalization of nontariff distortions, notably by Japan and some of the NICs and even by a few Third World debtors (including Mexico) under IMF and World Bank programs. The Uruguay Round was launched in 1986 in an effort to renew this momentum.

An increasing share of international trade flows has been subjected

13. Recommendations on how the US government should organize to achieve these results are in Chapter 8.

to quantitative restrictions (QRs), however. In the United States, the share of imports covered by QRs rose from 5 percent in 1980 to 18 percent in 1986.[14] European countries raised barriers to a number of manufactured imports, especially from Asia. Many Third World debtors tightened their import regimes to conserve hard currency. In agriculture, the World Bank estimates that weighted average prices paid to producers in the early 1980s were 2.5 times the world market price in Japan, 1.5 times the world price in the European Community, and slightly over the world price in the United States (a ratio of 1.16:1).[15]

As a result of these developments, the credibility of the liberal trade system has been jeopardized. Bilateral trade agreements are now more openly and widely considered, and a few (most notably the United States–Canada FTA) have been negotiated. Discussion of economic blocs, mostly disparaging and fearful but nonetheless serious, has reemerged. There is widespread concern outside the European Community that the completion of its internal market will raise new barriers against outsiders and perhaps even discriminate against companies based in other countries (McPherson 1988). The GATT, the institutional locus of the system, is under constant attack; by one calculation, it now has jurisdiction over only 5–7 percent of global economic activity.[16]

A similar erosion, with some reversal since late 1985, has occurred in the international management of macroeconomic and monetary policies. Countries did not always adhere perfectly to the rules of the Bretton Woods system, and there were frequent currency crises and conflicts over national responsibilities under that system during the 1960s. Yet a framework of rules existed and was largely adhered

---

14. See Bergsten, et al. (1987, 2).

15. See World Bank (1986, table 6.1). It has been estimated that the average nominal rate of protection (defined as the percentage of excess of domestic over world market prices) for 13 major agricultural products increased from 41.1 percent in 1960 to 83.5 percent in 1980 in Japan and from 32.8 percent to 35.7 percent in the European Community, while decreasing in the United States from already low levels (0.9 to 0.1) (Honma and Hayami 1986, 118).

16. Though it covers 80 percent of merchandise trade flows, the GATT's rules do not extend to agriculture, textiles and apparel, services, direct investment, and other capital flows (World Bank 1987, 154; Choate and Linger 1988, 88).

to (Michaely 1971). The institutional locus of the system, the IMF, had wide legitimacy.

The breakdown of fixed exchange rates in the early 1970s effectively destroyed the obligation of countries to conform their national policies to international standards.[17] The IMF, after a last hurrah due to the first oil shock, lost any significant role with the industrial countries. The creation of the European Monetary System (EMS) restored meaningful international obligations for its membership and represented the first serious effort to move back toward an effective international regime, but it further reduced the IMF's influence in Europe.

International policy cooperation reached its nadir during the 1981–85 period, when the first Reagan administration rejected the approach in principle. The major industrial countries, mainly through the G-5 and G-7 gatherings, have tried to restore a measure of effective cooperation since the Plaza Agreement of 1985 but they have not yet gotten very far (Funabashi 1988, 212). Nor have they been able to formulate a lasting solution for the Third World debt problem.

Over the past three decades, the major economic powers have demonstrated considerable ability to work together to manage crises. They developed these techniques originally to respond to currency runs during the era of fixed exchange rates, and they have used them subsequently to handle similar problems under flexible rates (such as the dollar declines of 1978 and 1987 and the dollar overvaluation of 1985) and the debt crises of individual Third World countries in the 1980s. They have been unable to translate these successes in firefighting into preemptive and system-building action, however, and therein lies the challenge for the future.

The one possible exception to this trend of systemic erosion has been the liberalization of international capital movements. Given the globalization of financial markets described above, most industrial countries have concluded that capital controls would simply place

17. This is not to say that the fixed-rate system was ideal, or that there should now be an effort to restore it. Indeed, as developed in Chapter 5, the contemporary need is to forge a new regime out of fixed rates (which turned out to be too rigid) and flexible rates (which turned out to be too unstable). The point here, also developed in Chapter 5, is simply that Bretton Woods (and the European Monetary System) constructed a coherent and fairly effective framework for policy cooperation, which flexible rates clearly did not.

them at too great a competitive disadvantage. Japan and the United Kingdom liberalized during the last decade. A number of smaller countries have done so subsequently. The European Community has decided to abolish all controls for internal flows by 1990.

The net effect of this freeing of capital movements is unclear, however. The sharp increase in money flows has helped drive exchange rates away from equilibrium levels, defined in terms of trade competitiveness, and thus has added to the pressures for new commercial barriers. But this may eventually induce countries to coordinate their policies more actively to counter currency misalignments, which may be the only way to maintain open markets for both capital movements and trade (see Chapter 5).

The open and multilateral economic system of the initial postwar period is in retreat at present. Its key institutions—the IMF, the GATT, and the World Bank—have lost a good deal of credibility. The fragility of the world economy is indicated by the precarious state of the dollar, the constant threat of protection, and the continued festering of Third World debt. As described in Chapter 2, a failure of the current and proposed macroeconomic strategies to correct the continuing international imbalances could further accelerate the erosion of the trading system. The process of policy cooperation has begun to make a comeback since 1985, when the United States began to support it again, but considerable further strengthening will be essential before the system can effectively cope with the complex and market-oriented world economy of the 1990s.

Reversing Systemic Erosion

Many historians and political scientists are skeptical about reversing this erosion because they believe that previous international economic systems have been coherent and stable only under the firm leadership of a hegemonic power—the United Kingdom for a considerable period prior to World War One, the United States for a generation after World War Two. By contrast, they argue, periods without such leadership—notably the interwar period, but also the years just prior to 1914—have been highly unstable (Kindleberger 1973 and 1981, Gilpin 1981).

However, critics of this "hegemonic stability thesis" argue that hegemony is neither a necessary nor sufficient condition for the creation and maintenance of international regimes. They believe that international cooperation was central to the stability of earlier periods, including the classic gold standard era, and is necessary even in the presence of a hegemon. They note that institutions like the IMF and the GATT, once created, can promote cooperation beyond the period of dominance of a hegemon (Keohane 1984, Eichengreen forthcoming).

In addition, it is important to recognize that the present and earlier nonhegemonic periods differ in a fundamental sense. During the 1920s and 1930s, and in the early years of this century, many of the key economic competitors were potential military rivals as well. Some of the rising economic powers had ambitious plans for territorial expansion. Germany and its allies of course went to war against the United Kingdom and its allies during both of these periods, and Japan attacked the United States in 1941. The economic conflicts during these periods thus carried enormous security and political overtones, and it is doubtful that any feasible changes in management structures could have provided significant systemic stability for the world economy.

Today, in contrast, the world's major economies are military allies. The United States has security ties with Germany and almost all of Europe in NATO, with Japan, and even with the key NICs (explicitly with Korea, implicitly with Taiwan). The putative military opponents of the Western Alliance, the Soviet Union and Eastern Europe (and also China, at least in earlier decades), remain minor participants in the world economy; there is little need to accommodate them in managing its affairs. In a nuclear age, territorial ambitions (and thus potential military conflict between the strongest countries) are muted in any event. And none of the rising powers, including Japan, display any desire to replace the United States, although they certainly seek to share its leadership position.

The contemporary effort to forge effective modes of pluralistic international economic management therefore takes place within a much more hospitable framework than was the case in earlier eras. Indeed, the need for continuing cohesion in response to the potential threat of the Soviet Union—and the opportunities implied by its recent policy changes—reinforces the political interest of the allies in avoiding internecine economic conflict. Security interests enhance the prospects for achieving effective "management by committee" in the 1990s, whereas they detracted severely from that possibility in the early part of the century and between the world wars.

It is nevertheless possible that US resistance to an enhanced role and status for the emerging economic powers, most notably Japan and Germany (or a truly united Europe), could sow the seeds both of economic instability and alliance erosion. The United States has not been reluctant to ask other countries to assume an increasing share of international economic responsibilities, and it should continue to do so. But it must be willing to confer a corresponding set of rights and privileges upon the countries that step forward, to attain lasting cooperation and the pluralistic leadership structure that is now required.

FOREIGN POLICY IMPLICATIONS

These considerations offer a pointed reminder of the importance of international economic issues to the foreign policy of the United States. Domestic political forces in the United States, operating mainly through the Congress, may increasingly insist that the United States "stop defending countries richer than we are." The fact that the United States is simultaneously defending itself, and that it remains considerably richer than most of those it defends, can easily be forgotten in such an environment. Troop withdrawals and other actions that would severely hamper American foreign policy, and even national security, could result.

Persistent macroeconomic imbalances could also intensify and politicize conflicts among the allies. Specific trade issues could continue to fester, as they have throughout the 1980s. The increasing American reliance on funds from its creditor allies has already begun to raise fears, and even suspicions, that those allies might use their financial leverage to blackmail the United States.[18] A failure to

18. As suggested in "From Superrich to Superpower," *Time,* 4 July 1988, 28: "The year is 1992. A local conflict has closed the Strait of Malacca, blocking Japanese tankers laden with Persian Gulf oil from entering the South China Sea. The Japanese Prime Minister places a call to the White House. 'Good evening, Mr. President,' he says. 'Would you consider sending the U.S. Navy to escort my ships through the strait?'

resolve the imbalances through the macroeconomic approach that has been pursued since 1985 could revive pressures for trade protection in the early 1990s, as described in Chapter 2, causing new clashes among the allies and considerable economic dislocation.

A failure to address these economic issues promptly and effectively could thus have significant adverse effects on America's international security position. This is especially the case because Japan and Germany are the linchpins of the Pacific and Atlantic security networks as well as America's largest creditors. The United States is the only superpower in both military and economic terms, but these countries play essential supportive roles in both spheres, and could jeopardize the realization of America's goals in both if they choose not to cooperate fully.

A weakening of the alliance as a result of economic disagreements would come at a particularly unfortunate time in light of General Secretary Gorbachev's apparent desire to ease global tensions. Alliance solidarity is essential on the eve of potentially historic negotiations on both strategic and conventional weapons. A successful American effort to get its own house in order and to work constructively with other countries on economic issues could provide a major boost to the overall foreign policy of the new administration and improve the prospects for successful negotiations with the Soviet Union. A demonstrated commitment to promote US interests through active international economic cooperation would dispel at least some of the suspicions of recent years and reduce the risk of declining political support for the alliance. The stakes of a successful resolution of the international economic problems confronting the new administration thus range well beyond economic affairs themselves.

Pause. The President is well aware that the request is coming from America's biggest creditor. 'Why, yes, of course,' he replies. The Prime Minister thanks him, adding, 'I am certain that your help will reassure our private investors enough so that they will buy their usual share of Treasury bills at next Tuesday's auction.' "

4

Eliminating the Current Account Deficit

The analysis in Chapter 2 stressed the central importance for the US economy, in both the immediate future and the long run, of removing the constant threat of financial and economic instability that stems from the huge current account deficit and the resulting need to attract foreign capital inflows of about $10 billion per month. We have emphasized the impossibility of avoiding an adjustment of such large external imbalances and the need for the United States to restore its international leadership position in part by putting its own economic house in order. To achieve both goals, the new administration and Congress should set a goal of fully eliminating the deficit in the American current account—and thus of halting the buildup of net foreign debt—over the course of the new President's term.

Some would be more ambitious, proposing that America seek to restore its traditional current account surplus in order to begin reducing the accumulated foreign debt (US Congress 1987, 3 and 26). Some believe that the United States, given its high per capita income and national wealth, should again become an exporter of capital to poorer countries. Some believe that the United States will be forced to run surpluses, for at least a while, to ensure confidence in the dollar.

Others take the view that the United States can readily sustain modest current account deficits for some time, perhaps on the order of $50–75 billion, or about 1 percent of GNP, stabilizing the relationship between its net foreign debt and its GNP (or exports) after 1992 or so (Williamson 1988a, 2). Some believe that the United States will never be able to eliminate its deficits, whatever it does, because other countries will not accept the required cuts in their counterpart surpluses.

The rough balance proposed here is thus a compromise goal, but anything less would seem to be extremely risky in light of the economic outlook described throughout this book. Stabilizing the foreign debt ratios is not good enough, because there is no basis for believing that the level at which stabilization would occur would be sustainable. Indeed, the runs on the dollar in 1987 indicate that the confidence of foreign private investors declined sharply with the ratios at much lower levels. It is true that those events occurred when the current account deficit was large and rising, but the only sure way to avoid continuing instability from a large stock of debt is to maintain balance in a country's flow position—the current account (Bergsten and Islam forthcoming).

Moreover, sustaining deficits at such substantial levels would require borrowing additional funds from abroad, in comparable amounts, to finance the servicing of the previously accumulated debt. Most LDCs were doing this prior to the onset of their debt crises, but quickly became unable to do so once confidence was shattered—with devastating effects on their economies for many years. As pointed out in Chapter 2, the US situation differs considerably from that of the LDCs in terms of mechanisms, but similar adjustments will ultimately be required. The United States can restore control over its own destiny, and avoid enormous and continuing risks to its prosperity, only by—at a minimum—stopping further buildup of its foreign debt.

There are also debates concerning the time frame over which the adjustment should be sought. One school of thought argues that a four-year current account deficit elimination program, implying a similar time path for eliminating the federal budget deficit (see Chapter 5), would be too rapid for the economy to absorb and might trigger a recession. Another view is that other countries cannot accommodate the American adjustment so quickly, and that they would be forced to choose between renewed inflation (by maintaining rapid domestic growth to promote the adjustment) or recession (if a further large dollar decline were part of the package).

Any program longer than five or six years would seem to be sufficiently uncertain as to undermine the credibility of the effort. No definitive judgment is possible, however, on the necessity of achieving the full correction in four years, rather than five or six, to ensure market confidence in the dollar and continued financing for the deficits. Several considerations support both the desirability and the feasibility of a quadrennium, however.

First, the Congress has already set a target (in the Gramm-Rudman-Hollings legislation) of eliminating the budget deficit over the next four fiscal years (by FY 1993). Second, we will argue in Chapter 5 that the trade improvement and lower interest rates induced by the fiscal action will sustain the expansion, and indeed that a credible program to correct the twin deficits is the best way to keep it going. Third, the advent of full employment and fears of renewed inflation, which would otherwise be heightened by the further fall required of the dollar, suggest such a fiscal contraction for purely domestic reasons. Fourth, some of the major surplus countries abroad, notably Japan and Taiwan, have already demonstrated that they can sustain (and even accelerate) economic growth while their trade surpluses are declining. Moreover, the required further appreciation of their currencies will provide an anti-inflationary antidote to any risks of overheating that might be generated by their maintaining rapid growth of domestic demand. Fifth, there is an obvious benefit in terms of credibility in setting an adjustment period that is coterminous with the new President's term—with respect to the markets and foreign governments, and for the purpose of sustained follow-through from the government itself.

THE MAGNITUDE OF THE ADJUSTMENT

Since the current account deficit will probably fall within the range of $130–140 billion in 1988, achieving full balance by 1992 will require average annual cuts of about $35 billion during the next four years (see table 2.2). Most models suggest that the first increment of this improvement was in the pipeline as a result of the decline in the exchange rate of the dollar and other developments that occurred between early 1985 and 1987. However, the rise of the dollar during 1988 and a possible slowdown of foreign growth in 1989 could disturb that prospect. More importantly, no plausible model shows the deficit falling much below $100 billion for any sustained period of time even with the dollar at the lower levels of late 1987. Virtually all analyses suggest that the deficit will start rising again by 1990 in the absence of further adjustment measures, and could return to at least $150 billion by the early 1990s (see table 4.1).[1]

To fully eliminate the current account deficit, the new policy package thus needs to achieve $100–150 billion in additional improvement. The swing in the merchandise trade balance will have to be considerably larger than the targeted improvement in the current account, however. This is because the continuing buildup of America's foreign debt, as the external deficit persists (even at a declining level), will produce a steady increase in the cost of debt service.

During 1987, when the net foreign debt of the United States reached $370 billion, the country continued to receive net investment income of about $20 billion because American assets abroad returned a higher total yield than did foreign assets in the United States. America's net earnings declined by only about $14 billion from their 1981 peak through 1987, despite an adverse swing of over $500 billion in the net international investment position over that period. The world's largest debtor country remained the world's largest net recipient of foreign investment income.

However, the sharp decline in the exchange rate of the dollar during 1985–87 produced a large one-shot rise in recorded income, measured in dollars, from American direct investment abroad in those years. In 1987, the rest of the investment income account deteriorated by over $10 billion. Even anticipating a further dollar decline of 15–20 percent we can expect an adverse swing of $25–50

1. The most widely used models are discussed in Cline (forthcoming). Also see Bryant, Holtham, and Hooper (1988). The models used throughout this volume are described in the Annex.

TABLE 4.1 Alternative Projections of the US Current Account Balance
(billions of current dollars)

Source	Approximate date of model run	Exchange rate as of:	Projections				
			1988	1989	1990	1991	1992
IMF	10-88	8-1988	−129	−129	n.a.	n.a.	n.a.
OECD	6-88	4-14-88	−150	−132	n.a.	n.a.	n.a.
DRI[a]	12-87	1987:Q2	−131 (−122)	−146 (−127)	−175 (−145)	−209 (−165)	−249 (−188)
WEFA	9-88	[b]	−143	−137	−138	−156	−161
Bryant	1-88	12-22-87	−125	−108	−113	−127	n.a.
Cline (HHC)	9-88	1987:Q4	−136	−105	−115	−137	−155
NB: 1987 = − $154 billion.							

n.a. = Not available.

Source: IMF (1988); OECD (1988); Gault (1987); WEFA (1988); Bryant (1988); Cline (forthcoming, table 3); also see the annex to this volume.

a. Figures in parentheses show the results without an adverse time trend.

b. Exchange rates are allowed to fluctuate in the WEFA model rather than being held constant as in the other models.

billion from the 1987 base by 1992.[2] The number could be toward the upper end of this range if American interest rates rise faster than rates abroad, or if it takes the United States longer than the proposed four years to eliminate the current account deficit.[3] The merchandise trade balance will thus need to improve by around $125–200 billion more to offer a strong probability of achieving the targeted elimination of the nominal current account deficit.

In real terms, the required adjustment is larger still. This is because a decline in the exchange rate of the dollar produces a deterioration in America's terms of trade, mainly by driving up the prices of imports. This swing will amount to at least $50 billion during the course of the correction, depending on how much further dollar depreciation is needed. Some of it had already taken place in 1987–88,[4] but further improvement of $150–250 billion will be needed in the merchandise trade balance in volume terms.

Such a swing would represent between 4 and 6 percent of real GNP at present levels ($4 trillion in 1982 dollars).[5] Elimination of the current account deficit in four years will thus require annual increments of between 1 and 1.5 percent of real GNP from 1989

2. The baseline projection in Cline (forthcoming) shows a swing of about $45 billion. The investment income account deteriorated at a seasonably adjusted annual rate of $20 billion in the first half of 1988, compared with the full year 1987, partly due to the renewed rise in the exchange rate of the dollar.

3. There is an important relationship between those two variables. Adoption in early 1989 of a credible program to eliminate the external deficit should produce lower US interest rates and hence lower payments on America's foreign debt, virtually all of which is dollar-denominated. Conversely, failure to adopt convincing cuts in both the internal and external deficits could trigger a sharp rise in interest rates that would further increase the magnitude of both problems.

4. By the second quarter of 1988, the deficit in volume terms had fallen by an annual rate of about $48 billion from its annual peak in 1986. The nominal deficit had declined by an annual rate of only about $14 billion. On this rough measure, the terms of trade had already deteriorated by about $34 billion.

5. As noted in the text, the targeted improvement in the merchandise trade balance is about $25–50 billion greater than the needed improvement in the current account—or "net exports of goods and services" as incorporated in the GNP accounts—because of the increase in the cost of servicing America's net foreign debt. On the other hand, if a pickup in inflation is to be avoided, resources must be shifted away from domestic spending to the external sector (see Chapter 5) to offset the decline in the terms of trade as well as to accomplish the improvement in "net exports" in real terms. Hence the volume shift required in the internal economy to accomplish the trade and current account improvements is about the same.

through 1992. Such improvements in the country's external position would provide a positive thrust to GNP growth of 1–1.5 percent annually in each year of the new President's term.[6]

THE PROGRESS TO DATE

Many observers wonder why the remaining correction should be so large. At its lowest point, the dollar had already fallen by an average of about 40–60 percent from its peak against the currencies of the other major industrial countries (figure 4.1). The decline began in early 1985, so it has now had almost four years to work its way into the trade flows. Japan and Europe, more recently and to a lesser extent, have been experiencing rapid expansion in their domestic demand, as urged by the United States. The sharp fall in the US budget deficit in 1987 should have contributed positively as well.

There are several reasons for the disappointing pace and magnitude of the adjustment as of September 1988. The most important technical factor is that the US external deficit had become so bad that substantial improvement was needed just to keep it from getting worse. Most models suggested that the deficit was headed above $200 billion when the dollar was at its peak in late 1984 and early 1985.[7] The modest decline since mid-1987 is thus a considerable achievement.

The trade improvement has been considerably greater in volume than in value terms, and two elements that offset part of the volume gains have already been cited: the deterioration in the terms of trade, which was inevitable because the adjustment required a large fall in the dollar; and the buildup in servicing costs on the foreign debt amassed by the United States. These two elements together will offset perhaps $75–100 billion of the real trade improvement by the early 1990s.

---

6. In the first half of 1988, net exports of goods and services improved at an annual rate of over 1.5 percent of GNP. They accounted for more than one half of real GNP growth during this period. The total increase in real GNP during this period could be accounted for by the trade improvement plus increased investment in producers' durable equipment, much of which presumably occurred in export and import-competing industries.

7. Marris projected a deficit of exactly $200 billion for 1987 (1985, p. 86, table 3.2).

FIGURE 4.1 The Dollar in the 1980s

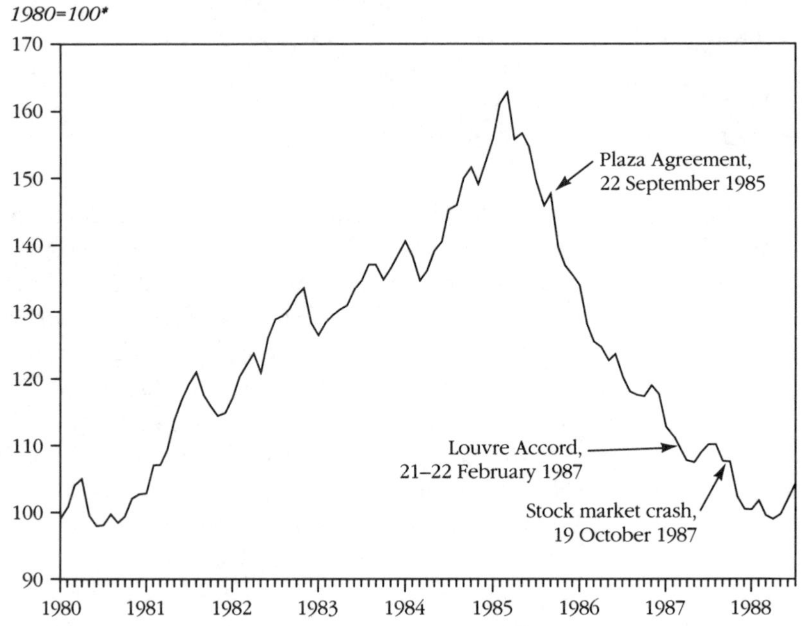

* Based on the IMF's MERM index.
Source: IMF, *International Financial Statistics,* various issues.

In addition, the starting point for the American correction was, to an historically unprecedented degree, unfavorable for a major industrial country (Marris 1987, 94). At the peak of the deficit, merchandise exports covered only about 60 percent of imports.[8] This meant that exports had to grow almost twice as fast as imports simply to keep the deficit from rising further. In fact, exports have grown two to three times faster than imports since mid-1986, and the "export cover" ratio had risen to about 70 percent by mid-1988. This has been enough to achieve only a modest reduction in the current account in dollar terms, however, because of the rapidly

8. This "export cover" ratio dropped only to 92 percent in France when it triggered the franc crisis surrounding the first Mitterrand government's "dash for growth" in 1982.

deteriorating trend at the start of the adjustment period, the highly unfavorable base, and the offsetting factors just cited.[9]

The good news is that American exports have boomed since the middle of 1986. They have been rising at annual rates of 20–30 percent since the middle of 1987. World trade volume has been growing at about 5–7 percent, so American firms are raising their market shares dramatically. The decline of the dollar seems to have restored a good deal of the price competitiveness of American firms.

THE TASK AHEAD

The US export expansion can continue at anything like recent rates, however, only if two further changes occur within the United States: considerable additional capacity is created in a number of export sectors, which will require substantial increases in investment in these sectors; and domestic demand slows to permit an additional shift of sales from US to foreign markets. On the import side, rapid growth continued until 1988 despite the improved domestic price competitiveness of American products resulting from the currency changes. The rise in domestic investment in 1988 has actually exacerbated the problem because about 30–35 percent of capital goods are now provided from abroad.

The clear implication, both from the standpoint of further expanding exports and limiting imports, is that the growth of domestic demand must be slowed. Since increased investment is

9. Several other elements have impeded more rapid US adjustment. The currencies of two of the smaller but important surplus countries, Taiwan and Korea, did not begin to appreciate until a year or so later than the currencies of the industrial countries. Growth in some of America's major export markets, notably Latin America but much of Europe as well until mid-1987, was modest. Exporting firms in some countries, particularly Japan, have apparently passed through less of their currency's appreciation to export prices than would have been expected from the experience of previous adjustment periods, such as the late 1970s. In part, this may be due to a phenomenon known as "hysteresis": Japanese and other foreign firms that invested considerable capital in establishing an export position in the American market while their currencies were undervalued will not withdraw simply in response to elimination of that undervaluation. We will suggest in Chapter 6 that a similar asymmetry may have limited, or at least slowed, the return to export markets of US firms that had dropped out of such competition when the dollar rose so sharply in the first half of the 1980s.

essential, to expand the availability of exports without causing large price increases and to boost productivity, demand restraint needs to be directed at the growth of domestic consumption (including government spending). Indeed, a further sharp increase in private consumption offset most of the cut in the budget deficit in 1987 and precluded the improvement in the current account (in dollar terms) that otherwise would have been expected. (The corresponding fall in the household saving rate offset much of the reduction in government dissaving and left little change in the relationship between total domestic saving and investment.) The main adjustment problem now seems to reside in the composition of US economic growth rather than in the exchange rate of the dollar.

Beginning in late 1985, the Reagan administration pursued a three-part program to reduce the external deficit: a decline in the dollar, faster growth of domestic demand abroad (especially in Japan and Western Europe) and substantial reduction of the American budget deficit. Secretary Baker never set a target for how much correction was sought, so we cannot assess with any precision whether the administration's efforts met its own goals. As noted above, it was a considerable accomplishment to stop the growth of the external imbalance. Further reductions of at least a modest amount can be expected. Exports are booming.

The bottom line, however, is that present policies show little prospect of cutting the current account deficit below $100 billion for any sustained period. Since the deficit was headed toward at least $200 billion in the absence of adjustment efforts, the correction has thus gone about halfway. This is reminiscent of the most extensive previous postwar adjustment, which occurred in the 1971–73 period. The initial phase of that effort, which culminated in the 10 percent dollar devaluation of the Smithsonian Agreement in December 1971, turned out to be only half as great as needed. Despite President Nixon's reference to the Smithsonian Agreement as "the most significant monetary agreement in the history of the world," market stability was short-lived and the dollar had to be devalued by another 10 percent in early 1973. The consequences of the inadequacy of the Smithsonian package included a sharp acceleration of global inflation, due importantly to the massive intervention of central banks vainly attempting to defend the new parities, and the final collapse of the Bretton Woods system of fixed exchange rates. The failure to complete the adjustment in a timely manner levied heavy and lasting costs on the world economy.

It is thus extremely important to carry the adjustment effort through to conclusion at the earliest possible time. However, the Baker program remains far from full implementation. The dollar declined sharply, but never far enough to restore full equilibrium, given the absence of other policy changes; its rebound in 1988 has even offset some of the adjustment gains that had been expected earlier. Domestic demand has boomed in Japan and picked up more recently in Germany and elsewhere in Europe, but it must continue at a rapid pace for several more years in both areas to support the full adjustment. The US budget deficit dropped by one-third in 1987, but it seems to have leveled off at about $150 billion. The other "Baker Plan," dealing with Third World debt, prevented a financial crisis but has proved inadequate to restore growth in the debtor countries and enable them to contribute to the global adjustment. As the new administration and Congress take office, it is clear that substantial additional steps will be needed to achieve the suggested target of full elimination of the current account deficit—or even a more modest objective.

It is important to set a target and announce it publicly for several reasons. Doing so would indicate, both domestically and internationally, the high priority that the new government assigns to the issue. American industry would be encouraged to take the steps needed to achieve the targeted outcome. The Omnibus Trade Act requires the President to submit a "trade projection report" by 1 March 1989. This would be an appropriate vehicle for publicly announcing the new administration's current account goal if an even earlier occasion is not chosen.

Setting an explicit target would also make clear the degree of accommodation required from other countries, and promote constructive discussions concerning how to distribute the American adjustment throughout the rest of the world without creating major new difficulties. National statements of medium-run current account targets are in fact required as part of the "indicators" exercise, launched at the Tokyo Summit in 1986, that is being used in an effort to foster more effective coordination of policies among the G-7 countries. A clear statement by the United States of its goal would compel the other countries to offer targets consistent with the

American objective. If they were unwilling to do so, they would have to explain why they would prefer to see the deficits continue and how they planned to finance them. The indicators exercise also calls for medium-run projections to see if the goals are likely to be realized.

About $30 billion of the foreign counterpart to the US current account improvement can be achieved through a series of measures, summarized in Chapter 1 and described in detail in Chapter 7, to reduce the "negative financial transfer" from the largest Third World debtors, enabling them to restore faster growth and finance a reduction in their trade surpluses. If the world price of oil were to fall sharply, as in 1986, the OPEC countries would also make a "contribution" to the global adjustment through further increases in their current account deficits. The bulk of the foreign counterpart will have to come from the handful of large surplus countries, however, roughly in proportion to the magnitude of their surpluses: Japan will have to cut its surplus by about $60 billion, Germany by about $40 billion, the smaller European surplus countries by about $10 billion, and the Asian NICs by about $20 billion (see table 1.2).

The willingness of the surplus countries to accept these changes in their external positions is a crucial variable in the equation. Their trade surpluses will have to decline more than their current accounts because all of them, as a result of their previous surpluses, are enjoying a steady rise in net income from their foreign investment portfolios.[10] Moreover, as with the United States, their adjustment in real terms—in this case, in a downward direction—must be larger than the shift in dollar terms because of the favorable impact of appreciation on their terms of trade. Since 1986, Japan and Germany have been experiencing declines in their external positions in real terms, retarding the growth of their economies, while their surpluses have remained at or near peak levels in dollar terms. These issues will be addressed in detail in Chapter 5.[11]

10. Korea is still a debtor country, but is reducing its external debt rapidly and its debt service payments are thus declining as well. Korea's central bank has announced its expectation that creditor country status will be attained in 1990.

11. Our emphasis is on the shifts needed in these areas' global current account positions to accommodate the targeted elimination of the US global current account deficit, rather than on shifts in bilateral balances between the United States and each country or region. This is partly because bilateral balances are even harder to estimate and

Whether or not the recommended adjustment targets are publicly announced, further action will be needed on all three components of the macroeconomic part of the strategy proposed in this volume: the exchange rate, foreign growth, and the American budget deficit. As noted earlier, the results to date suggest that American exports have regained a large measure of price competitiveness and that foreign growth has picked up. The priority now is therefore to foster a substantial shift in the composition of US economic growth, dampening the expansion of consumer demand and government spending in favor of exports and private investment. Our specific proposals will begin with this aspect of the adjustment problem.

---

achieve than shifts in global positions. But it is also because shifts in bilateral balances, such as between the United States and Canada, can occur with no deterioration in the global position of the partner country (in this case, Canada) as US exports compete more effectively with Japanese, Asian NIC, and European exports in that market. It is thus more illuminating to focus on those countries, primarily those in surplus, whose global deteriorations must mirror the US global improvement.

5

Macroeconomic Policy: The Heart of the Program

AMERICAN FISCAL POLICY

As argued in Chapter 4, the current account deficit can be eliminated over the next four years if the United States is able to shift 1 to 1.5 percent of its annual output into net exports. The output potential of the economy is increasing at about 2.5 percent annually, including expected expansion in the labor force of about 1.5 percent and productivity growth of about 1 percent. There is little if any slack to be taken up, since the economy is near full employment and full capacity utilization. The growth of domestic demand must therefore be limited to 1 to 1.5 percent per year to permit the required transfer to the external sector without an acceleration of inflation.

Under this strategy of export-led growth, about one-half of all US economic expansion during the adjustment period would come from improvement in the trade balance—as it did in the first half of 1988. Continued GNP growth of about 2.5 percent would provide jobs for new entrants to the labor force and prevent increases in the rate of unemployment. A steady improvement in the external position should minimize, and perhaps eliminate, the risk of a dollar plunge and a hard landing for the economy, the greatest threat to the continuation of the expansion.

Some portion of the "permissible increase" in domestic demand needs to be reserved for private investment. With the economy near full employment, capacity increases are essential to counter the risk of rising inflation. This is especially true for the export sector, where production bottlenecks are already apparent as a result of rapid growth since the middle of 1986. Over the longer run, higher rates of productivity growth are necessary to support both rising living standards and continued international competitiveness without a steadily declining dollar. This in turn requires higher rates of investment.

Increased spending by consumers and governments will thus have to be held to about 1 percent per year to make room for the essential growth of net exports and private investment. With the total population growing upwards of 1 percent annually, per capita increases in consumption would be modest. This would be the opposite of the pattern of 1982–86, when per capita consumption was growing by more than 3 percent each year.

As noted in Chapter 2, a unique feature of those years was the consistent excess of domestic spending over domestic production.[1] This excess grew by 0.5 percent to 1 percent of GNP annually and reached a peak of about 3.5 percent of GNP in 1986–87 (in both nominal and real terms). To reduce and eventually eliminate the current account deficits that resulted, the relationship between these two key variables had to reverse, as it did in 1987–88. This reversal must be maintained into the early 1990s.

The necessary shift in the composition of US growth over the next four years—in favor of exports and investment and away from consumption and government spending—can be achieved in four different ways.[2] First, private consumers might autonomously decide to cut back on the growth of their purchases and increase their saving

1. The advent of this phenomenon in 1982, a year of sharp recession, was the first sign of the onset of America's large external imbalance. The US trade balance normally strengthens sharply in a recession year, such as 1975, because demand for imports falls sharply. This particularly should have been the case in 1982, when recession was much sharper in the United States than in the other industrial countries. The appreciation of the dollar was already beginning to disrupt America's international competitiveness, however, and the deterioration of net exports accounted for more than one quarter of the decline in real GNP in that year (CEA 1988, 250–251).

2. In addition to its undesirability, recession is not a real "option" because, while it would cut private consumption and improve the trade balance (unless the rest of the

rate to rebuild their personal balance sheets, or simply to hedge against an uncertain future, especially with inflation concerns rising again. There appeared to be some movement in this direction in late 1987 and early 1988, perhaps in response to the crash in the stock market. But the household saving rate has been on a declining trend since the early 1980s and the American saving rate has been the lowest among the industrial countries for a long time (see tables 2.3 and 5.1). With GNP and personal incomes growing at 2.5 percent, the personal saving rate would have to at least double by 1991 to hold the rise in domestic demand to the required level by itself. It might be possible to achieve a modest part of the necessary shift in resources from this source, but it would be imprudent to count on it for substantial help.

Second, private business saving could rise autonomously. However, as a share of GDP, it has recently dropped back to the average for the 1980s (table 5.1). One reason is the increased tax burden on corporations resulting from the Tax Reform Act of 1986. Another is the slowing of economy-wide productivity with the approach to full employment, a trend that has not been offset by the continuing vitality of manufacturing.

Third, policies could be adopted that would stimulate an increase in private saving by individuals or companies. Unfortunately, the many previous efforts to do this have had little or no discernible impact. The "supply-side" approaches of the early 1980s have, to date at least, been associated with a decline in private saving instead. As noted above, the "tax reform" of 1986 seems to have cut into corporate saving without any offset in higher household saving.

The only reliable way to achieve the needed reorientation of the economy is to reduce the budget deficit of the federal government. The actual deficit is now running at about $150 billion. Since the economy is near full employment, the structural deficit is about the same. Chapter 4 argued that the elimination of the current account deficit will require a shift of resources within the United States of up to $150 billion in nominal terms. Coincidentally, the elimination

---

world went into recession too), it would also lead to cuts in private investment and a larger budget deficit. As noted in Chapter 2, however, recession would be the probable outcome—via a hard landing of the dollar—of a failure to pursue the approach suggested here.

TABLE 5.1 Net US Saving by Sector

	Personal		Net Business[a]		Federal Government[b]		Budget Deficit as a share of net private saving (percent)
	billion dollars	percent of GDP	billion dollars	percent of GDP	billion dollars	percent of GDP	
1980	110	4.3	32	1.2	−61	−2.4	43.0
1981	137	4.7	42	1.5	−64	−2.2	35.8
1982	154	4.9	20	0.6	−146	−4.7	83.9
1983	131	3.9	65	1.9	−176	−5.2	90.0
1984	164	4.4	94	2.5	−170	−4.6	65.7
1985	125	3.2	103	2.6	−197	−5.0	86.4
1986	122	2.9	104	2.5	−206	−4.8	91.1
1987	104	2.3	81	1.8	−158	−3.5	85.2
Annual average	131	3.7	68	1.9	−147	−4.1	74.1

Source: *Survey of Current Business*, July, various years, tables 1.7, 5.1.

a. Gross business saving less capital consumption allowances (with capital consumption adjustment).

b. National income and product accounts basis.

of the structural budget deficit could provide the bulk of the required resource shift.[3]

The internal American adjustment should be achieved by eliminating the structural budget deficit during the four years from 1990 to 1993. This will require average annual cuts of $35 billion to $40 billion, about the pace called for under Gramm-Rudman-Hollings.[4] According to the Congressional Budget Office, however, the outlook under current policy is for the budget deficit to remain in the range of $120 to $135 billion through FY 1993, even under favorable economic assumptions and without new spending programs (Congressional Budget Office 1988 and table 2.2). There are numerous reasons to expect a considerably less favorable outcome: the implausibility of five more years of continuous growth on top of the expansion of the past six years in the absence of further policy action; the buildup of pressures for new spending (including the potentially sizable costs of rescuing the savings and loan industry); and the unlikelihood of achieving lower interest rates without cuts in the budget deficit itself (Minarik and Penner 1988). It would be very risky to assume that the United States can "grow its way out" of the budget deficit. Significant additional policy steps are required.

Some observers would like to achieve "budget correction" by drawing on the continuing growth in the surplus of the Social Security Trust Fund, which is projected to continue rising until

3. The internal resource shift also needs to accommodate the deterioration in the terms of trade, described in Chapter 4, and so must match the improvement in the current account in real rather than nominal terms. Reductions in the budget deficit could also reduce the current account deficit directly if they were to produce a slowdown in the growth of the economy; our model shows an improvement of $15 billion in the external balance for every reduction of GNP by 1 percentage point per year. As indicated in the text, however, we believe that GNP growth will be maintained because sustained growth abroad and the lower exchange rate for the dollar will induce substantial further improvements in the trade balance once the budget cuts make the necessary resources available, and because private investment and other interest-sensitive expenditures will rise as a result of lower interest rates stemming from the budget cuts themselves.

4. The Balanced Budget and Emergency Deficit Control Act of 1985, amended in 1987 and popularly known as Gramm-Rudman-Hollings, requires the deficit, as defined slightly differently for its purposes, to be cut from $136 billion in FY 1989 to $100 billion in FY 1990, $64 billion in FY 1991, $28 billion in FY 1992 and 0 in FY 1993 (see table 2.2). The first budget of the new government will apply to FY 1990, which would be in time to support the proposed elimination of the current account deficit during 1989–92 because, as noted in Chapter 4, the 1989 component of that improvement may already be in the pipeline.

about 2010, when it could reach $500 billion. (The Trust Fund is consolidated with the rest of the budget, so its surpluses offset deficits in the rest of the accounts.) Such a strategy would be enormously short-sighted, however, leaving the fund short in the 21st century when the baby boomers will retire and the elderly will constitute an increasing proportion of the population.[5] Indeed, some knowledgeable observers recommend a course that would produce a budget surplus—aiming to eliminate the deficit *excluding* the social security surplus, which would require improving the rest of the budget by an estimated $236 billion in FY 1993. However, such an ambitious shift is not necessary to support the external correction. Moreover, if the economy were to turn down during the adjustment period, any resulting rise in the deficit should be considered cyclical and ignored (but the structural correction should be kept on course).

The advent of full employment and the likelihood of continuing economic growth in 1989 greatly enhance the feasibility of implementing a package to eliminate the budget deficit by FY 1993. Such budget cuts now carry much less risk of pushing the economy into recession than was naturally feared during the administration–Congress "summit" of late 1987 (in the wake of Black Monday), which effectively set fiscal policy for 1988 and most of 1989. In addition to the substantial improvement in the trade balance, interest rates would decline as a result of the budget cuts, thereby providing enough offsetting stimulus to prevent a downturn.[6] The greatest potential cause of a recession, a collapse of the dollar and the hard landing scenario laid out in Chapter 2, would in fact best be averted by such a policy.

The risk of renewed inflation suggests that such a package is needed for internal as well as external reasons. With the budget deficit still running at about 3 percent of GNP, and with the

5. See Morgan Guaranty (1988) and Greenspan (1988, especially 13). In addition, projections that the Social Security surplus will be able to cover even a fraction of the program's costs in the middle of the next century seem wildly optimistic (Peterson 1988, 639–42).

6. The WEFA econometric model of the US economy shows, for example, that the proposed budget program (with or without the other policy changes proposed in this analysis) would lead to a reduction of 1 to 1.5 percentage points in long-term interest rates.

economy at or near full employment, there is a strong case for substantial fiscal restraint in strictly domestic terms.[7]

Successful elimination of the budget deficit, because of its critical role in reducing the external deficit and avoiding renewed inflation, is more important than the specific methods through which that correction is achieved.[8] The interminable squabbles of the past six years, which produced frequent gridlock in the budget process, must be avoided. Several broad guidelines for the budget program follow logically, however, from the goal of restoring the United States to a strong and stable domestic and international economic position.

First, the required fiscal action must be wholly credible at the outset and phase into effect over the four-year target period. Immediate credibility is necessary to underpin market confidence in the dollar and the new administration, and thus to maintain the flow of foreign financing for the deficits—at least $200 billion—throughout the adjustment period.

This requires congressional action in 1989 that locks in the deficit reduction program at least through 1992. The budget actions themselves will need to be of a kind that can be put into place irrevocably (barring overt reversal by subsequent congressional actions) and that have an accelerating impact on the deficit. Examples include changes in the payments formulas of the large entitlement programs, such as Social Security, and most tax increases. Such a package would contrast sharply with the post-crash budget package of November 1987, which was wholly inadequate in magnitude—serving only to keep the deficits from rising further—and replete with asset sales, accounting changes, and other one-shot gimmicks, rather than substantial (let alone accelerating) savings.

Second, any changes in tax policy should aim to increase the

7. Some observers reject the view that the United States needs to cut its budget deficit on the grounds that the US deficit, as a share of GNP, is less than the deficits in a number of other countries. They ignore the fact that the American saving rate is much lower relative to most of these countries than is the budget deficit, so the United States is far less able to finance its deficit without crowding out private investment or building up foreign debt. For the period 1980–1987, the budget deficit exceeded total personal saving in the United States and absorbed over 70 percent of net private saving (table 5.1). See Friedman (1988) for more detailed analysis.

8. The counterargument that the method of reducing the deficit is at least as important as the magnitude, for reasons of equity, can be found in Faux (1988).

domestic saving rate and dampen the high national propensity to consume. This would free resources for an improvement in the external position and reduce US dependence on foreign capital in both the short and longer runs. Consumption taxes (across-the-board or on specific sectors, such as a gasoline tax[9]) would be superior to a reversal of the recent cuts in marginal tax rates on individual and corporate income, although equity concerns might suggest some blending of the two approaches.

Third, the budget program should not impair efforts to improve America's export performance. Modest increases in expenditures will be necessary for some export promotion efforts, including export financing through the Export-Import Bank (see Chapter 6) and new funding for the multilateral lending institutions, which promote US exports both directly and through their contribution to faster growth in recipient countries (see Chapter 7). Fortunately, these initiatives require very modest budget outlays and are thus compatible with the requirement of fiscal austerity.

This is not the place to lay out the details of a budget package that will meet these criteria, nor is it our comparative advantage to do so. Numerous cogent proposals for reducing the budget deficit have been presented elsewhere.[10] In both economic and political terms, however, the most desirable and most feasible program probably includes a continued leveling of defense spending (or additional cuts, if justified by arms reduction agreements or the elimination of cost overruns); further substantial cuts in domestic spending, particularly transfers of large benefits to higher-income citizens under the entitlement programs; and tax increases of the kind noted above. Whatever the composition of the package, the keys are its magnitude and credibility. With adequate size and certainty, it can be the cornerstone of an effective strategy to enhance America's international economic position. It would make possible all the other elements of the program.

Without early adoption of an effective adjustment program, a free

9. A gasoline tax could be adopted without raising prices at the pump if world oil prices were to decline. Several countries took advantage of such circumstances in 1986 and improved their budget situations considerably.

10. A detailed analysis of budget options appears in Minarik and Penner (1988).

fall of the dollar would be quite likely (as explained in Chapter 2). This would force the administration and Congress to implement a fiscal package like the one proposed here anyway, for that would be the only way to restore market confidence. Under such circumstances, however, the package might need to be much larger, and implemented much more quickly, to reassure the markets. The costs to the economy could be considerably greater than would have been the case if preemptive action had been taken to ensure confidence earlier.

FOREIGN GROWTH

Fiscal action by the United States lies at the heart of the solution to the global economic imbalances and the restoration of international financial stability. However, complementary macroeconomic policies are needed in the major surplus countries to maintain adequate rates of growth in their own economies as their trade surpluses decline; to thereby support continuing growth in the world economy (which is critical, among other things, for avoiding more protectionism and a renewed Third World debt crisis); and to provide enough market expansion to enable the American adjustment to succeed through export growth rather than import compression.

The model used in this analysis suggests that the US current account would improve by about $12.5 billion for each percentage point of annual GNP growth in the other industrial countries and the Asian NICs that was above the baseline rates assumed in the model (roughly 4 percent for Japan, 2–2.5 percent for Europe and Canada, and 4.5 percent for the Asian NICs). Higher surplus country growth averaging 1 percent per year over the four years of the recommended adjustment period would thus induce about $50 billion of improvement in the American current account position.[11]

11. Economists disagree on the extent to which faster growth abroad will speed the improvement of the US trade balance. This disagreement lies at the heart of the debate over whether the United States should actively seek international coordination of national economic policies. Those who see little US gain from faster growth abroad correspondingly place little emphasis on coordination aimed at achieving such growth (Feldstein 1988). The results of 12 models presented to a conference at the Brookings Institution in March 1986 are summarized in Fischer (1987, 9), who concludes that

Rapid foreign growth is also essential because the United States and the rest of the world will face an extremely delicate situation with respect to the exchange rate of the dollar as the adjustment process unfolds. A renewed depreciation of considerable magnitude is needed to complete the adjustment of current accounts, as we will see in the next section. Yet the recommended US budget cuts, which are also essential to that adjustment, could cause an appreciation of the dollar instead, as the markets react to America's "finally getting its house in order."

One way to resolve this conflict is for the surplus countries to ensure rapid and sustained growth of domestic demand at least through the four-year adjustment period, thereby attracting capital and supporting an appreciation of their currencies. Achieving this growth through fiscal expansion, as will be recommended, would reinforce the exchange rate effect by permitting the surplus countries to raise their interest rates. At a minimum, it would enable them to avoid an interest rate decline to match the one that should occur in the United States as a result of the proposed reduction in the American budget deficit.

These growth recommendations apply primarily to the three major surplus areas of the world: Japan, Western Europe (with a slightly above-average increase for Germany and the other surplus countries and somewhat lower increases for the rest of Europe), and the Asian NICs (notably Taiwan and Korea). Japan continues to run the largest external surplus in absolute terms. Western Europe is the world's largest market and thus has an enormous impact on the global economy. The European surplus is concentrated in four countries—Germany, Switzerland, the Netherlands, and Belgium—with a combined surplus only 25 percent less than Japan's in the first half of 1988. Germany's surplus has been higher than Japan's as a proportion of GNP since 1986, and rose to a record level (in DM

"the game theory literature on coordination makes a convincing case that coordination is generally superior to noncooperative policy making . . . (but that) calculations imply that the gains from coordination per se would be small, even if the current model of the economy were known." The models cannot capture the adverse effects of a breakdown in cooperation, however, such as the widely perceived rupture between the United States and Germany that was a major cause of Black Monday. Moreover, there are several other models, including Bryant (1988) and DRI (Gault 1987) that, like ours, show sizable gains for the US current account from faster growth abroad.

terms) in the first half of 1988. The external surpluses of the Asian NICs are far larger relative to these countries' total output—13 percent in Taiwan and 8 percent in Korea—than in Japan and Germany (3–4 percent in each). They are also perhaps the most inappropriate from an international standpoint, in light of the countries' relatively low levels of per capita income; their opportunities for expanding domestic demand (and standards of living) thus exceed those of the other surplus regions.

Japan has already shifted to domestic-led growth and its external surplus has been falling in real terms since 1986. However, Japan's surplus continued to rise in dollar terms in 1987 and will remain at $75 to $80 billion in 1988. Moreover, Japan's investment earnings are growing with the sharp rise in its international asset position. Hence it is essential that Japan maintain rapid domestic demand expansion, injecting further fiscal stimulus as necessary, and adopt additional structural reforms along the lines of the Maekawa Report (Balassa and Noland 1988, 177–180).

Japan's new Five-Year Plan (1988–92) projects GNP growth of 3.75 percent annually and growth in domestic demand of 4.25 percent annually. This would leave the current account surplus at or above 2 percent of GNP, however, probably in the range of $60 to $70 billion. Moreover, deficiencies in the Japanese standard of living, ranging from poor housing through inadequate social infrastructure, suggest that the potential for a sustained boom in domestic demand has only begun to be tapped. There are great prospects for improved productivity in the nontradeables sector, especially in services.

It thus seems both desirable and feasible for Japan to exceed the targets in the plan, perhaps maintaining growth of domestic demand at about 6 percent annually. In fact, domestic demand growth reached an estimated 7.4 percent in 1988. GNP would grow at about 5 percent. Together with the additional rise in the yen proposed below, this should bring the external surplus down by about 1 percent of GNP per year to about $30 billion (less than 1 percent of GNP) by 1992. The widespread domestic satisfaction with Japan's successful reorientation to date augurs well for such an outcome.

Domestic demand has also picked up in Europe, growing at 4 to 4.5 percent since mid-1987. Unemployment is still very high, however, so there is a strong case in purely domestic terms for trying to sustain this pace for several years. Europe had not, until now, had a growth spurt since the 1982 recession as would have been normal—and which the United States achieved, financed importantly by European (and Japanese) savings, in 1983–84.

It would thus be appropriate for Europe as a whole to move into current account deficit over the next few years to help finance the investment needed to put the unemployed back to work.[12] Sustained growth in Western Europe, the world's largest market, would also make a major contribution to maintaining growth in the world economy while the US trade deficit is being corrected. Because the external surplus of the region would be declining steadily, its GNP would be rising at about 3 to 3.5 percent—which is well within the region's growth potential.

A key problem, however, is that a major payments imbalance is developing within Europe. Four countries—Germany, the Netherlands, Switzerland, and Belgium—are running a combined current account surplus of over $60 billion, while the rest of Western Europe, which was in rough balance in 1986, is likely to have a combined deficit approaching $50 billion in 1988. This is partly because domestic demand has generally been stronger in the deficit countries (indeed, too strong in the United Kingdom).[13]

But a more important reason lies in the way in which the EMS has been operating. Each time a realignment has been necessary, attention has been directed largely to adjusting exchange rates for differences in national rates of inflation. Over time, however, a serious payments imbalance (reminiscent of the latter days of the Bretton Woods regime) has emerged because of other factors, such as differences in growth rates, industrial structures, and underlying competitive strength. This will require a major change in European exchange rates relative to one another.[14]

---

12. It was noteworthy that European members of the group of 33 economists from 13 countries convened by the Institute for International Economics after the October 1987 crash took the lead in arguing that, for this reason, "the Community could temporarily swing into external deficit for a period" (*Resolving the Global Economic Crisis* 1987, 10).

13. This is not a new phenomenon. From 1980 to 1987, domestic demand grew on average only half as fast in Germany (1 percent a year) as it did in the rest of Europe.

14. An EMS realignment could be triggered by a sharp fall in the dollar, which as described in Chapters 1 and 2 could occur at almost any time—especially in 1989 if the new American administration and Congress fail to launch a credible attack on the twin deficits. The EMS is directly affected because any significant fall in the dollar

This situation must be a matter of serious concern to the United States. By the closing months of 1988, it was becoming apparent that much of the foreign counterpart of the improvement in the US current account was coming at the expense of the deficit countries in Europe. But the US adjustment still has a long way to go and, if this trend continues, it is inevitable that the currencies of these countries will come under increasing pressure. They will then be forced to put on the brakes, bringing the encouraging pickup in European growth to a premature end and threatening to halt the American adjustment.

A complicating factor is that this payments disequilibrium is emerging at a time when Europe is taking major steps to integrate its goods and capital markets through the elimination of numerous internal barriers and regulatory inefficiencies. (These developments are also extremely important for the United States in terms of trade policy, as discussed in Chapter 6.) Under the right macroeconomic conditions, the "completion of the internal market" could help to sustain and broaden expansion in Europe, both directly and through the favorable effects on growth expectations in the business community (as occurred in the 1960s with anticipation of the completion of the tariff cuts under the original Common Market treaty).[15] Sustained and balanced growth would also help to ease political resistance to the measures needed to achieve full economic integration, just as it reduced resistance to the elimination of tariff barriers in the 1960s. As things stand, however, there is a clear risk that with a growing payments imbalance in Europe, resistance from the "losers"—who under present conditions are most likely to be found in the deficit countries—will become a major obstacle to success, and at the same time increase the danger that liberalization within Europe will come at the expense of the rest of the world.

Successful completion of the European internal market may thus not be possible without a major realignment of the European

---

means a rising DM, which would pull up the other European currencies against the dollar even though the payments position of several of these countries could not tolerate such appreciation.

15. The results of the Commission's analysis of the effects of completion of the internal market are summarized in the March issue of *European Economy* and in volume 1 of the multivolume analysis commonly known as the Cecchini Report (Commission of the European Communities, 1988). See also Pelkmans and Winters (1988).

currencies, accompanied by a significant recalibration of national monetary and fiscal policies (Marris forthcoming). The devaluing countries will need to tighten up to minimize the inflationary impact. The revaluing countries will have to take expansionary action to compensate for the drop in their external surpluses; this applies especially to Germany, where recent growth has been led largely by exports to the rest of Europe.

Where expansionary action is required, preference should be given to loosening fiscal policy to permit some further increase in interest rates if necessary to counteract a premature strengthening of the dollar or a pickup of inflation. Structural policies, particularly regarding agriculture, labor markets, and industrial subsidies, can help as well. There is legitimate concern in Germany and elsewhere over returning to the large budget deficits of the 1970s but, as Japan demonstrated in 1987–88, a well-timed fiscal boost to domestic demand can lead to smaller rather than larger fiscal imbalances.[16]

This complex situation in Europe poses a major challenge to US economic diplomacy. While in the first instance these are Europe's own problems, extremely important US interests are at stake. It will not be enough for the new administration to concentrate, as in the past, on the G-5 and bilateral pressure on Germany. Efforts should be made to mobilize support within the European Community for solutions compatible with US interests, in a way that will not be open to the accusation that the United States is "interfering" in internal European affairs. Several possible steps through which the United States can help foster an outward looking Europe are discussed further below.

Among the Asian NICs, the surpluses are greatest in Taiwan ($15 billion) and Korea ($10 billion). Taiwan is already one of the largest creditor countries in the world. Korea may become a creditor in 1990, having been the fourth-largest LDC debtor as recently as 1986, a reversal as stunning as America's in the opposite direction. Furthermore, as noted earlier, the exportation of domestic savings on this scale seems particularly inappropriate for countries with such relatively low per capita incomes (about $6,000 and $3,600,

16. Germany's present fiscal plans for 1989 are the most contractionary among the G-7 (IMF 1988, table A16).

respectively, in nominal terms at 1988 exchange rates) and enormous capacity for improving their standards of living.

Three adjustment techniques, all of which would promote higher living standards, commend themselves in these countries: increased government stimulus of domestic demand (employing both tax cuts and stepped-up spending on infrastructure), faster trade liberalization, and currency appreciation (Balassa and Williamson 1987). Since these countries have become so heavily dependent on export expansion for economic growth, they will have a special need for offsetting increases in domestic demand as their external surpluses decline. This is particularly true because they will need to open their markets further to imports, and let their currencies continue to rise, if adjustment is to occur at a sufficiently rapid pace.[17]

Sustained foreign growth is thus an extremely significant part of the adjustment strategy and the new administration should treat it as a high priority. The second Reagan administration did just that, and achieved substantial success with Japan (Funabashi 1988). Its capacity to win the necessary cooperation from Europe and the NICs was limited, however, by its inability to correct its own fiscal deficit. The persistence of the American internal imbalance led other countries to doubt that their export surpluses would drop very much, therefore relieving them of the need to pursue offsetting domestic adjustments. These countries also took the view that they were being asked to bail out the United States when its own policies were the major source of trouble. The American deficits provided a political excuse for avoiding actions abroad.

A new administration and Congress that convincingly attacked the US budget deficit would be in a much different position. Their actions would persuade the rest of the world that US domestic

17. Bergsten (1987b) analyzes the Taiwan case in some detail. The Group of Seven and the economic summits have recognized the international importance of the NICs since early 1987 and publicly called for changes in their policies. However, the industrial countries have not found an effective forum to discuss the issues directly with the NICs themselves; in practice, the United States has pursued the countries bilaterally on both trade liberalization and currency appreciation, although Korea succeeded in transferring at least the formal talks on exchange rates into the IMF. This approach is unsatisfactory, and it is therefore essential to bring these countries increasingly into the relevant multilateral fora, starting perhaps with the OECD. The unique political positions of Hong Kong and Taiwan should not be permitted to hinder this process.

demand, and hence the trade deficit, would be coming down, perhaps rather sharply, and that the world economy could slow markedly as a result. The surplus countries would then have to sustain their internal expansions both for domestic and international reasons. This kind of American action would also remove the concern (and the political excuse) that the United States was asking others to solve its problems. Again, responsible budget action at home is central to the success of the strategy. Foreign cooperation, however, is essential as well.

Latin America, and a few major debtor countries elsewhere, could also contribute to the adjustment of the global imbalances if there were a substantial and sustained increase in capital flows to them from the industrial countries. As a group, the heavily indebted developing countries (the so-called Baker 15) are now paying about $30 billion more in annual interest costs than they are receiving in new capital inflows (a "negative financial transfer"). Since their foreign exchange reserves have already been run down to minimal levels, they must generate sizable trade surpluses to avoid interruptions in the servicing of their debt. Such surpluses are wholly inappropriate for developing countries whose per capita incomes are still relatively low; they have contributed significantly to the sharp falls in per capita income that have occurred throughout the hemisphere during the "lost decade" of the 1980s (Cline 1987a, 63–67).

It would thus be highly desirable to reverse the negative financial transfer from these countries to help them restore more rapid growth, to further reduce the risk of financial disruption associated with their debts, and, most importantly from the standpoint of this analysis, to support the American trade correction. Japan and the other surplus countries should contribute a substantial portion of the required capital flows, which would enable them to avoid still larger reductions in their own current account surpluses. The bulk of the additional lending to the Third World debtors should be channeled through the international financial institutions, which are best able to encourage the policy reforms that permit effective use of new capital, using techniques described in Chapter 7.

THE EXCHANGE RATE OF THE DOLLAR

Exchange rate policy will be one of the most difficult challenges for the new administration. The rapid and sustained growth of American exports since the middle of 1986 suggests that the United States has regained substantial price competitiveness in the world economy. However, even if the United States adopts the fiscal stance proposed here, and the surplus countries maintain rapid growth of domestic demand, two key questions will remain for exchange rate policy in the new administration. Will a further decline in the value of the dollar be needed to complement the macroeconomic changes and reach a lasting equilibrium? What should be done if the dollar rises significantly after the launching of the recommended fiscal policy?[18]

Achieving a precise estimate of the "correct" equilibrium exchange rate is particularly difficult during the adjustment to such a prolonged and massive disequilibrium. It seems clear, however, that the dollar runup of 1988—as of early fall, about 5 percent above the dollar's average value in the fourth quarter of 1987,[19] and 12 percent from its trough at the end of 1987—will need to be reversed. In addition, our model shows that a further dollar depreciation of about 15 percent in real terms, during the course of 1989, will be required to fully eliminate the current account deficit by 1992 if other industrial countries achieve the faster expansion recommended above.

---

18. Further dollar depreciation would not be desirable in the absence of substantial cuts in the budget deficit, as proposed above. With the economy near full employment, the main result would probably be a considerable pickup in inflation—as with the hard landing scenario described in Chapter 2. In that circumstance, the exchange rate of the dollar would probably not even accomplish much depreciation in real terms. Even a successful further reduction in the external deficit, without *ex ante* assurance of a compensating slowdown in the growth of domestic demand, would be undesirable because it would push up interest rates (due to the corresponding fall in net capital inflows) and force the slowdown *ex post* by retarding private investment. In essence, the "crowding out" which many economists thought would result from the rapid growth of the budget deficit in the early 1980s, but was avoided by the parallel growth of the external deficit and capital inflow, would emerge in the late 1980s and early 1990s.

19. The fourth quarter of 1987 is used as the base for currency calculations in our model (which is the Helkie-Hooper model as modified by Cline; see Annex) because the late 1987 dollar decline and the subsequent runup through September 1988 largely cancelled each other out.

The dollar will thus probably need to fall by about 15–20 percent from its level in the early fall of 1988.[20]

An across-the-board fall of the dollar by another 15–20 percent, however, would transfer a significant part of the American correction to countries that are running deficits themselves and thus could not accept the losses. This group includes Canada and the deficit countries in Europe, including France, Italy, and the United Kingdom (Cline forthcoming). Their responses could forestall at least part of the adjustment and retard world growth. Pressures for new protectionist measures would increase, especially in Europe. A more targeted approach is needed.

If the bulk of the American correction were to be absorbed by the main surplus countries, their nominal exchange rates against the dollar would have to rise from the previous highs reached at the end of 1987 by considerably more than the average dollar depreciation (except for the Korean won, because it continued to rise against the dollar during 1988 despite the dollar's own rise). The nominal dollar rates that would emerge would be about 100 yen, 1.25 DM, 23 NT$, and 675 won.

A DM appreciation of this magnitude, even with parallel rises in the Dutch guilder and Belgian franc, would imply a realignment on the order of 20 percent within the EMS. Indeed, one of the objectives of this targeted approach is to limit the adjustment costs to the European countries that are already running external deficits. France and Italy would need to accept small appreciations against the dollar (as would Canada), but the DM and the currencies of the smaller surplus countries would rise much more.

The achievement of the necessary additional decline in the dollar's value could be frustrated, however, by successful implementation of another key element of the adjustment package: cuts in the US budget deficit. Conventional economic analysis suggests that expectations of steady reductions in the US budget deficit would lead to lower interest rates and thus a further depreciation of the dollar. If that were to happen, the only currency concern would be to keep

20. At that time, the dollar was worth about 128 yen and about 1.82 DM. On this point we are largely in agreement with Martin Feldstein, who called for a fall in the dollar of 10 to 20 percent in remarks to a Data Resources, Inc., conference in New York on 4 October 1988.

the dollar from falling too fast. Given the underlying fiscal correction that would be underway, however, the dollar's fall might turn out to be quite orderly, as in 1985–86. If intervention were needed, it should be relatively easy to work out under such conditions.

However, the psychological impact of the United States "finally getting its house in order," along with the prospects of lasting improvement in the external deficit and lower inflation, could induce sizable capital inflows and propel the dollar upward instead. This might be especially likely if it appeared that US growth would hold up well, and if Japan and Germany appeared ready to slow down because their domestic demand growth seemed inadequate to offset the further fall in their trade surpluses.[21]

It would be very tempting for both the United States and the surplus countries to let such a dollar rebound occur, and even to applaud it. The new administration's policies would appear to be vindicated by the markets. Other countries could avoid a painful policy choice, and indeed experience a renewed improvement in their international competitive positions.

Such a return to "benign neglect" would be a major mistake. As just indicated, further depreciation of the dollar is needed to restore equilibrium. It is quite clear that any significant dollar appreciation would move the world away from enduring international stability, especially after the appreciation of 1988. (Our model suggests that every 10 percent of sustained dollar appreciation against the currencies of the stronger countries and Canada affects the US current account adversely by about $60 billion after four years.) The deficit would never fall to a sustainable level, and the magnitude of the required adjustment would begin to rise again, building even larger future difficulties for the United States and its trading partners. Protectionist pressures would intensify again in the United States. As described in Chapter 2, a renewed deterioration of the current account deficit—which could easily occur within a year or two of any sustained rise of the dollar—might even discredit the entire adjustment effort and

21. Time lags are very important in this process (Marris 1987, 16–19). It takes about two years for currency changes to fully affect current account positions. Hence the markets could push the dollar up, sowing the seeds of future trade deterioration and renewed dollar weakness, in response to trade improvement generated by a lower dollar one to two years earlier. William Cline has warned of the "false optimism" that can result from ignoring this phenomenon, which was clearly present during 1988.

trigger a round of extensive trade controls and a further erosion of the open trading system.

The new administration must therefore avoid a renewed upward dollar surge. The US trade correction requires firm assurances to American industry that its export efforts will not be undermined by a premature rise of the currency. In particular, new investment in export capacity is needed to overcome the bottlenecks that were already apparent in 1988 and to sustain the export boom. Yet a number of major exporting firms have reportedly resisted expanding their productive capacity out of fear that the dollar will soar again, pricing them out of world markets by the time their new capacity comes on stream. The necessary improvements in the trade picture, along with the productivity and anti-inflationary benefits of such investment, could be seriously jeopardized unless it is clear that any premature appreciation of the dollar will be firmly resisted.

The authorities must take forceful action to avoid any appreciation of the dollar that threatens to postpone the restoration and maintenance of equilibrium in the US current account. At least some of the foreign central banks that acquired large dollar holdings while trying to limit the decline of the dollar during the 1986 to early 1988 period would probably welcome the opportunity to intervene on the selling side (more than was required during the dollar's 1988 rise) to unload more of their excess dollar reserves and to reduce any inflationary pressures that might build in their economies as a result of the proposed stimulus measures. By intervening to resist dollar appreciation, the United States would also benefit by building the reserves of foreign currency it will need to defend the dollar during its next period of excessive decline.[22]

But intervention alone, in light of the hypothesized fiscal tightening in the United States, may not be enough to halt a renewed rise of the dollar. American interest rates should be falling, however, and monetary policy could push them down even further, if necessary

22. It will be especially important for the United States to augment its holdings of foreign exchange, which are quite modest by comparison with all of the other major countries, if the world decides to adopt a full target zone system to stabilize currencies in the future, as recommended in the next section. US nongold reserves ($25.3 billion as of July 1988) are less than half as great as those of Japan, Taiwan, and Germany, and are at about the same level as those of the United Kingdom, Spain, France, and Italy.

and if consistent with keeping inflation under control. The maintenance of rapid foreign growth as proposed is also essential, because it will attract capital flows to the surplus countries. If that growth is achieved through fiscal stimulus, it will enable them to raise their own interest rates as well.

This combination of intervention and monetary policies should be able to stop any renewed rise of the dollar. Given the premise of US fiscal correction, the central banks should not fear that capping the dollar's rise will produce a renewed dollar slide, as it did in April and August of 1987. (This experience helped induce the central banks to permit the unwarranted dollar rebound of 1988.) They will in fact be more likely to need to nudge the dollar down to achieve the required depreciation, using official intervention to "lean with the wind" whenever the markets move in that direction, as they did after the Plaza Agreement.[23]

Given the possibility that the proposed budget program could push the dollar up when it still needed to fall considerably farther, the best strategy might be to seek the needed further depreciation before the fiscal program is put in place. This would require rapid and deft management of the situation between the election and the early weeks of the new administration, when the budget is submitted. Alternatively, if negotiations between the new President and the Congress over the budget package took several months to work out, a dollar fall could be permitted (or even encouraged) at the same time—with the desirable side effect of adding pressure on the negotiators to agree on a credible program. In either case, the announcement of the fiscal program should stop the dollar's slide and provide the internal US adjustment needed to translate the slide into a lasting improvement in the current account. The monetary authorities might still have to take action to avoid a substantial rebound, but they would be operating much nearer the long-term equilibrium level and could then launch the new target zone system (see below) to help them do so.

23. The case for "leaning with the wind" was outlined by Bergsten (1984).

INTERNATIONAL MONETARY REFORM

By setting the stage for the elimination of the massive international imbalances that the new administration will inherit, the adoption of appropriate macroeconomic measures and further exchange rate changes by the United States and the other major countries would also set the stage for an effort to maintain long-run currency stability through decisive reform of the international monetary system. If a stable pattern of exchange rates could be established and ratified by the markets, the foundation will have been laid for the installation of new forms of systemic cooperation. A new monetary system could help prevent the severe misalignments that have occurred periodically since the advent of floating rates, and could provide an orderly basis for needed currency adjustments in the future.

It is clear that the system (or nonsystem) of unmanaged flexibility in exchange rates is no longer viable (Williamson 1985). Currency misalignments have grown in frequency; most notable was the overvaluation of the dollar by 40–60 percent in trade terms at its peak in early 1985. This disequilibrium was twice as great as the dollar overvaluation of the early 1970s that triggered the collapse of the fixed-rate system of Bretton Woods. Largely as a result of these currency misalignments, protectionism has grown and the entire international system has eroded (as described in Chapter 3). The monetary regime has failed in its basic task of providing a foundation for open trade (Bergsten and Williamson 1983, Pelkmans 1988).

Moreover, the advent of floating rates effectively voided any meaningful obligations on the part of national governments to coordinate their economic policies, or even to take external factors into consideration in devising their domestic strategies. But the early hopes that floating would insulate national economies, enabling governments to adopt policies with a high degree of effective autonomy, have been totally dashed (Fischer 1987, 43).[24]

The new administration should thus seek to devise, with its leading economic partners, a system of target zones as a framework within which to stabilize currencies and to achieve more effective

24. This is a further reason, beyond the structural considerations cited in Chapters 2 and 3, why benign neglect is an unviable strategy for the United States in the 1990s (Marris 1984, 7–8).

international coordination of national economic policies. This system should be installed as soon as a pattern of sustainable equilibrium exchange rates is established. Such a step would represent a natural evolution from the reference ranges adopted by the G-7 in the Louvre Accord of February 1987. It could also draw on the "indicators" approach adopted at the Tokyo Summit in May 1986 and elaborated since that time, employing, in particular, the comparable data bases and medium-term targets and projections for the countries' key economic variables that have recently been developed in that context (Mulford 1988). From a longer-run perspective a target zone regime would represent a synthesis of the positive elements from the Bretton Woods system, whose fixed rates became far too rigid, and the nonsystem of unmanaged flexibility, with its excessive gyrations and huge misalignments.

This extension and formalization of exchange rate management would be desirable for several reasons. The current reference ranges are kept secret and hence give uncertain guidance to the markets. The participating countries have made no firm commitments to defend them, have apparently failed even to discuss such key tools as monetary policy when setting currency targets, and have in practice tended to "rebase" rather than resist when pressures arise (as in April and December 1987, though not in January 1988). There seems to be little operational interaction between the indicators, which relate to underlying macroeconomic policies (and, since the Toronto Summit in June 1988, to microeconomic measures as well), and the currency ranges. The enterprise has been conducted entirely on an ad hoc basis, with no recording of decisions, let alone institutionalization in the IMF or elsewhere.[25]

All these shortcomings in the present regime are understandable, given the massive imbalances—and the absence of adequate policies to correct them—that have been present throughout the period. Former Treasury Secretary Baker, his American colleagues, and other G-7 officials deserve enormous credit for even attempting systemic improvement in such a context; their progress over the past three years provides a valuable base from which to proceed. Further

25. Details of the G-5/G-7 efforts "from the Plaza to the Louvre" can be found in Funabashi (1988).

institutional improvement is needed to achieve lasting stability, however.

A full target zone system would have several basic features. The key countries (and later, perhaps, much of the IMF membership) would first agree on sustainable and internationally consistent current account outcomes. They would then devise a set of exchange rates thought to be consistent with these outcomes over the medium term, and set a range (extending perhaps plus or minus 10 percent around the targets at the outset) within which their exchange rates would be allowed to fluctuate. They would establish procedures for altering the ranges to reflect changes in underlying economic relationships—quasi-automatic alterations to offset inflation differentials, judgmental alterations to accommodate changes in "real" economic variables (such as productivity growth) and major systemic shocks (such as large upward or downward movements in oil prices).

The countries would also commit themselves to the adoption of policy changes, as needed, to prevent their currencies from moving outside the ranges. They would start with direct market intervention and jawboning, in most cases, but turn to monetary policy if necessary. The determination of responsibility for action would depend on the outlook for the world economy: countries with currencies rising to the top of their zones would ease monetary policy if there were risks of global recession; countries whose currencies were moving to the bottom of their zones would tighten if the main international problem were inflation. If the changes in monetary policy required to defend the zones ran counter to the needs of a domestic economy, fiscal policy could be altered in an offsetting manner. Over time, the IMF should assume an increasingly central role in managing the new system, both to endow it with political legitimacy and to make sure that the global economic outlook was taken fully into account when individual adjustment decisions were made. And it would be essential to ensure consistency between the new global arrangements and the EMS.[26]

---

26. An alternative to target zones is to seek better coordination of national economic policies directly, with exchange-rate stability expected to result from such an effort rather than providing its focal point. Proponents of this approach argue that targeting exchange rates per se will be ineffective unless such policy coordination is achieved, so it should be addressed forthrightly. Conceptually, the two approaches represent

Finally, government officials should announce their target ranges and policy commitments publicly. This would help induce stabilizing private capital flows, once it became clear to the markets that the officials would implement the system effectively. The huge flows of international capital would then support, rather than undermine, underlying trade and economic objectives.[27]

If public announcement of the zones themselves was not feasible at this early stage of the process, the reforms should still proceed. In this case, it would be desirable to have maximum disclosure of the procedures involved and the policy commitments being undertaken, to maximize the market impact and credibility of the enterprise. But if the major countries, or even the United States alone, as recommended in Chapter 4, were to publicly announce their current account goals, there would be a strong case for announcing their exchange rate targets as well, to provide convincing evidence that they know how they are going to reach those objectives.

The new administration will have a major interest in installing such a system of currency management and policy coordination as soon as conditions permit. In the short run, it would help significantly to avoid renewed dollar appreciation—which, as noted above, could choke off much of the needed trade adjustment and limit the gains of the entire strategy proposed in this volume. Indeed, the G-7 might want to announce an agreed set of ceiling exchange rates for the dollar before they worked out a full set of target zones.[28] In the longer run, a system of target zones would help to avoid the huge swings in the dollar—sharp depreciation with substantial inflationary

alternative tactics for achieving similar ends. Historically, however, there are no examples of successful international arrangements to coordinate policies directly whereas there are several cases—including the Bretton Woods system and the EMS as discussed here—in which a currency focus has proven reasonably effective. This may be because the exchange rate approach is much simpler: there is no need to coordinate all policies at all times if the goal is "only" to defend currency levels.

27. The details of these proposals are in Williamson and Miller (1987). They respond to critics of the original target zone approach on pages 46–63.

28. They already came close to doing so in their communiqué of 22 December 1987, which, after repeating the usual language about "excessive fluctuations of exchange rates" and "a further decline in the dollar," added that "a rise in the dollar to an extent that becomes destabilizing to the adjustment process could be counterproductive . . ." (Funabashi 1988, 291–292).

consequences as in the early and late 1970s, excessive appreciation and subsequent trade deterioration and protectionism, as in the late 1960s and early 1980s—that have had such adverse effects on the US economy during the past 20 years.

History suggests that international arrangements that promote policy coordination induce all countries, including the United States, to adopt more sensible domestic policies. International commitments to pursue coordination, or at least to avoid undesirable unilateral policies, were included in the Bretton Woods charter of the system of fixed exchange rates and are now included in the EMS. Neither Bretton Woods nor the EMS worked perfectly. Nevertheless, "the Bretton Woods system unquestionably enforced policy coordination ... (and) imposed significant constraints on policy, including on occasion policy in the United States" (Fischer 1987, 31, 43).[29] Both systems established frameworks that constantly reminded countries of their international obligations, forced them to make conscious decisions if they were going to ignore those obligations, and often (as with France in 1983) pulled them back to international consistency.

The restoration of a meaningful international monetary system should be of particular interest to countries outside the United States because it could help deter new American administrations from lunging toward the extremes of benign neglect or aggressive unilateralism that have been typical during the past two decades (figure 5.1 and Bergsten 1986). A systemic constraint would also be desirable for the United States itself, since America's policy extremes have always turned out to be deleterious to its own fundamental national interests—with considerable costs incurred before the inevitable forced return to pluralistic cooperation (as with Nixon at the Smithsonian in 1971, Carter at the Bonn Summit and with the dollar support program in 1978, and Reagan at the Plaza and Louvre). The creation of a meaningful system would maintain pressure on the Europeans to retain a global perspective, rather than turn

29. Some observers (R. Solomon 1987) argue that the current international imbalances derive from the failure of governments to adopt sensible policies rather than from the shortcomings of the monetary system. Our analysis fully concurs in the indictment of many recent policies. But this is a false dichotomy: any international system worthy of the name, as pointed out by Fischer (1987) and many others, has consequential effects on national policies and tilts them in the direction of greater international consistency.

inward as they rely increasingly on the EMS and possibly move toward a European central bank. (A similar problem in the trade area is addressed in the following chapter.)

It would be desirable to implement a target zone system as soon as possible. However, it may take a while for the hypothesized new policies to be put in place. It may take even longer for the markets to settle on a stable set of exchange rates, given those policies. The most urgent task of international monetary management—avoidance of a renewed rise of the dollar—could (as noted above) be accomplished without the installation of a new system. And it would be a serious mistake for the United States, both for substantive and tactical reasons, to agree to a new system that would stabilize the exchange rate of the dollar before it was clear that the current account deficit was well on its way to elimination. The United States made such a mistake at the Louvre in February 1987, when the dollar was still far away from the level needed to restore equilibrium in the current account; the reference ranges adopted there had predictably short lives.[30]

The proper course for the new administration is thus to indicate clearly its desire to move to a full target zone system, to promptly commence negotiations on its components, and to deploy the system as soon as it is agreed that appropriate economic policies are in place and the dollar has fallen enough. Conditions will never be perfect for such an initiative. But the key countries should be ready to move as soon as their new policies win the confidence of the markets, and the resulting pattern of exchange rates and policies shows good prospects of restoring and maintaining international payments equilibrium.[31]

---

30. The effort was understandable in tactical terms, however, because of the need at that time to stop the sharp slide of the dollar and thus the risk of a hard landing (as described in Chapters 1 and 2). Moreover, as noted in the text, the systemic implications of the Louvre Accord were highly desirable and it may turn out to have been the first step toward a historic reform of the international monetary system.

31. It is sometimes argued (Feldstein 1988, 10–11) that the United States is constitutionally incapable of participating in effective international policy coordination because the executive branch cannot make binding commitments on fiscal policy and the Federal Reserve has independent authority over monetary policy. Concerning fiscal policy, the same problems existed with respect to trade policy before 1934: the executive could not negotiate because the Congress had constitutional authority to act. That problem was resolved, after the Smoot-Hawley disaster in the early 1930s, by

FIGURE 5.1 US International Economic Cooperation: 1960–1988

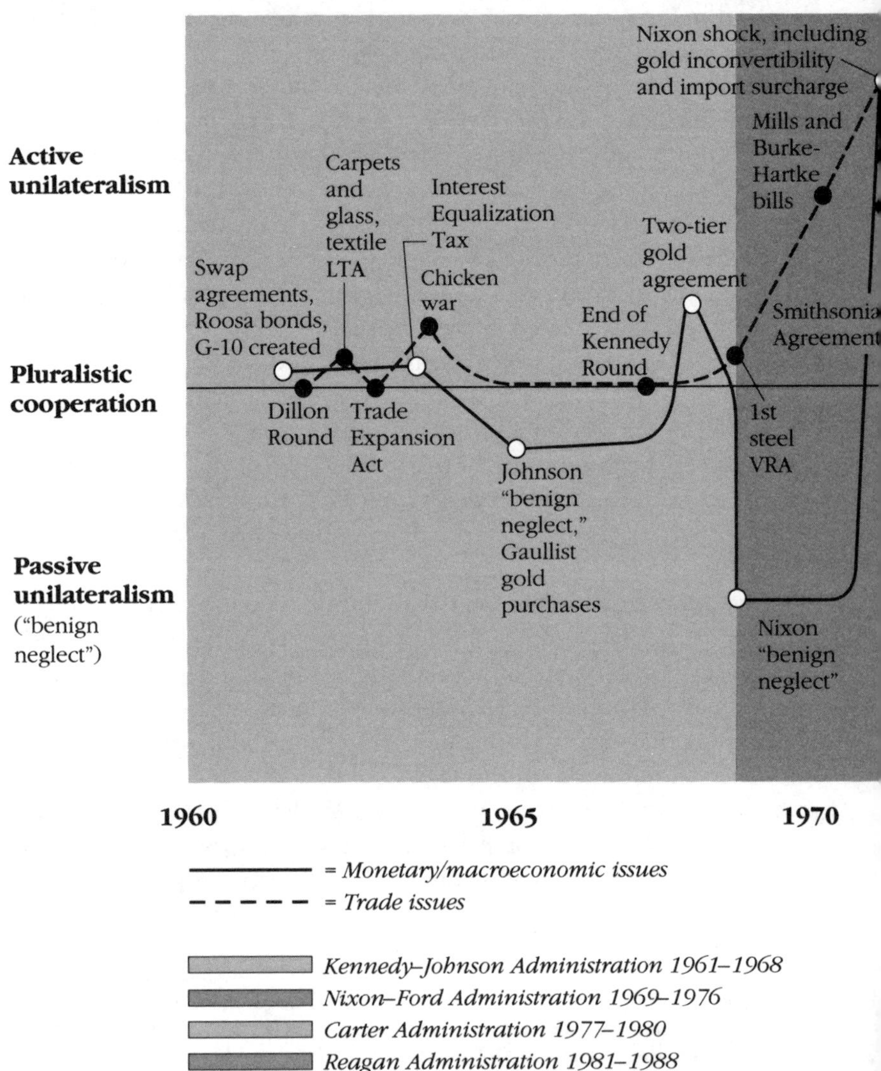

LTA Long-Term Agreement on International Trade in Cotton Textiles
VRA Voluntary Restraint Agreement

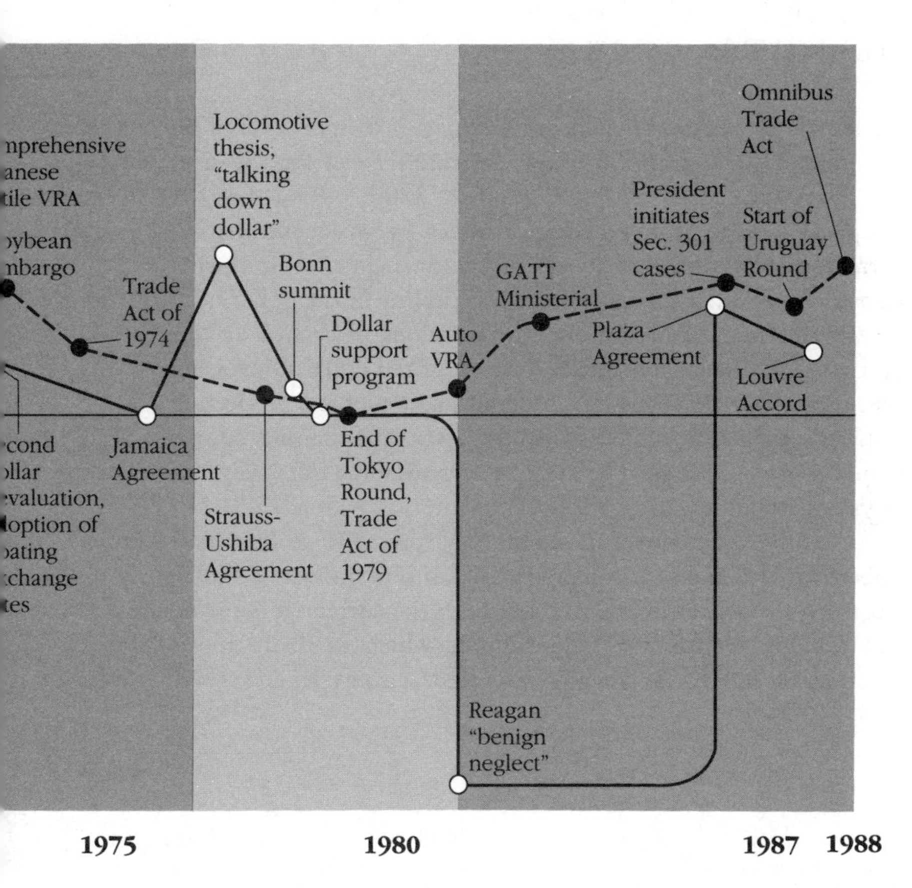

Locomotive thesis, "talking down dollar"
Omnibus Trade Act
President initiates Sec. 301 cases
Start of Uruguay Round
Bonn summit
GATT Ministerial
Trade Act of 1974
Dollar support program
Auto VRA
Plaza Agreement
Louvre Accord
Jamaica Agreement
End of Tokyo Round, Trade Act of 1979
Strauss-Ushiba Agreement
Reagan "benign neglect"
1975
1980
1987
1988

FINANCING THE REMAINING DEFICITS

Under the best of circumstances, American's current account deficits will remain at a sizable (though declining) level for the next few years, accumulating at least another $200 billion before they disappear. There is a potential conflict between eliminating the current account deficit and obtaining financing for it during the transition period: a further substantial decline of the dollar is needed to achieve the adjustment, but expectations of such a decline can deter the needed capital inflow (and cause the dollar to overshoot on the downside). Nevertheless, a combination of dollar decline and stable funding was achieved in 1985–86. The coming adjustment period must be managed in a way that maintains the foreign capital inflows without aborting the adjustment.[32]

A credible adjustment program that promises to eliminate the imbalances within a reasonable period might induce a sufficiently large private capital inflow to cover both the current account deficits and the gross outflow of US capital, which is likely to remain substantial. Indeed, as already discussed at some length, there is a

congressional decisions to delegate authority to the executive to change tariffs and later to negotiate on nontariff barriers under limits and procedures (the fast track authority) that fulfilled its constitutional responsibility. If the executive and Congress cannot find more effective ways to work together on fiscal policy, a similar delegation of authority—which already exists in major countries such as Germany and the United Kingdom—may be needed. As to the Federal Reserve, effective cooperation with the Treasury has been the rule rather than the exception and the problem is certainly no more acute in the United States than in Germany, where the independence of the Bundesbank has proven to be compatible with the extensive exchange rate and intervention requirements of the EMS. These issues will be addressed in Destler and Henning (forthcoming).

32. The standard theoretical reconciliation of the dilemma is for the exchange rate to complete its needed fall with extreme rapidity so that the market will expect its next move to be upward and therefore provide the required capital while the currency changes are working through to the trade flows to obviate the need for more foreign borrowing (Dornbusch 1976). In practice, unfortunately, sharp currency falls and market expectations can never be calibrated. Officials therefore always fear, perhaps correctly, that the rates will overshoot far beyond the equilibrium level and generate expectations of further decline (as well as considerable inflationary pressure) rather than stabilization or recovery—thereby exacerbating rather than resolving the financing issue.

risk that such a program could induce excessive capital inflow—pushing the dollar up when it needed to decline further. Yet financing problems might remain, and they could require continued official attention. One result of credible expectations of American budget correction should be considerably lower interest rates in both nominal and (even more so) in real terms. This will help both to promote the needed depreciation of the dollar and (along with the trade improvement) to maintain economic growth in the face of the fiscal contraction. But lower interest rates could also discourage the needed inflow of private capital, especially if rapid growth in Japan and the key European countries (as recommended above) places upward pressure on their money markets.

In addition, currency runs sometimes occur very late in an adjustment process (Marris 1987, xxxviii). Indeed, they can begin well after the current account has begun to improve (as was the case in the last major American correction, during the late 1970s). It would be surprising if this were to happen in the wake of effective budget action, as posited here, but we are not able to predict market attitudes toward investing in a key currency whose issuing country is the world's largest debtor and whose gross liabilities to foreigners approximate $2 trillion (as they will in the early 1990s). Hence it is prudent to anticipate the need for further official financing, beyond the $150 billion or so provided during 1986–87, even if the adjustment strategy proposed here is adopted.

Given steadily falling American internal and external deficits, foreign central banks might be willing to support the dollar on their own. The ultimate outlook would be for a stable or even stronger dollar, so their financial risk would be minimal. (This favorable outlook would be further enhanced by the proposed reform of the international monetary system.) The United States would be taking the needed adjustment measures, so there would be no reason to withhold finance to encourage policy changes. The inflationary risk of dollar purchases could pose a problem, particularly if these countries are pursuing rapid demand growth. But the declining US trade deficit would be imparting deflationary pressure to the surplus countries, and any inflationary risk to them should be modest given the scale of intervention necessary under the proposed adjustment program.

If the US authorities nevertheless needed to work more actively than in the recent past to acquire the necessary funding from abroad, they could do so rather confidently under this scenario. With a falling current account deficit, they could issue foreign-currency bonds (like the Roosa bonds of the 1960s or the Carter bonds of the late 1970s) with a good deal of confidence that this would stabilize the currency (and avoid losing money for the United States government) once the dollar had reached its equilibrium level. There are two basic criteria for issuing such securities: the existence of an effective adjustment program, so that the bonds will be viewed as a means of financing a genuine transition to a new equilibrium, rather than as a desperate attempt to borrow rather than adjust; and a favorable outlook for the dollar, to avoid the risk of heavy currency losses. Under our proposed program of fiscal correction and related steps, both criteria would be met after the dollar had completed its downward movement.[33]

The United States will face an immense financing problem if the new administration and Congress fail to launch an effective and credible adjustment program. There would be a need for very high interest rates, and probably substantial sales of US reserve assets and large quantities of foreign currency borrowing. We do not dwell on this scenario because it would almost certainly doom the entire economic strategy of the new administration. Avoiding such an outcome is perhaps the most compelling reason for adopting the program proposed here.

33. Details can be found in Bergsten (1988). The acceptance of new foreign-currency liabilities would probably be better for the United States under such circumstances than sales of reserve assets (gold, SDRs, the IMF reserve position). Such assets are better held against the next period of downward pressure on the dollar, when adequate adjustment measures are not yet in place and when the acceptance of additional foreign-currency liabilities would be both risky financially and ineffective psychologically.

6

An Activist Trade Policy: Promoting Exports and Opening Markets

STRATEGIC GOALS FOR TRADE POLICY

US trade policy in 1989 and the early 1990s should aim primarily to support the elimination of the current account deficit. This will require active promotion of US exports and persistent international negotiations to open foreign markets further to American goods. The trade strategy, like the budget strategy, must be worked out in close collaboration with the Congress. The new administration could launch its effort in this area with the first set of trade policy reports required in early 1989 by the new Omnibus Trade Act.

The United States still faces a marketing reentry problem, despite the rapid export growth of the past two years. As described in Chapter 2, American firms displayed an impressive ability to compete abroad in the late 1970s. After the enormous rise of the dollar in the first half of the 1980s priced many firms out of world markets, however, some lost interest. Other companies have been reluctant to build additional export capacity because of fears that the dollar will climb again before this capacity comes on stream—a fear validated to an extent by the events of 1988.

American industry must realize that its fortunes will be largely tied to export markets for the next few years because the growth of domestic demand, especially consumption, will have to be quite modest to free resources for the trade correction. In contrast, foreign growth should be rapid, which augurs well for foreign sales and profit expansion. American firms should target those foreign markets where demand will be especially buoyant—Japan and the Asian NICs; Europe, as it completes its internal market, and especially if it adopts the policies for sustained expansion proposed above; and perhaps Latin America again, at least to a degree, if the steps proposed in the next chapter help resolve its external debt problems. The new administration and Congress should thus adopt a series of measures to promote the export consciousness of American industry.

As pointed out in Chapter 4, the United States must achieve an improvement on the order of $200 billion in its merchandise trade balance (from the 1987 base) to restore balance in its current account. This means that other countries will have to accept an aggregate decline of about $200 billion in their trade balances—perhaps $85 billion in Japan, $70 billion in Western Europe (mainly Germany), $20 billion in the major Third World debtors, and $25 billion in the Asian NICs (mainly Taiwan and Korea).[1] As awareness abroad of the magnitude of the needed correction grows, protectionist pressures will inevitably grow (except among the Third World debtors, who desire larger current account deficits if sustainable financing is available). This will be especially true in countries whose surpluses fall more through exchange rate appreciation than through faster domestic economic growth.

Protectionist pressures will become particularly acute if the US adjustment also hits deficit countries, such as Canada and some European nations, to a significant degree.[2] These pressures will be eased if it proves possible to target the currency and other adjustment

1. These are the trade balance components of the changes in current accounts shown for these areas in table 1.2. The net investment earnings of all these countries (except the Third World debtors) are rising, so the shifts needed in their current account balances are about $25 billion less for Japan, $20 billion less for Europe, and $5 billion less for the Asian NICs.

2. The US–Canada Free Trade Agreement, if it enters into force, could thus be of particular value to the United States by barring the imposition of new protectionist measures in Canada against American products.

measures largely on the surplus countries, as recommended in the previous chapter. The pressures could be substantial even in this case, however, and we cannot of course be confident that such targeting will always succeed.

Prospective internal developments in Europe are quite important in this context. The leaders of the European Community (EC) have made a political commitment to "complete the internal market" by 1992. Their laudable goal is to eliminate all remaining intra-European barriers and create a truly integrated economic unit. A number of initiatives have already been undertaken, and several decision-making bodies are working to meet the target date.

A key issue for the United States (and the rest of the world) is whether this process will limit the ability or willingness of the European Community to liberalize externally, or whether it could even lead to the creation of new barriers against countries outside the Community. The European leaders have stated unequivocally that their efforts will conform strictly to their international obligations, including those of the GATT. However, they have also asserted that they will insist on "full reciprocity" from other countries on issues where no international rules now exist, such as services (Cockfield 1988). Even in areas for which GATT obligations exist, such as government procurement and state subsidies, there are widespread fears that the tough intra-European decisions that will be necessary to erase internal barriers will generate new barriers against outsiders or discrimination against European subsidiaries of foreign-based firms (which could also adversely affect US exports and economic interests). Even if the additional trade created by faster EC growth were to exceed the volume of trade diverted by any new discrimination of this type, along with the trade diversion inherent in the elimination or further reduction of barriers only for member countries, conflicts could arise and protectionist momentum will be accelerated.[3]

The Europeans will thus be undergoing two simultaneous developments that could push them toward new trade protection: a substantial deterioration in their current account positions, as part of the counterpart to the reduction in the US deficit, and the

3. The United States made its first official statement of concern about this issue in August 1988 (McPherson 1988).

development of a single internal market. The risk of protectionism may be especially great because a considerable portion of the US adjustment could fall on European countries with weak external positions, such as France, Italy, and the United Kingdom (Cline forthcoming, Chapter 3).[4] The pressures felt by these deficit nations could push the European Community toward protectionist measures against the outside world, notably Japan and other highly competitive East Asian nations, but against the United States as well.[5] At a minimum, the Community could become extremely reluctant to liberalize simultaneously vis-à-vis outsiders. Since Europe is the world's largest market, the adoption of protective policies there would have two harmful effects: slowing the required adjustment in trade balances, and adding considerable momentum to the erosion of the global trading system.

By hampering the American effort to eliminate its external deficit, protectionist measures abroad could frustrate the payoff from budget correction and other politically difficult steps taken by the United States. In contrast, the liberalization of foreign trade barriers would assist the US adjustment effort. This is partly because foreign barriers, in and of themselves, block substantial quantities of US exports.[6]

---

4. These trade policy concerns reinforce the need to focus the cut in European trade balances on Germany and the smaller surplus countries in Europe, as emphasized in Chapter 5.

5. New European protection against Asian products could also hurt the US adjustment effort by deflecting those products toward the American market or, at a minimum, deterring the needed diversification of Asian exports away from the United States.

6. Bergsten and Cline (1987) estimated that Japanese barriers, tangible and intangible, were reducing US exports by about $6–8 billion annually in 1985—10 to 15 percent of the bilateral imbalance at that time. Lawrence (1987) and Balassa and Noland (1988) suggest higher numbers. All of the analyses of this topic conclude that substantial amounts of money are involved, however, and it is clearly important that US policy make a major effort to eliminate as many of these barriers as possible as part of the overall strategy suggested in this volume. On the other hand, it is hardly possible to blame the increase in the US trade deficit in the 1980s on trade barriers because that deficit ballooned at a time when America's own barriers were rising and barriers in most areas abroad were either falling (as in the Asian NICs) or remaining roughly constant. (Bergsten and Cline noted that US import barriers were limiting Japanese sales in the United States by about $5 billion in 1985, so that an elimination of barriers on both sides would have little net impact on the bilateral balance.) In addition, the US deficit increased sharply with every region of the globe and there are no allegations of such a generalized rise in foreign barriers.

Even more to the point, however, is the importance to the United States of open markets abroad at a time when exchange rate changes have created an enormous improvement in the US international competitive position, and when the shift in relative growth rates of domestic demand will place a premium on foreign markets for American industry. Export-oriented strategies can be far more effective in a world of open markets. Indeed, American firms would hesitate to undertake the new investments needed to expand export capacity if they foresaw a risk of foreign market closure, just as they would hesitate if they thought a renewed rise in the dollar's exchange rate would again price them out of overseas markets.

This emphasis on export expansion as the main route to the required current account correction for the United States rests on the view that the alternative course of seeking to reduce imports through trade restrictions would be largely ineffective and even counterproductive. To be sure, import growth must decline as part of the adjustment process, and the absolute level of imports may even fall for some periods of time. The proposed exchange rate changes and the dampening of domestic demand growth in the United States are intended to have precisely these effects.

But an effort to limit imports through new trade restrictions would be a major mistake. Such restrictions would have the usual unfavorable domestic economic consequences. By restricting supply, they would add to inflationary pressures, especially with the economy near full employment. They would remove competitive pressures on American industry at a time when every effort must be made to maximize competitiveness. They would harm export performance directly by driving up the costs of imported inputs; this could be especially damaging for capital goods, where imports now account for over 30 percent of the volume of productive inputs.

It is doubtful that import restrictions could make any net contribution to the required improvement in the trade balance. This is because any significant import reductions resulting from such restrictions would probably generate losses of American exports that would offset, or even exceed, the import decline. Some countries, notably in Latin America, would simply be unable to buy as much from the United States if new American barriers (and those adopted by countries that emulate the United States) trimmed their export earnings.[7]

Import restrictions would also be likely to fail because many countries would emulate the American restrictions and/or retaliate against them. The European Community has already adopted a "New Commercial Instrument" that is the mirror image of Section 301 in US trade law, and its new emphasis on sectoral "reciprocity" was inspired in large part by the American authors of that concept. The ultimate result of the adoption of new protective barriers by the United States—which is now enjoying a prolonged export boom and has been the world's most successful creator of new jobs over the past six years—would almost surely be a proliferation of trade barriers throughout the world.

One trade policy proposal that has received extensive attention is an import surcharge, which would seek to attack the twin deficits simultaneously by cutting imports and raising budget revenues through "taxing the foreigners" (although the surcharge's tax burden would fall mainly on American consumers). This particular device would have the same adverse effects mentioned above, but it is even more likely to trigger retaliatory foreign responses because of its breadth and its obvious rejection of international cooperation. If applied to Third World debtor countries, an import surcharge would almost certainly cause a financial crisis; they and Canada (because of the Free Trade Agreement [FTA] if ratified) would have to be exempted, thereby reducing the maximum coverage of the device to about two-thirds of total US imports.

The effect of an import surcharge on the economy would be perverse, because the implied US effort to escape from responsible domestic measures and international cooperation could drive the dollar down sharply in the exchange markets and bring about a hard landing.[8] Its fiscal impact would also be perverse, because, as a

---

7. Any adoption of substantial new US trade barriers against Latin American products would be likely to reignite the debt crisis, both because it would impair these countries' ability to service their borrowings and because of the political implications of such a step by the country whose banks were receiving much of the debt service. Protectionist action by the United States would thus risk renewed financial instability as well as undercut the trade adjustment effort.

8. The surcharge adopted by the United States for four months in 1971 was aimed at achieving devaluation of a clearly overvalued dollar within a system of fixed exchange

temporary measure that would almost certainly be phased out over time, it would make a declining contribution to budget correction, whereas steps are needed that will provide increasing returns over a period of several years.

Another recent trade proposal calls upon other countries, notably Japan, to reduce their bilateral surpluses with the United States to a specific level within a fixed period of time (US House of Representatives 1986; Kissinger and Vance 1988; Prestowitz 1988). In addition to generating the usual costs of trade restrictions, this "results rather than rules" approach would force the "partner" countries to cartelize their entire economies to control trade flows in a way that would enable them to comply—hardly a desirable outcome for the United States. It would also greatly enhance the credibility and frequency of "managed trade," an international game which the United States is peculiarly ill-equipped to play against Japan and other far more homogeneous societies that have been engaged in such activities for a considerable period of time (Lawrence 1988). And even if it were successful in reducing US deficits with the countries in question, it has the fatal flaw of any bilateral approach—leaving other countries free to improve their positions with the United States, which would obviate any net gains in the American trade balance.

The United States needs a world of expanding markets to eliminate its current account deficit, and it is now primed to take full advantage of them. Achieving such an outcome will require the use of tough American negotiating tactics to open markets, including the carefully targeted use of threats to close US markets on a selective basis. But the objective must be clear: maintenance and expansion of an open trading system to permit the US correction to succeed.

EXPORT PROMOTION MEASURES

The marketing reentry component of the trade policy strategy will require a series of specific policy steps by the administration and

---

rates where it was widely perceived that dollar devaluation was possible only with the agreement of the major foreign countries. This is very different from today's environment of flexible rates with the United States near full employment and facing a pickup of inflation concerns, where the United States can push the dollar down quite easily whenever it wants to do so but must avoid a sharp depreciation in the absence of complementary policy changes at home and abroad.

Congress, along with a large dose of exhortation by top officials, including the President. The goal is to get American industry to focus on the great opportunities presented by foreign markets following the currency changes, particularly markets in surplus countries that maintain rapid growth of domestic demand, as proposed above. The potential of foreign markets needs to be contrasted with the likely modest growth of American domestic demand during the years ahead.

One potentially important tool for effective government support of the export drive is the Export-Import Bank (De Rosa and Nye 1980). It can provide liquidity for export finance, especially to buyers in Third World and Eastern European countries where private lenders have largely withdrawn because of the debt problem. It can provide attractive interest rates to help induce American firms to resume their export efforts. It can help ensure that American exporters are not at a disadvantage because of the aggressive financing programs of other trading countries.

The programs of the Bank were severely truncated by the Ford administration in the mid-1970s, but a four-fold expansion of its lending activities during 1977–81 undoubtedly contributed to the American export boom of that period.[9] The Reagan administration sought to abolish the Bank and succeeded in again turning it into a very minor actor (Stockman 1986, 113–114). The Bank in fact ran out of new lending authority in mid-1988 and had to suspend its direct loan program in the middle of an export boom. Hence a major export promotion tool was shelved just when it became most essential, and when it could do much to enhance further the competitiveness of American industry.

The new administration and Congress should substantially expand the role of the Export-Import Bank. First, its lending program should be sharply increased. Expanded authority for direct loans would enable the Bank to extend lines of credit to major foreign buyers, as the Japanese and some European export finance agencies do, strengthening the competitive position of American suppliers.

---

9. The Export-Import Bank has played major roles in promoting US trade (and foreign policy) objectives during several periods in its history. See Rodriguez (1987), especially Chapter 1.

Second, the guarantee program of the Bank—where a large amount of unused authority exists—needs to be utilized much more aggressively and creatively. Many US banks need to be encouraged to enter (or reenter) export financing activities, which will in turn encourage more companies to focus on export markets. New sources of funding can be drawn into export finance, and new techniques for using the guarantee authority need to be developed. Third, the Bank should play a major public and private role in conveying the export message to the business community. It thus needs to be provided with dynamic leadership, along with increased and more professional staff, during the coming period.

There has been considerable tightening of the Agreement on Guidelines for Officially Supported Export Credits, the international "consensus" or "gentleman's agreement" to limit export finance subsidies. But there remains a problem of subsidization through mixed credits, which blend export finance and concessional foreign assistance to provide extremely attractive terms to potential customers. The administration and Congress set up a "war chest" in 1986 to defend US exports against this practice for the next two years, and extended the program for a third year in the Omnibus Trade Act. But the size and duration of the program are far too limited to deter Japan, France, and others from using mixed credits, which have a major impact on many large capital projects around the world, where the absence of competitive US finance has often discouraged American firms from bidding for the business. Elimination of mixed credit subsidies should rank near the top of the trade negotiating agenda of the new administration. This effort will succeed, however, only if Congress approves a sharp expansion in the "war chest," thereby providing convincing evidence that the United States will no longer give up such business without a serious effort.

Changes in the budgetary treatment of the Export-Import Bank would facilitate this set of proposals. Congress now authorizes and appropriates annual lending levels for the Bank, and loans are counted as budget outlays even though they are almost always repaid. Conversely, losses due to effective interest-rate subsidies are not revealed in the budget (although they can be found in the annual reports of the Bank itself). This budget treatment needs to be reversed, to focus on the Bank's net profits (or losses) rather than on its gross lending level, in an effort both to reveal real costs (if any) to the taxpayer and to avoid accounting barriers to desirable program modification.[10]

It would also be desirable to move Eximbank out of the "foreign affairs" part of the budget (function 150), creating instead a new "export support" function in which the Bank's programs would be grouped with similar efforts of the Department of Commerce, the Commodity Credit Cooperation, the Overseas Private Investment Corporation (OPIC), and other agencies scattered throughout the government. Setting up a separate category for export promotion would indicate the high priority attached to it by the administration and Congress. It would also more accurately characterize the Bank, which is no longer primarily an instrument of foreign policy. Since the Bank would be the largest element by far in such a function, it would be placed in a strong position to assert leadership of the export promotion campaign.

The United States can also promote its exports effectively by significantly increasing the role and funding of the international financial institutions—especially the World Bank, Inter-American Development Bank, and International Monetary Fund. These institutions serve a number of key US policy objectives, as developed in detail in Chapter 7. In particular, they promote faster economic growth, relaxation of acute shortages of foreign exchange, and more liberal trade policies in the large debtor countries in Latin America. These countries are major markets for US exports, and can become even better markets once their debt problems are resolved and steady growth resumes. The international institutions can play a central role in this effort, and they can do so in an extremely cost-effective manner with very small budget outlays from the United States.

In addition, the new administration and Congress can take a large stride toward improving the American trade position by launching a concentrated attack on the numerous export disincentives that continue to pervade US law and practice. These disincentives include explicit export controls that have been imposed for reasons of national security, foreign policy, environmental protection, and short supply

10. In FY 1986, estimated subsidies were 2 percent of guaranteed loan commitments and 11 percent of direct loan obligations for a total estimated cost of $178 billion. See Office of Management and Budget (1987, F-35/37).

(which is sometimes an excuse for pure protectionism, as when the domestic maritime industry won controls on Alaskan oil exports). Other disincentives include the use of economic sanctions in pursuit of foreign policy goals, such as the grain embargoes of the 1970s and the gas pipeline effort of the early 1980s. These sanctions have hurt US exports and have reinforced the reputation of the United States as an unreliable supplier, generally with modest if any foreign policy payoffs (Hufbauer and Schott 1985b). The results are sometimes the same with policies that seek to punish foreign corrupt practices or restrict arms sales to certain countries, and perhaps also with some tax policies (such as those affecting income earned by Americans working abroad).

The goals of these various measures are defensible when viewed individually and in their own special contexts. However, taken together, and weighed against the imperative of external adjustment for the United States in both the short and longer runs, policies like these can do considerable harm to US national interests. The Omnibus Trade Act eliminated some of these self-imposed barriers, particularly by restraining the use of export controls for foreign policy purposes (Bonker 1988). But much more should be done, and the scheduled renewal of the Export Administration Act in 1990 provides a natural opportunity.

The new administration should adapt its own policies and procedures accordingly, and work closely with the Congress to devise an "Export Promotion and Removal of Disincentives Act." This legislation could include the proposed increases in Eximbank and other export promotion programs, and revisions of current limitations on US export capacity. A logical successor to the Omnibus Trade Act, such an initiative would stress what the United States could do on its own to promote its international competitiveness.

In addition to spurring exports through its own institutions, the new administration will need to continue the aggressive effort launched in September 1985 to attack foreign barriers to American exports. Numerous such barriers continue to exist, some in violation of existing GATT rules. Attacking them through both bilateral and multilateral channels—including in the Uruguay Round, as discussed in the next section—must be an integral element of any comprehensive adjustment strategy for the United States. In particular, the United States must make it unambiguously clear that it will respond immediately to the threat or the imposition of any new barriers against its exports. The United States can only keep markets open for its export drive if it is willing to retaliate in all cases in which a country contravenes the international rules or fails to pay full compensation through an offsetting reduction of other trade barriers.[11]

In addition to their substantive merit, these export promotion efforts link directly to another key objective of the overall strategy: a successful Uruguay Round. The linkages come from the domestic political reality that administrations can carry out open trade policies far more successfully if they are able to mobilize outward-looking "export politics" to counter domestic interest groups committed to inward-looking "import politics" (Destler 1986, 15–16, 96, 208). As noted above, import suppression would be a wholly ineffective (indeed counterproductive) alternative to export expansion in the current context. However, the two are frequently seen as alternative strategies. Hence a major export push by the administration will be helpful, perhaps essential, in achieving the domestic consensus necessary to support a trade strategy of opening rather than closing markets.

There is also an important international reason for an explicit American export campaign. There is a widespread view around the world, perhaps most prevalent in Asia but apparent in Europe and elsewhere as well, that the United States does not care about exports and is unwilling (or unable) to make a major effort to acquire and maintain foreign markets. This view sometimes leads to two conclusions: that the United States "will never be able to balance its books" and that it is thus futile to take steps to help it do so; and that the United States is basically trying to get others to initiate measures to achieve the correction instead of taking responsibility itself. Chapter 2 argued that this first conclusion is wrong, and that the underlying competitive position of the United States is quite strong. The second conclusion would be countered by the adoption of the program recommended in this book.

Nevertheless, both views persist and must be countered if the United States is to obtain the foreign cooperation that is necessary

11. Due to its consensus method of decision making, the GATT almost never formally authorizes retaliation (because the offending party can veto action against itself). The United States should therefore retaliate unilaterally whenever a GATT panel finds that a violation has occurred. The GATT system should be modified in the Uruguay Round to make such a practice universally applicable.

for the proposed strategy to succeed. Export campaigns have been standard practice in most nations for many years. The adoption of a serious export program in the United States would be an innovation, despite previous rhetorical gestures in its direction, and it would earn the United States increased respect abroad. It would thereby enhance US chances of earning the cooperation of others and restoring American leadership more broadly, as well as provide some support for the trade correction itself.

NEGOTIATING TRADE LIBERALIZATION

The second key part of the trade policy strategy is maximum liberalization of trade around the world. History demonstrates the validity of the "bicycle theory": if trade policy does not move toward the greater openness that is in the general interest, it will topple in the face of protectionist pressures.

As noted above, these pressures will be especially acute during the next few years in countries whose trade surpluses are coming down (or whose deficits are rising) as the counterpart to the American current account improvement. Protectionist sentiment could be strong in the European Community, as its members take the difficult steps to "complete the internal market" while experiencing a sharp fall in their external balances. The pressure to protect will also remain severe throughout Latin America, as countries there search for additional ways to earn and save foreign exchange. Resistance to liberalization has even begun to grow in Korea and Taiwan, given the rapid pace of adjustment required there because of the magnitude of their surpluses (as a share of GNP).

The United States thus needs to generate liberalizing momentum simply to avoid the risk of increased barriers abroad—which would frustrate its own trade correction—as well as to pursue the increased market access that would enhance its export push.[12] The central tactical issue is whether to focus primarily on the multilateral

12. Implementation of the Free Trade Agreement would achieve that objective with Canada, the largest trading partner of the United States, which would be precluded from putting up new barriers to US exports even if its total external position were to deteriorate sharply.

negotiations of the Uruguay Round or to devote further attention to bilateral agreements like the United States–Canada FTA (or perhaps regional arrangements, notably in the Pacific).

A successful Uruguay Round is essential. Key US export sectors, particularly agriculture but also a number of high-technology and services industries, simply could not obtain the scope for increased export opportunity they need even with an extensive series of bilateral pacts. Key functional issues such as subsidies cannot be handled adequately on a bilateral basis, as the United States discovered in the successful negotiations with Canada, its largest trading partner (Schott 1988). It is also essential to engage the European Community in a process of global trade liberalization to remove any temptation it might have to pass on the price of internal deals to outsiders.

In any event, it is doubtful that other bilateral FTAs comparable to the one with Canada are feasible. Perhaps a few sectoral arrangements with Mexico, and consultative mechanisms with Japan and others, could be negotiated. There is a possibility of broader arrangements, notably a "G-2" between the United States and Japan, to deal with macroeconomic and monetary coordination (Bergsten 1987a; Baucus 1988). But there is little possibility of meaningful trade liberalization through this approach. The United States should put its major international trade emphasis on a successful Uruguay Round.[13]

The basic strategy in the Uruguay Round should be the same as in past rounds: "reciprocity at the margin." Concessions are traded, and roughly quantified, in terms of reductions in protection from

13. By contrast, Choate and Linger (1988, 91–93) argue for a "tailored-trade approach [that] would elevate bilateral and plurilateral negotiations from a secondary to a primary role." They recommend seeking immediate bilateral negotiations with Japan, South Korea, Taiwan, and Germany, which with Canada account for two-thirds of the US trade deficit, with the aim of reducing the current imbalances. However, their use of the US–Canada FTA as a model for reducing bilateral imbalances is simply a misreading of the agreement; that issue was never even discussed, let alone included in the aims of the agreement. Moreover, while Choate and Linger concede that "a system of global trade based exclusively on bilateral or plurilateral relations could easily create so much fragmentation and discrimination that net global trade would be reduced," they ignore the inevitability of retaliation against agreements that simply rearrange trade flows for the benefit of participants to the detriment of those excluded—such as those proposed in some quarters in Korea and Taiwan for the explicit purpose of shifting those countries' imports from Japan to the United States, which its proponents hope would remove the pressure to reduce their global surpluses.

levels that applied at the outset of the negotiations. As in the past, trade-offs among sectors will be necessary to achieve substantial liberalization. This is because different countries, depending upon their competitive abilities and domestic politics, are willing and able to liberalize further in some sectors than in others, so the sectoral patterns of liberalization will differ from country to country.

The alternative approach of "sectoral reciprocity," in which similar degrees of market access are sought for individual industries, would be far less likely to achieve the degree of market-opening that is now so important to the United States. This approach would limit the magnitude of the total package to the extent of liberalization agreed upon within each sector, which would reflect the wishes of the least competitive country in each. This reduces opportunities for larger intersectoral trade-offs. Sectoral reciprocity can ultimately be achieved by a total freeing of trade across the board, and the traditional emphasis on "reciprocity at the margin" provides by far the most promising route to a "level playing field."

The primary objectives in the talks should remain largely similar to those originally pursued by the Reagan administration: reduced barriers and distortions to trade in agriculture; new rules for services, intellectual property, and foreign direct investment; improvements in the existing codes, especially those covering subsidies and government procurement; and a sharp improvement in the effectiveness of the GATT in managing the trading system. The new administration will have to establish clear priorities in each of these areas, deciding what it wants and what it is willing to pay for foreign concessions. In agriculture, for example, the Congress will be loath to accept liberalization of the current US quotas until the President outlines what he might realistically expect to get in return.

The new administration, working closely with the Congress to establish US negotiating priorities and potential concessions, could profitably make a few changes in the US negotiating stance for the talks. On agriculture, it could seek a less sweeping and thus more widely acceptable arrangement than the current goal of total elimination of all government supports.[14] In contrast, it should propose the elimination of all tariffs on trade in industrial products among

14. See Hathaway (1987); *Reforming World Agricultural Trade* (1988); and Paarlberg (1988).

the developed countries by 2000—which is a realistic goal. To induce greater liberalization by key developing countries, the United States should propose giving them subsequent credit in the GATT for any unilateral reductions in barriers adopted as part of structural adjustment programs worked out with the IMF and the World Bank, as long as the trade liberalization is maintained (Hufbauer and Schott 1985a, 8–11).

Most importantly, the new administration could give a dramatic boost to the US bargaining effort by offering to begin a gradual long-term liberalization of the international Multi-Fiber Arrangement (MFA). It should indicate a willingness to phase out its import controls on textiles and apparel, perhaps over 10–15 years, if the textile exporting countries would provide reciprocal liberalization of their own import controls, initially in the textile sector itself and then more broadly, and if the other major importing countries did likewise. Normal attrition in the industry would offset most of the employment losses that would result, and substantially increased government assistance—self-financed by auctioning rather than giving away the quotas as they are phased down, as described below—could further ease the transition for affected workers. The bicycle theory is nowhere clearer than in textiles: in the absence of efforts to liberalize this sector, protection steadily increases and bills calling for even more restrictive quotas continue to pass the Congress despite the extensive regime already in place and the improved conditions in the industry.[15]

By putting textile restrictions, its most extensive program of protection, on the table, the United States could trigger a quantum leap in the substantive content of the Uruguay Round and assert a strong leadership position. The American negotiating effort would be further bolstered if the United States also worked to ban "voluntary" export restraint agreements and other "gray area" protectionist

15. The underlying analysis and proposal are in Cline (1987b), who shows that the present textile quotas cost US consumers about $20 billion annually, much of which falls on lower-income groups and thus has a regressive impact on the country's income distribution. His conservative estimates suggest a consumer cost of about $82,000 for each job saved directly in the apparel industry and $135,000 per job saved directly in textiles.

devices. Such a ban would be very much in the interest of the United States itself, as described below.

These steps would challenge both the industrial countries and the LDCs to up their antes as well. In particular, agreement on a phased elimination of the MFA and elimination of "gray area" controls should permit the negotiation of a meaningful Safeguards Code during the round.[16] Such a code is a high priority for most LDCs, so its completion could unlock the door to concessions from them on "special and differential" treatment. The "S&D" provisions have enabled LDCs to apply far-reaching restrictions of their own, and they have frustrated all GATT efforts to achieve meaningful liberalization of LDC trade barriers. Since many LDCs represent large and potentially growing markets for US exports, inducing them to liberalize would be a major gain for the United States (as well as for them and for the world trading system as a whole).

The United States should also continue to press for improvement in the functioning of the GATT system. The United States has a major stake in the better operation of the international institutional framework because of its growing inability to resolve disputes unilaterally—especially in the trade area, where the European Community accounts for a much larger share of the world's activity. If most trade disputes could be handled effectively in the GATT, there would be much less pressure, both internationally and within the United States, for overt trade management by governments. The record of the GATT in recent years is not bad.[17] However, it has

16. The goal of the Safeguards Code is to limit all import controls to measures that are temporary and degressive, outlaw "gray area devices" such as "voluntary" restraint arrangements—of which the most egregious is the MFA—and ban discrimination in the application of trade restraints. LDCs are the major targets of most such practices, and successful completion of such a code is therefore at or near the top of the priority list for most of them in the Uruguay Round (as it was in the Tokyo Round).

17. In 1984, GATT members agreed on guidelines of 30 days for the establishment of a dispute settlement panel and three to nine months for it to complete its work. According to Horlick, Oliver and Steger (1988), GATT panels since then have become faster even though the guidelines are not binding. In the first half of 1988, GATT dispute settlement panels recommended liberalization or elimination of Canadian barriers to certain types of fishing in the Pacific, Canadian provincial taxes on beer, wine, and liquor, and Japanese barriers to 12 categories of miscellaneous agricultural products. Canada and Japan eventually accepted the GATT reports and either implemented the recommended liberalization or negotiated a compromise acceptable to all parties (*International Trade Reporter*, various issues).

failed to resolve several major trade conflicts, particularly in agriculture, where the rules themselves are inadequate. There is a close relationship between improving the rules and strengthening the institution, and the two goals should be pursued together in the Uruguay Round.

The timing of the round is important, and is comparable to that of the Tokyo Round of the 1970s. That effort was launched with the Tokyo Declaration (1973). The United States received congressional authorization to negotiate in 1975, but the round could only be completed three years later (1978) by a succeeding administration because other countries would make meaningful concessions only to the American team that would be there at the conclusion. The Uruguay Round was launched in 1986, preparatory work and a midterm review will be concluded in 1988, negotiating authority has been obtained from Congress, and a major push by the new administration could result in a similarly successful outcome.

A target date of 1990 has been set for completion of the round. This may be feasible, and it would be highly desirable to complete the negotiation on agriculture before Congress writes the new American farm legislation, scheduled for 1990. However, this would require the completion of most or all of the entire package, because agriculture is such a central element. On the other hand, the likely acceleration of the European integration effort as 1992 approaches suggests the merit of continuing the GATT talks (and keeping the bicycle in motion) at least until that year. This would maintain the pressure on the Europeans to avoid internal bargains that would be inconsistent with global liberalization.

The best outcome for the United States would be a two-part Uruguay Round, including an initial package dealing mainly with agriculture, largely finished by early 1990 (with enough progress made during 1989 to have a substantial effect on congressional deliberation on the farm bill), and a final deal in 1992 (to ensure ratification by Congress during the term of the same administration that negotiated it, as in the Tokyo Round). The agricultural component could develop in two stages: agreement in 1990 on short-term measures and a framework for the full package, and completion of the package by 1992 (*Reforming World Agricultural Trade* 1988). This would essentially postpone by two years both the "early harvest" envisaged for 1988 and the completion of the final package, but it would maintain the comprehensive outcome sought by the United States and agreed upon by the other Uruguay Round participants from the outset.

Needless to say, full achievement of US goals in the Uruguay Round will require important concessions by the United States, and will not be easy in any event. It would therefore be prudent to continue to explore the possibility of additional bilateral or regional arrangements, both for their potential substantive benefits and to remind other countries that there are alternatives to the multilateral approach if it does not succeed. Given the high payoff from a successful Uruguay Round and the limited scope for substantive bilateral outcomes, however, the policy focus should be on completing the multilateral effort.

DOMESTIC POLITICS

Two related domestic political requirements must be met if the new administration is to implement a trade policy of the kind suggested here, rejecting pressures both for new protection at home and excessive mercantilism abroad. First, the President will have to reassert leadership of American trade policy. He must do so in full consultation with the Congress, but presidential leadership is essential for an effective and sustained trade policy, and, despite occasional signs to the contrary, this leadership is desired by the Congress itself (Destler 1986).

President Reagan and his Treasury Department abdicated trade leadership during their first term by virtually ignoring these issues and by helping to create the massive external deficit with their budget deficits and their "benign neglect" of the exchange rate. This led directly to an upsurge of protectionism (Baker 1987). For the first time in over fifty years, Congress felt compelled to try to fill the leadership vacuum. The result was a virtual stalemate between the two branches, with the administration belatedly seeking to reassert authority after September 1985, but never able to gain the full confidence of the Congress or of key constituency groups. The struggle over the trade bill lasted more than two years, and resulted in over 1000 pages of legislation that will have little impact on the core trade concerns of the United States addressed throughout this analysis. The bill even moves in a counterproductive direction to some extent by enhancing the prospects for more "process protection," which would undermine rather than promote US competitiveness if future administrations do not guard vigilantly against it. These developments have raised further doubts, both at home and abroad, about the ability of the United States to mount a consistent and constructive trade policy.

It will thus be a matter of the highest priority for the new President to promptly restore the authority of the executive branch in the management of trade policy. Rapid and deft implementation of the program outlined here should enable him to do so. Early appointment of highly respected and qualified officials to the key trade policy positions—especially that of United States Trade Representative (USTR)—is also necessary. Just as with fiscal policy, full consultation with the Congress will be needed both to achieve substantive agreement on trade policy and to assure faithful implementation. The combination of an effective program and full consultation offers the best prospect of restoring order to US trade policy.

The second domestic political requirement for a successful trade strategy is closely related: reestablishment of a stable coalition of constituencies that will support the program politically. The business community has played a largely positive role in recent years, after the second Reagan administration began to address trade issues seriously, and the existing network of USTR and Commerce Department advisory committees provides a valuable foundation on which to build. The emphasis on "export politics" outlined earlier should help retain the allegiance of agriculture and most of the corporate community, and perhaps even win some help from labor. The improved program of adjustment assistance described below should promote the latter goal as well.

Several new measures could further enhance the prospects of success. Systematic government publication of "trade barrier impact statements," which indicate the costs of proposed new restrictions both to consumers and to affected groups, such as industrial users of imported components, could help mobilize resistance to protectionist proposals. The preparation of "retaliation hit lists," through which each major trading country would indicate each year what foreign industries it would most likely hit in any future trade conflicts, should help galvanize opposition to new import barriers both in the United States and abroad.[18]

DOMESTIC ADJUSTMENT AND IMPORT RELIEF

Even a strategy based on export expansion, as proposed here, must obviously address the problem of import relief. The rapid pace of global economic change will continue to threaten industries in the United States (and elsewhere). The new administration must be prepared to deal effectively with their problems.

The chief objective must always be effective adjustment by the endangered industry. In a few cases, this may mean the restoration of a former competitive position and market share. In most cases, however, it will mean downsizing through the shedding of inefficient product lines and the closing of obsolete plants, enabling the industry to compete without relying on quasi-permanent import relief.[19] The challenge is to achieve adjustment in the most efficient and humane manner, avoiding excessive costs both to the individuals involved and to the economy as a whole.

The basic goal of such a program should be to provide a wide array of financial assistance and adjustment services to displaced workers, thereby reducing the interest of labor in trade protection. Such services would include education and training, job counseling, and relocation advice. The trade adjustment provisions of the Omnibus Trade Act provide financial assistance for up to 52 weeks, contingent upon a worker's taking advantage of education or retraining programs. Since the adjustment problem largely involves experienced and older workers, the program should experiment with a variety of training and relocation efforts geared specifically to their needs; finance early retirement (perhaps at age 55–60) at a reasonably generous level, perhaps 65 percent of previous wages (Hufbauer and Rosen 1986,

18. Both ideas are developed in Destler and Odell (1987).

19. See Hufbauer and Rosen (1986) and Hufbauer, Berliner, and Elliott (1986). None of the 31 cases analyzed in the latter study revealed an industry with "phoenix" ability to regain its previous market position without lasting protection. (The one-firm motorcycle industry has subsequently displayed such resilience.)

83–84); and provide temporary supplemental wage allowances for workers who experience large earnings losses after becoming reemployed (Lawrence and Litan 1986, 112–113).

Temporary import relief can play a constructive role in this process if it supports rather than discourages adjustment, and if it is supplied in ways that avoid creating pressures to continue the relief indefinitely. Current law permits both of these criteria to be met, and the Omnibus Trade Act requires a much clearer adjustment effort from firms that receive relief under the "escape clause" (Section 201). However, current law also permits these criteria to be evaded, as happens in practice all too often, especially through the use of so-called "voluntary" restraint arrangements (VRAs) to circumvent legally prescribed relief routes. Moreover, there are now added incentives for industries seeking protection to avoid Section 201 precisely because of its greater emphasis on adjustment. The key issue, then, is how the new administration chooses to administer these laws in the context of its overall trade and economic policies.

Three related changes in import relief policy could simultaneously help to fulfill both of the key criteria. First, all industries seeking relief should be required to petition formally under one of the channels provided in trade law: the "escape clause" (Section 201), the national security clause (Section 232), or the unfair trade statutes (Section 301 and the dumping and subsidy provisions). No end runs to Congress or the executive, leading to imposition of restraints outside these channels, should be permitted. The administration should make a clear statement of policy to this effect, and it should have its adjustment requirements ready when the first relief case arises.

The administration could be assisted in this by the development of a mechanism to provide projections of the outlook for key industries in the United States. This would provide a benchmark against which to judge petitions for import relief (or other types of "industrial policy" assistance). The US government has historically had no basis for deciding whether the prospects for an industry were satisfactory, or even what constituted a "satisfactory" outlook in terms of national economic and security objectives. Most import relief decisions—particularly those that ignored the legally prescribed channels and thus did not have the benefit of the analyses of the International Trade Commission—have therefore been made largely on short-run, highly political grounds. It would also be useful for this new mechanism to analyze the impact of foreign government policies on American industries, especially in the high-technology and other "sunrise" sectors, so that any "targeting" practices could be identified before damage was done and redress was impossible.[20]

A second valuable change in import relief policy would be to eschew any further use of VRAs to restrict imports into the United States.[21] Such arrangements, which are used in seven of the eight major sectors that now "enjoy" quantitative import relief,[22] may actually hurt the position of the protected American industry. The VRA approach, by giving the quotas to the exporting countries and allowing them to parcel out market shares among their firms, enables America's chief competitors abroad to set higher prices for their products, upgrade the value added of their output, and seize the scarcity rents generated by the trade restriction. These rents have amounted to billions of dollars annually in such major industries as textiles and apparel, steel, and autos. The foreign firms are then able to reinvest their windfall earnings, substantially enhancing their long-run positions.[23]

---

20. See Bergsten (1983). The Competitiveness Policy Council created by the Omnibus Trade Act might be able to play such a role. More extensive forays into this dimension of "managed trade" would be undesirable, however, for several reasons. The US government has a demonstrably poor record of picking "winners" and "losers" (and other governments that allegedly excel at the practice, such as Japan and France, have championed numerous losers as well). The payoff from most industrial policy proposals is highly uncertain; the widely heralded export trading companies authorized in 1979, for example, have provided no evident boost to the trade balance. Budget constraints will of course limit the scope for extensive steps in such a direction. And it would be folly for the United States to endorse an approach at which other countries are much more expert, thereby justifying their resort to greater protectionism as well. See the skeptical analyses of Schultze (1983) and Krugman (1986).

21. Whether they are labeled VRAs, "voluntary" export restraints (VERs) or "orderly marketing arrangements" (OMAs). There are technical and legal differences between these techniques but they can be grouped together for most purposes.

22. Automobiles, carbon steel, machine tools, meat, specialty steel, sugar, and textiles and apparel. Only the dairy quotas are implemented through allocation to the domestic industry.

23. See Bergsten, et al. (1987), which estimates that the annual quota rents seized by foreign exporters have totaled as much as $9 billion for the industries now covered. One leading Japanese consultant to many of his nation's top exporting firms told me that "we Japanese love your American trade restraints because they have been enriching us for so many years." But American negotiators also love VRAs because their ability

One result of the use of VRAs is that foreign exporters end up joining US importers in supporting them; the exporters value their windfall profits and assured market shares as much as protected industries value their market security. The result is an unusually strong international coalition for protection. With VRAs so firmly in place, there is little incentive for the domestic industry to adopt serious adjustment measures. Moreover, as noted above, administrations have frequently decided to seek VRAs for an industry that has not completed any of the prescribed legal avenues for relief (as with autos, steel, and textiles and apparel). No linkage to adjustment is required, and there is little reason to expect early termination of the restraints.

It would be desirable to eliminate VRAs by statute from the array of devices available to the President. A new administration could achieve the same outcome by rejecting them as a matter of policy. As suggested in the discussion of the Uruguay Round, it could then seek to achieve broad international agreement on such a self-denying measure. The step would be highly valued by most LDCs and many industrial countries as well, and it could make possible the negotiation of a meaningful GATT Safeguards Code. This in turn would help strengthen the GATT's ability to limit import barriers (as prescribed by its Article XIX) and to win meaningful liberalization from the LDCs. The United States could achieve significant market liberalization and rulemaking concessions in return for a step that promoted its own interests in any event.

Instead of resorting to VRAs, the new administration should adopt a third policy reform: using either tariffs or auction quotas to implement all cases of import relief (Lawrence and Litan 1986; Bergsten, et al. 1987). These techniques provide far greater transparency than VRAs or even quotas administered through domestic firms (as with dairy products), so they should help to keep the relief temporary. In addition, they generate revenues for the Treasury (not for foreign exporters) that can be earmarked to finance adjustment

to use the technique to pass the windfall profits to the affected foreign industry "induces" the other countries to accept the quota arrangements, solving the negotiators' domestic political problem and enabling them to avoid GATT requirements to provide formal compensation. The irony is that the compensation paid by conceding the windfall profits is probably larger and considerably more damaging, certainly to the "protected" domestic industry, than if GATT procedures were followed.

measures for the industries and workers that are being protected. Any remaining funds could help support programs to promote the overall competitiveness of the American economy or to reduce the federal budget deficit.[24]

This method of self-financing for trade adjustment would be superior to the additional import fee voted by Congress in the Omnibus Trade Act. This fee, which the President is directed to try to negotiate over the next two years, and which the United States might then implement unilaterally anyway, imposes an additional (if small) trade barrier. The proposal here would simply alter the method of implementing given levels of protection to generate funds for adjustment.

Self-financing would further enhance the prospects of phasing the relief down and fully out within a defined period of time. The result would be similar to a user fee levied on consumers of imports, who would pay a moderately higher price for a temporary period to support their continued access to an imported product and to help the domestic industry adjust; they would again receive free access to the product when the adjustment was completed. (Users of imports also pay a higher price for protected products under VRAs, but that price would be much more transparent under tariffs or auction quotas and the United States would receive the revenues.) Tariffs are preferable to auction quotas, because they leave the price mechanism intact (albeit with a government-imposed distortion). But when political forces dictate a resort to quantitative controls, as they will on occasion, quotas should be auctioned rather than given away to the foreign competition.

The more difficult question concerns whether the VRAs that have been protecting several large sectors for extended periods of time should also be converted to tariffs or auction quotas. The answer

24. The President currently has the authority to auction quotas under a variety of circumstances in section 1102 of the Trade Act of 1979. The Omnibus Trade Act added auction quotas explicitly as an option under Section 201 but did not mandate their use in cases where the USTR recommends quantitative restraints as the form of relief. Bergsten, et al. estimated that a conversion to auction quotas of existing QRs in the textile and apparel, carbon and specialty steel, machine tools, sugar, and dairy sectors could have raised as much as $5 billion in new revenues for the Treasury in 1986–87 at the restraint and price levels of that period (1987, 49). The Congressional Budget Office, using slightly different assumptions, estimated in 1987 that the revenue gain would have been $3.7 billion.

should be negative in the case of automobiles, where the VRA with Japan has become nonbinding (given the present import ceiling and the recent level of Japanese car imports) and should simply be allowed to lapse. The other key cases are textiles/apparel and steel, both of which must be addressed by the new administration within its first year in office.

Considerable adjustment, including substantial downsizing, has already occurred in the steel and textile/apparel industries. As already suggested, the textile/apparel controls should now be phased over a period of ten to fifteen years. At a minimum, these quotas—and those for steel, if the current restraints are continued beyond September 1989—should be converted from VRAs to tariffs or auction quotas, with the resulting revenues dedicated to the adjustment of the industry itself, facilitating a gradual phase-out of the protection.[25]

These measures would have to be negotiated with the exporting countries since the restraint agreements are international compacts. The exporters should be willing to give up their present rents in return for an opportunity to increase their market shares over time, if the United States is willing to commit itself to phase out the controls, and makes that pledge credible with an expanded domestic assistance program.[26] Indeed, an offer to reform these arrangements and phase them out should enhance the US negotiating position in the Uruguay Round and accelerate the reduction of import barriers in other countries.

FOREIGN DIRECT INVESTMENT IN THE UNITED STATES

The final "trade policy" issue concerns foreign direct investment (FDI) in the United States. The continuing rise of inward FDI, in

25. An alternative is tariff quotas, as suggested by Cline (1987b, 257–262), perhaps with the quota portion to be auctioned (Sampson 1987; Sampson and Takacs 1988).

26. Feenstra (1988) argues that exporting countries would suffer net losses from a US shift to auction quotas, especially in textiles and apparel, and that they would therefore reject the proposal. He suggests that the United States instead adopt tariff quotas in the industries now protected by VRAs to achieve some of the same goals, including the generation of considerable revenue from the tariff element of the approach, but leave the exporters no worse off.

particular the growing presence of Japanese firms and the occurrence of several major takeovers launched from abroad, has triggered proposals for new US policies to limit, regulate, or more closely monitor foreign investment. Initiatives of this type produced some of the most heated debate on the Omnibus Trade Act in 1988, and they will clearly remain on the policy agenda as long as FDI continues at anything like recent levels. And it is quite likely that FDI will continue to expand for some time to come, in part because income levels abroad will be increasing as a result of the rapid growth and further currency appreciations that are essential components of the adjustment process.

Much of the concern about FDI in the United States represents fear of increased foreign influence over the American economy (and the society more broadly) as a result of greater participation by foreign-based corporations. Some worry that national security could be jeopardized by the presence of foreign firms in industries that either supply the military directly or whose technology will be important to the defense effort in the future. Concentrations of FDI in a few locales (such as Hawaii and California) and a few sensitive sectors (such as real estate and semiconductors) have heightened these concerns.

As stressed throughout this study, the United States is indeed at risk from its heavy dependence on foreign financing, the product of the huge deficits that the country has developed in its external economic position. But FDI in US plants and real estate is probably the most desirable method of obtaining such funding.[27] This is partly because FDI is "serviced" only when the investment generates profits. Even more importantly, direct investments are much more likely to remain in the country permanently than are liquid holdings of Treasury bills and other short-term assets, which could be repatriated on literally a moment's notice and cause a financial crisis of the type described in Chapter 2. Most broadly, FDI gives foreign companies (and, presumably, their governments) a greater stake in the US

27. Capital inflows for FDI purposes were recorded in the balance of payments data at $34 billion in 1986 and $42 billion in 1987—amounts equal to about one-quarter of the entire external financing required for the current account deficit. This percentage increased to about 30 percent in the first half of 1988. About one-third of the total increase in FDI assets in the United States in recent years appears to have been financed from abroad (with the rest supported by local borrowing).

economy than trade and other arms-length transactions, and probably reduces the possibility that they would take steps to hurt it.

Furthermore, the risks from "control" by foreign firms seem remote. The share of American industries, real estate, or farmland owned by foreigners remains small.[28] Investment in sensitive sectors is banned or limited by law and the Exon-Florio Amendment to the Omnibus Trade Act provides far-reaching authority to review the national security implications of any new direct investments. The United States retains full authority over all investments within its legal jurisdiction, including the authority to block exports of any objectionable product or, in extremis, to nationalize firms.

Most other countries are exposed to greater potential for foreign control than the United States, because of the much larger role of (mainly American) FDI in their economies.[29] None of them seems to have suffered very much, if at all. Some Latin American countries (and other LDCs) did seek to "maintain their sovereign independence" by limiting the role of foreign firms in their economies in the 1960s and 1970s, but they wound up heavily indebted to commercial banks and dependent on the IMF and the World Bank—hardly a reliable path to domestic autonomy as revealed so graphically in the 1980s. Recently, many countries (including Canada and Mexico) have been liberalizing their foreign investment rules to a considerable degree.

More subtle concerns about FDI focus on the fact that many other host countries, both industrial and developing, seek to manipulate such flows through the use of performance requirements. These policies attempt to avoid excessive dependence on foreign companies by requiring, for example, that a majority of the shares be owned locally. They try to maximize the foreign investors' contribution to the local economy, particularly by requiring them to increase exports and reduce imports. Similar concerns may soon be expressed in the United States, in the latest incarnation of the demand for "reciprocity."

---

28. US affiliates of foreign parents account for 12.1 percent of total assets in US industry and less than 1 percent of privately owned farmland. See *Survey of Current Business*, May 1988, p. 64.

29. Raymond Vernon, probably the closest observer of these issues over the past three decades, notes that "when Americans begin frowning on foreign direct investment one cannot help thinking of the missionary turned cannibal" and that ". . . if foreign-owned subsidiaries in the United States may sometimes play the role of Trojan horses, they are as likely to play the role of hostages" (1988, 2 and 17).

It is indeed reasonable to ask why Japanese and other foreign-based multinationals should be able to pursue their corporate strategies by investing freely in the United States if US-based firms cannot do so in their home countries. If one accepts the view that FDI abroad by American-based multinationals helps the US economy on balance, it is clear that those benefits would be even greater in the absence of foreign limitations and performance requirements. If one is convinced that inward FDI is also advantageous on balance, it is tempting to believe that even greater benefits could be obtained by more active direction of its composition and character.

It would be a mistake, however, for the administration and Congress to erect new barriers or screening devices against foreign direct investment in the United States in an effort to redress perceived imbalances. No one has demonstrated that inward FDI hurts the American economy, or even has the potential to do so (Graham and Krugman forthcoming). Indeed, many state and local governments find FDI highly desirable and compete aggressively to attract it.[30] Restrictive steps by the United States would be likely to trigger increased foreign manipulation of US-based FDI abroad, risking a reversal of the highly favorable deregulation trend of the past few years. It would thus be doubtful that the United States could receive net benefits from enactment of such measures.[31]

Most importantly, any attempt by the United States to restrict FDI would both impede the needed improvement in the current account and discourage foreigners from investing in the dollar—undermining the overall strategy proposed in this book. This is partly because Japanese and other foreign-based direct investors can help expand US exports and substitute for imports, perhaps considerably, over the coming years.[32] It is also because many of the new

30. Thirty-seven governors reportedly visited Tokyo during the past year in an effort to attract Japanese investment to their states.

31. See Anthony M. Solomon in the *New York Times*, 31 May 1988 and "Restoring America's Independence: An Exchange" (with Felix Rohatyn) in the *New York Review*, 12 May 1988. There would be little harm in requiring the submission of additional data by foreign-based firms, as sought by the Bryant Amendment, which was included in the Omnibus Trade Act until its final stages, but most of the relevant information is already available and the main issue is which officials of the US government (including Congress) may have access to it.

32. The US subsidiaries of foreign-based firms have traditionally accounted for about one-quarter of US exports, and thus are already heavily involved in that activity. They also have accounted for about one-third of US imports, however, so have contributed

restrictions that foreign host countries would inevitably place on US-based firms in response to US action would further limit their imports and require additional expansion of their exports, adversely affecting the US adjustment effort.

The main problem, however, is that any new US embrace of protectionist policies gives a major boost to (and excuse for) increased protection abroad. This would be particularly true for new US limits on FDI, an issue that is far more sensitive in most other countries (due to their far greater exposure) than in the United States, and in which the United States has traditionally championed liberalization. As we have seen earlier in this chapter, increased protection abroad would undercut the fundamental US interest in increasing market access around the world and preventing a trend toward market closure. New US restrictions on inward FDI could have an especially strong effect on events in the European Community, whose possible implementation of new discriminatory measures against foreign-based firms in the move toward the internal market is already a source of concern.

Any new US limits on FDI would also jeopardize all forms of foreign investment in the dollar. If one major class of dollar holdings were subjected to new limitations, the utility of all would be reduced. Such a move would signal that the United States failed to appreciate the importance of maintaining foreign confidence in its currency and policies. It could be read as a step toward exchange controls, additional trade barriers, or both, and thus as a new form of American isolationism and a retreat from the open world economy. This would raise doubts about the fundamental will (and even the ability) of the United States to compete.

Any new controls on FDI would also raise the prospect of renewed clashes between the United States and its major trading and financial partners—notably Japan, its main banker, which clearly wants to continue increasing its FDI in the United States. It is noteworthy that the dollar fell in early 1987 when Fujitsu felt compelled to withdraw from its proposed takeover of Fairchild largely because of

---

substantially to the overall trade deficits in recent years. See the *Survey of Current Business*, May and June 1988. But the nature of these firms is changing rapidly, with the drop in the dollar, toward import-substitution (as in autos) and even toward viewing the United States as an "export platform." The further currency and macroeconomic changes suggested in Chapter 5 would enhance this effect.

the negative jawboning of a single American cabinet officer. The imposition of major restrictions on FDI by the United States, like the adoption of any far-reaching restrictions on trade, could cause a run on the dollar and thus undermine the entire international economic policy of the new administration.

The new administration, instead of adopting new domestic restrictions, should instead launch a major international initiative to reduce foreign barriers to, and manipulation of, FDI. This would be an investment analogue of the "bicycle theory" of trade policy outlined above. It would in part be a continuation of the efforts of the Reagan administration to address trade-related investment measures (TRIMs)—particularly export performance requirements and value-added requirements that limit imports—in the Uruguay Round and through Section 301 cases against specific countries. Such an initiative would also expand upon the World Bank's new Multilateral Investment Guaranty Agency (MIGA) and on the efforts of the United States and some other countries to address international investment issues through bilateral investment treaties (BITs).

However, it will be difficult to address some of the key investment issues through the GATT or by improving the OECD Guidelines for Multinational Enterprises (issued in April 1986). Right of establishment and national treatment, for example, bear at best an indirect relationship to trade flows. Topics such as taxation and antitrust raise difficult jurisdictional questions, and they are unlikely to be addressed effectively in any of the existing institutional frameworks.

The new administration, working closely with Congress, should carefully explore the possibility of launching a major international initiative to create a "GATT for Investment."[33] Such an arrangement would include rules binding both on governments and on firms, and an institution to enforce those rules. Like the GATT itself for trade, it would seek to limit governmental intervention in market decisions. Like the existing network of bilateral tax treaties and agreements on national bank supervision, worked out over the past decade or so among most of the industrial countries, it would be based on the recognition both by governments and firms that international ar-

33. Such proposals have been made by Goldberg and Kindleberger (1970); by Bergsten, Horst, and Moran (1978, 487–492); and by Shultz (1981).

rangements were essential to overcome jurisdictional conflicts or vacuums.

Where governmental intervention could not be totally barred, the new rules would set standards for such intervention, the violation of which would require offsetting compensation or justify foreign retaliation (which might include trade measures). Since it is clear that many host countries will be unwilling to give up their present domestic regulations and leave FDI decisions entirely to "the market," especially when the market is often comprised of large oligopolists, the limitations on governmental intervention would almost certainly have to be coupled with binding rules on corporate behavior if the package is to be successfully negotiated. These limitations could build on, but would have to go beyond, the current OECD and other voluntary codes.

FDI is one of the most politically contentious of all the avenues of international economic exchange. This is clearly indicated by the alarm expressed by many Americans about a degree of penetration that would appear trivial to most other countries. Largely because of its political volatility, it is the only major form of international economic exchange that is not effectively covered by institutionalized arrangements. Its potential will never be fully realized, nor threats to that potential decisively countered, until such arrangements are put into place.

Negotiation of a "GATT for Investment" would be extremely difficult and would probably take many years. It should not be permitted to deter an active and successful attack on TRIMs in the Uruguay Round, which would move international policy in this area in the right direction and help resist the pressures for counterproductive reactions within the United States (and elsewhere). But a sweeping initiative on FDI would be a dramatic supplement to the renewed emphasis on international institutional arrangements discussed above in relation to the GATT, and emphasized in the chapter on the international financial institutions, which follows. It would promote the further opening of the world economy, a central theme of the proposed strategy. It would reassert American leadership in an area where such leadership is natural, since the United States is now the largest host as well as home country for FDI. It would begin the process of resolving the interminable debate on FDI. It thus commends itself to the new administration and Congress as a potentially major US objective for the 1990s.

7

Third World Debt and Burden Sharing: Mobilizing the International Financial Institutions

A third major cluster of international economic challenges facing the new administration and Congress can best be addressed by substantially enhancing the role of the international financial institutions (IFIs). Three such challenges are of greatest importance: Third World debt, burden sharing, and the possible reentry of the Soviet Union into world economic affairs. Two other considerations strongly support a renewed American commitment to these organizations: budget constraints on spending for international economic purposes, and the need to forge a new leadership role for the United States within the pluralistic power structure of the contemporary world economy. The institutional focus of this discussion will be the World Bank, the IMF, and, to a lesser extent, the Inter-American Development Bank (IDB).

THIRD WORLD DEBT

The most important of these issues is Third World debt. A much more effective response to this problem must be an integral part of the proposed strategy for several reasons.

First, a revival of Third World markets, especially in Latin America, can make an important contribution to the necessary US trade correction. US exports to Latin America declined by almost $20 billion from 1981 to 1983, because of the sharp decline in the import capability of the region, and they still have not climbed back to their earlier level; the region's total imports remain $30 billion below their previous peak. The Baker 15 highly indebted nations must now generate trade surpluses of about $30 billion annually to service their debts, given the sharp decline in new capital flows to them.[1] If they could reverse or even substantially reduce this "negative financial transfer," they could restore faster economic growth and increase their imports. A relaxation of the debt constraint would also enable these countries to carry out faster and more extensive liberalization of their import controls, thereby enhancing US adjustment prospects.

Second, a more effective response to Third World debt is needed to prevent instability in the US and global banking systems. American banks have substantially strengthened their capital positions since the debt crisis erupted in 1982, and they have considerably reduced their exposure to debtor countries as well (see table 7.1). Nevertheless, some major money center banks remain at risk.

No single debtor country, even Brazil or Mexico, could now cause a major financial crisis in the United States, even with a total default. But simultaneous defaults by the three largest debtors (Argentina, Brazil, Mexico), let alone Latin America as a whole or the entire group of major debtors, could still cause enormous disruption. The US financial system has already been jeopardized by the crisis in the savings and loan industry, and by continuing bank problems in some regions. This further highlights the importance of avoiding shocks from abroad.

There are two (perhaps related) situations under which Third World debt could trigger major financial disruption. One would be a simultaneous resort to radical policies in the key debtor countries, despite the admitted failures of such strategies undertaken to date (such as Alain Garcia's 1986 ceiling on debt service payments in Peru, or Brazil's repayment moratorium in 1987). The other would

1. Over 80 percent of the trade surpluses and debt-service costs of the Baker 15 are located in Latin America.

be if the world economy sank into recession, shrinking export markets for the debtors and thus further limiting their access to foreign exchange. If the recession were caused by a sharp rise in real interest rates, as occurred in 1982, the double blow to the debtors could tip many of them into default. We have argued throughout this volume that a recession with high interest rates is possible if the United States and the other industrial countries fail to take decisive action to resolve the huge imbalances among them. The possible reigniting of the Third World crisis thus supplies yet another reason for those nations to take such action, but the risk of such an outcome also counsels more effective steps on Third World debt itself.

Successful implementation of the strategy proposed in this volume would provide substantial help to the debtor countries of the Third World. Faster world growth would enhance their export opportunities. Renewed liberalization of trade, especially if it included a phase-out of controls on textiles and other products exported by LDCs, would have a similar effect. Most directly, the reduction of dollar (and perhaps world) interest rates that should result from a decisive reduction in the US budget deficit would substantially reduce the costs of debt service. Every drop of one percentage point in market interest rates saves the debtors about $5 billion annually, and, according to the WEFA model of the US economy, a decline of a full percentage point or more should be possible if the proposed adjustment strategy is followed.

The third reason the Third World debt problem must be handled better, by far most important to the debtor countries themselves, is to restore their economic growth. The 1980s have been a lost decade for most of these countries, with per capita incomes lower now than a decade (or, in some cases, even two decades) ago.[2] The encouraging democratization of countries throughout Latin America, and in the Philippines as well, could be jeopardized if growth is not restored soon.

Third World debt can be stabilized over the long run only with better policies in the debtor countries, a sharp and sustained increase in the availability of external resources, and a new leadership structure

2. The World Bank estimates that per capita consumption declined 1.6 percent annually from 1980–1987 for the 17 heavily indebted countries (the Baker 15 plus Costa Rica and Jamaica). (World Bank 1988; xiv, and Balassa, et al. 1986, 52–53).

TABLE 7.1 Exposure of US Banks in Developing Countries and Eastern Europe
(end of calendar year)

	Amount owed to US banks (million dollars)				Ratio of exposure to capital (percent)			
	1982	1985	1986	1987	1982	1985	1986	1987
All Banks								
Baker 15[a]	91,085	90,526	86,172	81,695	129.0	85.9	74.2	63.2
Argentina	8,231	8,411	8,524	8,812	11.7	8.0	7.3	6.8
Brazil	20,438	22,796	22,404	21,275	28.9	21.6	19.3	16.5
Mexico	24,377	24,934	23,654	22,722	34.5	23.7	20.4	17.6
Non-OPEC LDCs	103,180	98,186	90,492	84,761	146.1	93.2	77.9	65.6
Eastern Europe	6,278	4,358	3,571	3,239	8.9	4.1	3.1	2.5
Sum	109,458	102,543	94,063	88,000	155.0	97.3	81.0	68.1

9 Largest Banks[b]								
Baker 15[a]	55,868	58,851	56,383	54,566	192.6	139.1	120.7	106.0
Argentina	5,125	5,875	5,927	6,295	17.7	13.9	12.7	12.2
Brazil	13,296	15,550	15,358	15,007	45.8	36.8	32.9	29.1
Mexico	12,862	14,087	13,353	13,351	44.4	33.3	28.6	25.9
Non-OPEC LDCs	64,148	62,801	58,308	55,762	221.2	148.5	124.9	108.3
Eastern Europe	4,045	2,931	2,354	2,271	13.9	6.9	5.0	4.4
Sum	68,193	65,732	60,662	58,033	235.1	155.4	129.9	112.7

Source: Board of Governors of the Federal Reserve System, "Country Exposure Lending Survey," Statistical Release no. E.16, Washington, various issues.

a. The Baker 15, so named because they are the countries targeted in the Baker Plan for dealing with the debt crisis, are Argentina, Brazil, Mexico, Bolivia, Chile, Colombia, Ecuador, Ivory Coast, Morocco, Nigeria, Peru, Philippines, Uruguay, Venezuela, and Yugoslavia.

b. Bank of America, Citibank, Chase Manhattan, Manufacturers Hanover, Morgan Guaranty, Chemical, Continental Illinois, Bankers Trust, and the First National Bank of Chicago.

for the handling of the problem. The Baker Plan has encouraged most of the debtor countries to begin adopting necessary reforms, but most of them still have a long way to go. The commercial banks and other external lenders, while responding to new adjustment programs in the largest countries, have failed to provide adequate resources to support the strategy; negative financial transfers from the Baker 15 have totaled about $30 billion during each of the past two years. Voluntary debt relief schemes have begun to help a few countries (such as Bolivia and Mexico), but to date they have been modest in scope.

The core of any strategy for dealing with each of these three components of the debt problem must be a sharp expansion in the role of the IFIs. Because of their multilateral status and proven expertise, these institutions are in the best position by far to encourage the debtor countries to pursue effective policies to deal with inflation, their underlying fiscal imbalances, and structural problems like excessive governmental regulation and state ownership of enterprises, all of which hamper their adjustment.[3] But the ability of the IFIs to persuade the debtors to change their policies has been limited by the modest level of resources that they have been able to offer as inducements. Indeed, the three major international financial institutions—the IMF, the World Bank, and the IDB—are now "contributing" to the negative financial transfer: over the past year, each of them withdrew about $1 billion from the Baker 15.

This negative flow resulted in part from a slowdown in the disbursement of funds already committed as a result of project cutbacks in the debtor countries, a consequence of debtor efforts to reduce their budget deficits. Some of the slowdown quite properly reflected the absence of effective economic policies or projects worthy of support. Some also results from the accounting treatment of the recent changes in the value of the dollar, the currency in which the World Bank and the IDB keep their accounts.

3. Brazil publicly admitted in early 1988 that external debt was not its main problem when recognizing that its moratorium of 1987 had been a costly failure. The details of the policy changes required for adjustment in Latin America can be found in Balassa, et al. (1986, 13–15, 24–32).

Nevertheless, there has been a sharp diminution of the contribution of these institutions at a time when a significant rise in their support is needed instead. Increased lending can induce better policies in recipient countries by easing the costs of those policies (for example, the increased foreign exchange expenditures that result from import liberalization) and by providing tangible rewards for the implementation of such policies, which strengthens the position of the officials who pursue them. A significant expansion of the role of the IFIs offers the best prospect for achieving the major policy reforms required in the debtor countries.

The IFIs also provide the only real hope for achieving substantial increases in new lending to the debtor countries. The multilateral development banks, as intermediaries in the world's capital markets, can borrow substantially larger amounts for lending to the debtor countries than private investors would be willing to transfer on their own. This is partly because these institutions can attach policy conditions to their credits, maximizing the chances that new funds will be used productively. But it is also because the development banks' own bonds are backed by their member governments, which include the industrial countries. The World Bank and the IDB obviously should not increase their lending (and borrowing) so much that they jeopardize their own credibility and credit ratings, but it seems quite feasible for them to expand substantially the size of their commitments and the pace of their disbursements.

At least $20 billion of additional new lending to the major debtors is needed each year for the foreseeable future (Balassa, et al. 1986, 40; Lessard and Williamson 1985, 27–28). The commercial banks may still be dragooned by the authorities into "involuntary lending" through new money packages for a few major borrowers, but it is clear that they are reducing rather than expanding their exposure (see table 7.1). Very little flight capital is likely to be repatriated soon—although the debtor countries must make every effort to attract it—and the adoption of better domestic policies is the only practical way to do so over the long run (Lessard and Williamson 1987). Direct investment and nonbank financial lending also have considerable potential over the long run and are quite responsive to changes in host country policies; they can make a modest contribution now, but will not occur on a major scale until the debt problem itself appears much closer to a lasting resolution.[4] Export credit agencies in industrial countries should expand their programs, as recommended for the United States in Chapter 6, but governments in those countries are not likely to provide much direct assistance because of their budget problems. Hence the IFIs, backed by their wealthiest member countries, are the only viable source of significant flows of new money to debtor countries.

Debt relief is an additional possibility. It is now clear that a number of the poorest countries, particularly in Africa, have little prospect of fully servicing their debt—let alone repaying it—and that they will require extensive debt relief. Most of the credits to these countries have been issued or guaranteed by governments in the industrial world, rather than by commercial banks or other private lenders, so many of the complications involved in providing relief from private credits are not relevant. The largest industrial countries agreed at the Toronto Summit in June 1988 to step up these efforts. Working primarily through the Paris Club, they now need to do so as expeditiously as possible.

The issue of relief for the large debtors in Latin America is much more complex, however, both because of the greater magnitudes involved and because most of the debt is owed to commercial banks. Such relief can come from only two sources: the public purse and the lenders themselves. However, the potential role of governments in the industrial countries (including the United States) is severely limited by budget constraints and the need to provide relief for the poorest countries—the priority recipients of such concessional assistance according to traditional aid criteria.

As for the private lenders, there is no way to require them to participate. Sweeping relief schemes that propose creating new international institutions to buy current debt at a discount and pass

4. Detailed proposals for expanding such flows can be found in Lessard and Williamson (1985). For example, host-country liberalization of restrictions on foreign direct investment could encourage substantial increases in this type of transfer—which is particularly appealing in the debt context because it is "serviced" only when the investment itself is profitable. Liberalization of host-country rules governing foreign access to domestic equity markets can also trigger significant inflows as shown recently in Brazil, India, Thailand, and others (Hale 1988, 24). In addition, country-specific mutual funds have considerable promise; the Brazil Fund was successfully launched in March 1988 and attracted $150 million (International Finance Corporation, Capital Markets Department, Emerging Markets Data Base).

on the benefits to debtor countries in return for new policy commitments are therefore almost certainly infeasible. Any truly comprehensive relief scheme, covering all lenders and all countries in one fell swoop, would also reduce the pressure to adopt better economic policies and could leave the debtor countries worse off once the short-term benefit of the relief itself had passed.[5]

The most promising approach is therefore to try to induce the private banks to offer relief on a voluntary basis. Most of the banks are now able to do so, at least to some extent, because they have strengthened their capital positions considerably and have set aside substantial reserves against their loans to the Third World—in the range of 25–30 percent of exposure for the money center banks, and 50 percent or more for the regional (and most foreign) banks. Actual write-offs of credits up to the levels reserved would eliminate any prospect of returning those reserves to reported earnings in the future, but would not generate additional losses on the income statement because the reserves themselves were deducted from current income reported to shareholders when they were set aside. Write-offs would, of course, reduce bank capital by a corresponding amount, although, as losses are actually realized, such write-offs can be deducted from income assessed for tax purposes. The losses are thus shared by the Treasury.

Some banks have already indicated a willingness to provide modest relief by selling loans back to debtor countries at a discount or by buying discounted exit bonds that exempt them from any future "obligation" to participate in new-money packages. It is likely that a number of banks would go further down this road if the inducement to do so were greater, and negotiations between creditors and debtors on the price that will provide such an inducement are now under way for some countries.

The IFIs should attempt to accelerate this process by offering guarantees of new debt instruments that would confer meaningful relief. A specific scheme for that purpose is developed in the section

5. For examples of broad relief schemes, see Peter Kenen in the *New York Times*, 6 March 1983, Felix Rohatyn in *Business Week*, 28 February 1983, and the recent proposal by James Robinson of American Express (1988). The proponents of these approaches generally argue that they could be carried out on a case-by-case basis, and insist on sound adjustment policies, but it is hard to see how relief could be denied to all or most countries once granted to any major debtor.

below on the World Bank. The governments of the industrial countries could also make changes in regulatory, accounting, and perhaps tax practices that would encourage the banks to offer additional relief. Banks that do not wish to exit the process through discounted bonds should be pressed hard to provide a proportional share of new-money packages that support policy reforms ratified by the IFIs—perhaps through interest capitalization, which provides cash flow relief if no actual reduction in the debt itself.

The objective of these several elements of a new debt strategy is to eliminate or begin to reverse the $30 billion annual "negative financial transfer" from the Baker 15 by the end of the four-year adjustment period in 1992. About $15–20 billion could come from increased lending by the IFIs, $5–10 billion from the lower interest rates resulting from industrial country adjustment, and the rest from voluntary debt relief and new flows of capital from private sources and export credit agencies (see table 1.1). Such an outcome would permit at least a modest increase in growth in the debtor countries, further reduce the risk of global financial instability, and make an important contribution to the international adjustment process. If better policies and performance in the debtor countries were to justify even larger increases in the flow of new capital and the reduction of existing debt, the United States and the other industrial countries—working mainly through the IFIs—should make every effort to provide such assistance.

The IFIs, particularly the World Bank, in view of the long-term nature of the debt problem, also must be given a much stronger leadership role in managing the issue. The IMF, quite properly (and effectively), took the lead role in the first phase, when the problem appeared to be a short-term one and had to be dealt with in crisis terms in any event. But the early rationale for Fund leadership has now disappeared, and the revolving nature of Fund loans limits its potential for financing longer-term adjustment. Furthermore, the Fund's essential role in the international monetary system—a role that needs to be substantially enhanced, as described below—demands that it limit the riskiness of its own portfolio and hence reduces its ability to lead the next phase of the debt strategy. The Fund's imprimatur will continue to be of critical importance to private lenders. But its constitutionally defined short-term focus and its image as a purveyor of austerity—however unfair, since Fund-related financing tends to reduce the degree of austerity needed to extricate countries from their largely self-imposed straits—make it quite difficult for the Fund to lead a successful growth-oriented debt strategy.

No single country can provide effective leadership for such a global problem. Strong US support will be needed for any lasting solution, but US interests would probably be served by a less aggressive role than was characteristic of the Baker Plan. Such a prominent role reinforces the view of some lenders in other countries that Third World debt "is an American problem" and that the United States should provide most of the new money and necessary policy concessions, despite the fact that only one-third of the bank debt is owed to American institutions.

A clearly designated leader is badly needed, however, to forge agreements among the debtor countries, private lenders, governments of the creditor countries, and the several IFIs themselves. The World Bank could naturally accede to this role by sharply expanding its own lending activities and sponsoring policy initiatives to facilitate voluntary debt relief. Proposals to that end will be offered below.

The United States would benefit, in particular, from a significant easing of the debt problem in Mexico. The United States has numerous interests in a speedy and substantial revival of the Mexican economy: a reduction in the incentive for Mexicans to migrate north; Mexico's pivotal role in the financial problems of a number of American banks; its market potential as America's third-largest trading partner; and a stable resolution of the political uncertainties following its latest national elections. It is difficult, however, for the United States to provide substantial bilateral assistance to Mexico, given the hostility engendered by a donor-client relationship on both sides of the border (as well as the usual budget constraints). For many years, Mexico has been one of the largest recipients of funding from all three of the main IFIs. A further substantial increase in their engagement with Mexico, aimed both at supporting additional policy reforms and expanding the inward flow of resources, would be of particular interest to the United States.

IMPROVED BURDEN SHARING

The second major issue that can best be addressed through the IFIs is the development of a better distribution of the costs of maintaining global security, including the prosperity and stability of the world economy. Efforts to devise a precise formula for "fair shares" are conceptually difficult, and would take an inordinate amount of time to negotiate. The United States spends a considerably higher proportion of its GNP on defense and foreign assistance than do its allies,[6] however, and will probably need to level off, or even cut, its military expenditures as part of the effort to eliminate the budget deficit by FY 1993 as called for by Gramm-Rudman-Hollings (and this book). There is thus a strong case for increased contributions from Europe and especially Japan (table 7.2).

There is widespread agreement that it would be a mistake to permit this problem to disrupt alliance security arrangements, especially given the potentially historic opportunities for greater stability now presented by the new leadership in the Soviet Union. Moreover, the United States has considered the defense of Europe and Japan to be an integral element in its own security throughout the postwar period, and there is no reason to alter that belief now. There is also widespread agreement that it would be a mistake for Japan to undertake a massive rearmament effort and enlarge its military role in Asia.

There is also wide agreement, however, that there have been sharp changes in relative economic capabilities in the period since the present security structure was put in place in the 1950s. The rapid progress of other countries and the associated relative decline of the United States during the past three decades, described in Chapter 3, now require some revision of national contributions to international security, broadly defined to include its economic component. Such a revision should be accomplished through a shift in relative financial obligations, rather than through any major restructuring of the security arrangements themselves.

In this context, most of the allies agree that some of them—obviously Japan, but perhaps some Europeans as well—should be doing more to support international public goods such as foreign assistance and debt relief. Just as the United States did when it was the dominant surplus country during the Marshall Plan period, Japan

6. It should be noted, however, that the United States ranks next-to-last among all OECD countries in shares of GNP devoted to concessional aid alone ("official development assistance," or ODA).

TABLE 7.2 Defense and Economic Assistance Expenditures in the Western Alliance, 1986 *(percentage of GDP)*

Country	Defense expenditures	Economic assistance	Combined expenditures	Index of effort (US = 100)
United States	6.7	0.2	6.9	100
NATO Allies				
Belgium	3.0	0.5	3.4	50
Canada	2.2	0.5	2.6	38
Denmark	2.0	0.8	2.9	41
France	3.9	0.7	4.6	67
Germany	3.1	0.4	3.5	51
Greece	6.1	0.0	6.1	88
Italy	2.2	0.4	2.6	38
Luxembourg	0.9	0.0	0.9	14
Netherlands	3.0	1.0	4.0	58
Norway	3.1	1.1	4.3	62
Portugal	3.2	0.0	3.2	47
Spain[a]	2.0	0.0	2.0	28
Turkey	4.8	0.0	4.8	69
United Kingdom	5.0	0.3	5.3	77
Non-US NATO Weighted Avg.[b]	3.3	0.5	3.7	54
Japan[a]	1.0	0.3	1.3	19

Note: Detail may not add to totals because of rounding.

Sources: Congressional Budget Office computations using data from NATO Press Service, "Financial and Economic Data Related to NATO Defense" (December 1987) for defense expenditures; data for gross domestic product from International Monetary Fund, *International Financial Statistics* (January 1988); and from Organization for Economic Cooperation and Development, *Development Assistance* (December 1987), for economic assistance.

a. Defense expenditures for Spain and Japan use the national, not NATO, definition as reported in International Institute for Strategic Studies, *The Military Balance 1987–1988* (London: IISS, 1987).

b. Using 1986 gross domestic product shares.

should "reverse tie" its aid—that is, prohibit it from being used in Japan. Europe and Japan will only do more, however, if they receive full credit for their new capabilities and contributions, just as the United States will want to retain predominant control of allied security arrangements because of its superior contributions in that sphere. Deals of this kind can best be worked out and implemented in the IFIs.

An alternative is to address the burden-sharing issue in the defense context, linking economics and security explicitly in an effort to determine a preferred distribution of expenditures.[7] However, the compartmentalization of security and economic issues among the allies that has characterized most of the postwar period has worked well for both sets of issues, and it should be preserved if at all possible.[8] Security-related discussions will inevitably be dominated by defense and foreign policy officials, at least in the United States, raising doubts about the efficiency and domestic sustainability of any economic decisions that might be taken. Perhaps most importantly, it would be very difficult to engage Japan—the major target of the effort—meaningfully in the defense context, and it would be virtually impossible to multilateralize such discussions with Japan and Europe simultaneously.

---

7. It has been proposed (Hale 1988) that the United States should explicitly return to the "military offset" arrangements of the 1960s. Under these agreements, Germany (and a few other European allies, to a much lesser degree) committed itself to buy a large quantity of military equipment from the United States and to invest in special Treasury securities to cover any remaining net foreign exchange cost to the United States of its military programs in Germany. In addition, Germany committed itself in 1967 not to buy US gold with its dollar reserves. The United States itself decided to drop the offsets, however, because they destroyed the compartmentalization of security and economic issues and thus raised major political problems abroad (and were widely viewed as causing the downfall of German Chancellor Ludwig Erhard in 1966). Moreover, today's linkages among issues must extend much more widely than in the 1960s—into foreign assistance, debt relief and other matters that would be extremely difficult to tie to troop levels and sales of military hardware. The more far-reaching approach suggested in the text would appear more desirable. Increased military spending by the allies would, however, simultaneously contribute to better burden sharing and stimulate domestic demand in the surplus areas as proposed in Chapter 5.

8. By contrast, the United States has consistently linked security and economic issues vis-à-vis the Soviet Union (and, to a lesser extent, vis-à-vis Eastern Europe and China). Japan and the Europeans have been much less inclined to do so, and this has been a frequent source of discord within the alliance.

The better course is therefore for the United States to make clear that the heavy costs of its own security commitments must be taken fully into account when new international economic arrangements are devised. Those arrangements should be negotiated between the United States and the other countries (notably Japan) within the framework of the existing IFIs. The basic approach would be to seek a sharp increase in the relative contributions to economic management from Japan, several European countries, and some "graduating" NICs. In return, these countries would be accorded a greater voice in managing the IFIs both through personnel changes and alterations of voting structures. The United States would retain its basic defense commitments. Specific proposals for each of the key institutions are made below.

ENTER GORBACHEV?

The international financial institutions can also play a useful role in addressing another potentially important issue, the possible reentry of the Soviet Union into the international economic system. The USSR opted out of the system shortly after participating in its creation at Bretton Woods in 1944, and since then it has remained a virtual nonparticipant in the world economy, both because of its ideological hostility toward the market-based exchange that characterizes relations among most nations of the world, and because of its autarkic and inefficient economic system.

The Gorbachev reforms, however, could produce a fundamental change in Soviet attitudes toward the world economy and even some changes in their international economic capabilities. But internal liberalization and the restoration of a price mechanism, however halting and limited, can only succeed if leavened by at least some exchange with the outside world. The desperate economic and political need to improve living standards in the Soviet Union will require the infusion of goods, technology, and money from the West. The experiences of China and several East European countries illustrate the essential linkages between internal liberalization and external exchange.

These precedents also indicate the role that the IFIs might be called upon to play vis-à-vis the USSR. The IMF, and especially the

World Bank, have helped to influence the economic leaderships in China and Hungary, and to guide those nations' increasing interactions with the West. Similar developments may now occur in Poland. One of the great (if unheralded) diplomatic successes of the past decade has been the quiet movement of China into closer contact with the world economy, partly through its involvement with the international financial institutions.

The Soviet Union has now put out feelers toward the IMF and the World Bank, and, after applying for observer status at the GATT's Uruguay Round, it has stepped up its efforts to join that organization.[9] To date, the response of the United States and the other members of these organizations has been negative: noting that the Soviet economic system is fundamentally incompatible with the operating premises of these organizations, which are based largely on market forces, the members have essentially rejected any overtures until the Soviet system has been radically transformed. Beneath this concern lie deep worries that Soviet entry—particularly to the Bretton Woods institutions, with their weighted voting arrangements—would require wholesale restructurings that would take considerable time and could politicize these largely technical bodies.

All such concerns are understandable, as are doubts that the Soviet Union really wants to join the IFIs for constructive purposes (or that Gorbachev's reforms will last). Nonetheless, even a partial integration of the USSR into the world economic system would represent a potentially historic breakthrough in political and security terms. The case of China, in particular, demonstrates that the IFIs could play an important role in such a development. The precedents of all the Communist countries indicate that the "entry fee" issue is manageable, though complex (especially in the GATT), and that fears of politicization have been unfounded.

Indeed, it would seem highly desirable to channel toward the IFIs any credible effort by the USSR to begin engaging in extensive economic exchange with the West. This is the least political, and hence most effective, way to get accurate data on its economy; to bring outside influence to bear both on its internal reforms and its

9. Increased interest in joining GATT was indicated by Soviet Foreign Economic Relations Minister Konstantin Katushev in an interview with the Japanese newspaper *Kyodo*, 22 August 1988.

internationalization; and to avoid, or at least coordinate, the inevitable scramble among western countries seeking to gain a competitive foothold in this "vast new market."

This is another potentially important role for the IFIs, reinforcing the case for the new administration to work to strengthen them. Seizing the opportunity offered by the Gorbachev reforms to begin to engage the Soviet Union in the world economy could have a significant impact on the international orientation of that country and thus enhance the prospects for world peace.

BUDGET CONSTRAINTS

Another important reason why the United States should support the IFIs is their cost-effectiveness. The United States must carry out the ambitious strategy proposed in this volume in the context of substantial overall cuts in government spending. Hence the need for efficient policy instruments is greater than ever before.

The IFIs fully meet this test. The United States can support the expansion of these institutions' Third World debt program with very modest budget outlays. In the latest General Capital Increase (GCI) for the World Bank, for example, only 3 percent of members' subscriptions is actually paid in. The remaining 97 percent is provided in the form of callable capital, a guarantee against the Bank's repayment of its borrowings in the international capital market. (These borrowings provide the actual resources that the Bank lends to debtor countries). Under congressional rules worked out in the 1970s, only the paid-in portion of World Bank capital subscriptions requires budget outlays. Callable capital is included in appropriations legislation (and requires full authorization), but would count as an outlay only in the unlikely event that the capital was ever called.[10]

Since the US share in the Bank's total capital is now under 20 percent, and only 3 percent of new subscriptions are paid in, every

10. Even if one doubted the creditworthiness of new World Bank loans and the adequacy of its reserves of $8.5 billion to handle any repayment problems, over $85 billion of callable capital is already available to the Bank from its past capitalizations and would be drawn before new callable capital would be tapped.

dollar of US contributions supports over $165 of new Bank credits. To the extent that the Bank can use its guarantee and financing programs to generate additional lending from private sources, this leverage is even greater. The ratio is not quite as impressive in the regional development banks, but it is still about 1:40 in the IDB. The IFIs provide a great deal of "bang for the buck" in terms of nonconcessional lending to debtor countries and others in the Third World.[11]

The resources of the IMF consist of member country quotas (the General Account) and Special Drawing Rights (SDRs; the Special Account). Increases in either require no budget outlays by the United States at all. Under the guidelines developed in the late 1970s, quota increases (like World Bank callable capital) are included in appropriations as well as authorizing legislation, but no outlays are recorded.[12] Legislation from the early 1980s requires the administration to consult with the Congress before approving new allocations of SDRs, but these are not included in the budget at all—quite appropriately, since they represent newly created international money that carries no liability for any of the member governments.

Increasing program levels in the IFIs is thus a uniquely attractive policy approach from a fiscal perspective. Given the likely budget stringency of the 1990s, especially for the United States but also for many other countries, the IFIs deserve special attention.

AMERICAN LEADERSHIP

An overarching theme of this analysis is the need for the United States to develop a new leadership role that corresponds both to its own increased dependence on the world economy and its reduced,

11. Each of the IFIs also has a concessional lending window for its poorest member countries, such as the International Development Association (IDA) of the World Bank. All contributions to these programs require full budgetary appropriation, and thus have much less financial leverage. They are still quite useful in this respect when compared with bilateral programs, however; the US share in IDA is about 25 percent so every dollar of US budget outlays there triggers $4 in total assistance to poor countries.

12. The reason in this case is that the United States receives a claim on the IMF in return for its "contribution" of dollars, which entitles it to draw hard currencies such as yen and DM when needed, so the transaction amounts to an exchange of assets rather than a net payment.

though still potent, ability to influence international economic events. It is clear that the new economic management structure of the world must be multilateral, with at least Japan and Germany (or a united Europe) at the core of the directorate. The United States will find it increasingly difficult to pursue its objectives effectively through unilateral or bilateral steps, although such approaches may work on occasion and small steering groups (such as a G-2 arrangement with Japan or a G-3 with Japan and Germany) will often be needed to guide the course of the formal institutions (Bergsten, Berthoin, and Mushakoji 1976).

Because of their multilateral nature and weighted voting, the IFIs provide a ready-made framework within which the United States can pursue its new leadership role. These institutions may frequently represent the best channel to pursue direct US interests, such as avoiding an international financial crisis or increasing import capabilities in Third World countries. They may also be the best places to pursue indirect but important US interests, such as more sensible economic policies in LDCs. The two goals will often fuse: the United States has a major developmental as well as export interest in trade liberalization in LDCs, for example, so support for IFI efforts to achieve policy reforms in return for new credits can be a valuable element in the overall strategy suggested here.

The European situation also supports the case for an American effort to boost the role of the international institutions in finance and trade. As the European Community moves toward its "single internal market," closer policy coordination, and possibly even a European central bank, it will inevitably tend to emphasize regional issues at the expense of global ones. This would be ironic, since the achievement of greater internal cohesion would strengthen Europe considerably and enable it to play a larger international role, a development that would be very much in America's interest. The United States thus has a special incentive to launch initiatives that will foster a larger role for the global institutions, challenging Europe to participate in them fully rather than turning inward to its own organizations. An effective system of pluralistic economic management requires Europe to play a central role, and the present period is extremely important in ensuring such an outcome for the 1990s and beyond.

The IFIs are not by any means perfect, either from the standpoint of the national interests of the United States or those of other nations. But they have achieved considerable success under extremely difficult circumstances through several decades of rapid change in the world economy. They would have to be invented now if they did not already exist. The United States, which led the creation of all of these institutions (except the African Development Bank) during its hegemonic period, can now use them to great advantage as it seeks a new and more complicated leadership role. To achieve the US policy goals that have just been elaborated, new initiatives are needed in the World Bank, the IDB, and IMF, in particular.

THE WORLD BANK

The World Bank needs to take several important initiatives to lead a more effective response to the problem of Third World debt. Most importantly, it needs to increase sharply the level of credits that it can make available to the main debtor countries. This would help induce those countries to adopt better policies, reduce the negative financial transfer from them, and enable the Bank to solidify its leadership on this issue for the foreseeable future.

Under current plans, the Bank intends to expand its annual new commitments to all borrowers from about $15 billion in FY 1988 to about $21 billion by FY 1992. This increase requires additional resources, and the membership voted in early 1988 for a General Capital Increase (GCI) of $75 billion. The Congress approved in September 1988 the US subscription to the GCI, which will require budget outlays of only $420 million over the entire six-year period.

The currently planned increase in Bank lending under the GCI, however, will make only a modest contribution to reducing the $30 billion annual negative financial transfer from the Baker 15, to which the Bank "contributed" over $1 billion in FY 1988. The Bank should thus take three additional steps. First, it should be prepared to raise its annual commitments to at least $25 billion as soon as possible (rather than $21 billion by 1992). Its actual ability to lend such amounts will depend on whether borrowing countries can provide enough worthy projects and policy reforms, and no arbitrary lending targets should be set. But the Bank should stand ready to offer generous support for worthwhile projects and programs at considerably higher levels than now planned.

Second, the Bank should make much larger amounts available through "structural adjustment loans" and sector loans, to support more far-reaching policy changes by borrowing countries. This would help to increase the level of its transfers and speed their disbursement, as well as respond to the major development needs of many of the Bank's largest borrowers during this period. Instead of lending $1 billion to Mexico to facilitate its substantial steps toward trade liberalization (along with another $1 billion for sectoral reforms) in FY 1988, for example, the Bank could offer to lend $2 billion to finance even more sweeping liberalization (including on inward FDI) and some of the internal adjustments that would be required as a result.

Third, the Bank should launch a temporary program under which it would guarantee exit bonds issued by debtor countries with effective adjustment programs to banks that are prepared to convert their existing loans at a considerable discount. Mexico's arrangement with Morgan Guaranty in early 1988 sought to persuade banks to undertake such a conversion, but the result was modest because the lenders did not see much greater assurance of interest payments on the new paper than on the old. A Bank guarantee of such payments could transform such arrangements, enabling even the largest debtors to cut their outstanding liabilities significantly. This would give the Bank a major role in inducing commercial banks to reduce their claims on debtor countries, as a number of its congressional critics have advocated.

If exit bonds were sold at an average discount of 50 percent from the face value of existing bank loans (in accord with current prices in the secondary market), and were paid off in eight years, as much as one-third of the bank debt of the 17 highly indebted middle-income countries could be converted. This would reduce the value of the debt by as much as one-sixth, or about $45 billion, at the cost of a contingent claim on the Bank's newly available callable capital that would not compete with its traditional lending program because the new claims would begin falling from their peak after four years. The main problem would be to provide adequate cash flow to the debtor countries in the interim, enabling them to service the bonds as well as meet their other foreign exchange payments.

This could be done partly by persuading the banks that did not exit to offer sufficient new capital to facilitate the substantial improvement in the countries' long-term positions (and thus the value of the banks' own claims).[13]

These new uses of the Bank's resources would have two important financial consequences. First, they would require the United States and the other key donor countries to speed up the timetable under which they actually pay in their subscriptions under the GCI, thereby providing the Bank with the capital it needs to accelerate its lending and guarantee programs as proposed here.[14] The United Kingdom, the first of the major donors to fulfill its subscription, did in fact pay the total amount in a single installment. Second, the changes proposed here would also require a modest advance of the date on which another GCI would have to be considered—perhaps from 1993 to 1992. Given the small costs of Bank capital to the donor countries, and the high payoff from its programs, these changes should be acceptable.

An additional source of funding for the Bank could be an early Selective Capital Increase (SCI), through which the major creditor countries would further augment the Bank's capital in return for a corresponding increase in their voting rights. Japan would certainly participate, and the NICs and perhaps a few Europeans should do so as well. This would be an effective way to increase the contribution of newly wealthy countries to the stability of the international economy. Relative shares could be determined at least in part through the discussions on improved burden sharing proposed above.

An alternative to using the Bank's regular capital to back the new program of exit bond guarantees is to create a separate window in the institution for this purpose. Such a facility could be mainly or

13. This proposal is developed in Williamson (1988b). The exit bonds could also be structured with much longer maturities, at the cost of adding to the potential net use of IBRD resources. On the other hand, the Bank could limit its exposure by guaranteeing the bonds partially rather than fully.

14. The United States may need to accelerate its payments, in any event, to keep its voting share in the Bank from falling below the level required to maintain veto power over charter amendments and a few other major decisions. This will certainly be the case in the event of a substantial Selective Capital Increase with rapid pay-in, as proposed below, through which Japan and other countries would fund an increased share of bank capital as part of the broader reallocation of economic burden sharing advocated throughout this volume.

entirely capitalized by those countries, led by Japan, that have experienced a rapid improvement in their relative income positions and that have also been running external surpluses. This approach would thereby also contribute to the objectives of correcting the current imbalances—because these countries' funds would help finance expanded US exports to the debtor countries—and to better global burden sharing. The facility might be able to leverage its capital to a substantial extent, guaranteeing exit bonds valued at five to ten times its own resources. (The Bank's Articles of Agreement prohibit this kind of leveraging of the capital of the Bank itself.) Backing the new guarantees through a separate facility would free the Bank's resources for the proposed expansion of its lending program without any need to accelerate payments under the present GCI or advance the date of the next one. Such a facility would take longer to start up, however.

After these new initiatives were under way, the only significant constraint on Bank programs would be its ability to use its money wisely and elicit meaningful commitments from borrowing countries. The debt crisis is already pushing many of the large borrowers toward policy reforms, and expanded Bank lending can be made available with greater confidence than in the past. But it will be essential that the Bank insist on effective structural reform programs in fashioning its loans, and that it use its increased resources to induce such efforts. The Bank will have to demonstrate that it means business by withholding funds from countries that fail to implement their policy commitments faithfully, or by denying loans in the first place to those who will not make meaningful commitments. There can be no arbitrary fulfillment of lending targets, simply to achieve a desired level of capital transfer.

With these additions both to the quantity of its lending and the breadth of its programs, the Bank will be in a strong position to assume leadership in managing the debt problem. The debt issue now approximates a three-ring circus—comprising the governments of the debtor countries, commercial lenders (mainly banks), and the governments of lending countries (independently and working through the IFIs)—without a ringmaster to direct the participants in a cohesive performance. The IMF, as noted above, can no longer lead. Former Secretary Baker succeeded in filling part of the vacuum and avoiding a financial crisis during the past three years, but his Baker Plan has fallen far short of success, and no single country can organize a successful debt resolution effort. Since the problem is now clearly of a long-term character, and is thus intimately linked to the development prospects of the Bank's borrowers, Bank leadership is appropriate. This further supports the case for enhancing its programs through the measures proposed here.

If Japan were willing to provide a sufficiently large part of the increased capital needed by the Bank, it should receive in return not only the normal increase in voting power, but serious consideration for its nationals for the presidency of the institution. The original rationale for an American president for the Bank, in addition to the dominant shareholder position of the United States at the time, was that virtually all the Bank's borrowing occurred in the US capital market. But Japanese investors have reportedly been buying up to one-half of all new bonds issued by the Bank in the world's capital markets. If Japan, now by far the world's largest creditor country, is willing both to provide the bulk of the Bank's funds and to back its capital with considerably larger governmental guarantees, the Bank's traditional criteria would suggest that the next president should be Japanese if a qualified candidate is available.[15]

The markets and the other countries will want the United States to maintain full support for the Bank at the same time, to ensure that the institution will in fact be able to play its new key role. For its part, the United States can only retain the leadership role advocated throughout this volume if it fully supports the activities of the Bank. This will require accelerated payment of its subscriptions under the GCI and efforts to convince other governments to do the same; support for an SCI that increases the share of Bank capital made available to Japan and others, as they increase their financial contributions; advocacy of a larger and faster disbursing lending

15. Current Vice Minister of Finance Toyoo Gyohten would be a strong possibility. Similarly, the time has come to end the anachronistic reservation of the top management positions in the IMF and GATT for Europeans. An eminent American, such as Paul Volcker or William Brock, should certainly be eligible to head the Fund or GATT. An effective leader from outside the Big Three, such as Prime Minister Bob Hawke of Australia after he leaves office, could lead the GATT. These institutions will be so important in the 1990s and beyond that the best person available should be sought to run them regardless of nationality or implicit political deals from the 1940s. The member countries will have to make their most qualified people (including government officials) available for both top staff positions and as Executive Directors, which they—notably including Japan and the United States—have not always done.

program and new guarantee authority; acceptance of a lead role for the Bank in managing Third World debt; and support for a more diversified leadership structure in the organization.

These changes in US policy toward the World Bank would form an important part of the overall shift in the international economic role of the United States in the 1990s. They would also help to achieve two of the core objectives of America's foreign economic policy: a correction of the external deficit (by promoting the expansion of US exports to Third World markets) and a reduction of the risk of financial instability (by providing a more effective response to the debt problem).

THE INTER-AMERICAN DEVELOPMENT BANK

Similar changes are needed at the Inter-American Development Bank. The starting position there is more complex, however, because the United States has brought the institution to a virtual halt over the past three years by insisting on near-veto power on individual loans as a quid pro quo for supporting the capital increase needed to permit increased lending.[16] New loan commitments dropped from $3 billion in 1986 to $2.4 billion in 1987, and the IDB is now on balance withdrawing funds from the hemisphere (about $1 billion in 1987 and 1988 from Argentina, Brazil, and Mexico).

The American demand for greater power in the Bank obviously runs counter to the more pluralistic management strategies recommended throughout this book. The futility of this course is demonstrated by the refusal of the other members of the Bank, including nonregional donors (from Europe and Japan) as well as the Latin Americans, to accept it, despite the dire economic straits of the borrowing countries and their need for IDB capital. The US initiative

16. A somewhat similar, if less damaging, sequence has occurred in the Asian Development Bank (ADB). Japan has proposed a sharp increase in the Bank's capital, but the United States has opposed the idea in part because of a fear that it would lose voting power if it failed to match the Japanese subscription. The ADB is in fact a very useful vehicle for channeling Japan's surplus funds to developing countries in Asia, and an increase in its share in that institution would promote better burden sharing among the allies.

should be quietly shelved, in return for firmer commitments from the Bank's new management on the quality as well as the quantity of future lending.

There are valid concerns about the efficiency of the IDB, however, so US strategy there should be more limited in magnitude and more cautious than in the World Bank. The main goals should be similar: larger loan commitments to encourage recipients to adopt more effective policies; expeditious approval of a capital increase (of perhaps $25 billion), to enable the Bank to increase its level of new commitments (perhaps to about $6 billion per year); and more rapid disbursements through increased emphasis on program and, especially, sector loans.

Because of concerns about the performance of the IDB, its loans should be offered in conjunction with those of the World Bank whenever possible. The IDB has several unique advantages, however, that the United States should seek to exploit. As an inter-American institution, with majority participation by Latin Americans, it has greater legitimacy than the Bretton Woods institutions among the governments of some of the chief debtor countries and can thus be especially effective in eliciting their cooperation on policy reforms. The IDB could take the lead in coordinated efforts with the World Bank in some cases, while deferring to its primacy in others.

THE INTERNATIONAL MONETARY FUND

Like the World Bank and the IDB, the Fund must make a larger contribution to the resolution of the Third World debt problem.[17] In addition, it must play a central role both in the proposed adjustment of the massive international imbalances among the industrial countries and in the reform of the international monetary system. By addressing these tasks, the IMF can also be an important

17. It has recently taken two useful steps in this direction: creation of the Enhanced Structural Adjustment Facility to provide longer-term assistance to its poorest member countries, and creation of the Compensatory and Contingency Finance Facility to provide credits to offset, inter alia, the impact of higher interest rates on borrowing countries (as originally proposed by Cline 1980).

vehicle for improved burden sharing and a new international economic leadership role for the United States.

On debt, the IMF can provide major assistance in achieving the policy reforms required of the debtor countries. Its programs should increasingly emphasize structural adjustment for the longer run through such steps as trade liberalization, the removal of restrictions on foreign direct investment (to enhance the utility of debt-equity swaps among other things), and the liberalization of domestic capital markets. As the World Bank moves toward more active leadership of the debt problem and the Fund's loans become more oriented toward structural adjustment, IMF approval of country programs should increasingly be coordinated with those of the Bank. In fact, it would be desirable to create a joint Bank–Fund unit to develop and monitor at least some of the country programs in which both institutions are involved, or for the two institutions to at least prepare joint policy strategies for key borrowers from both.[18] However, the Fund's independent imprimatur will remain extremely important to the commercial banks and other private lenders regarding the financial soundness of country programs and potential new loans.

The fact that the IMF is a revolving fund is exacerbating the debt problem because some of the major debtors are now repaying Fund loans drawn during the first stage of the crisis in the 1982–84 period, creating a negative financial transfer of about $1 billion to the Baker 15 in 1987. By contrast, the Fund extended net new credits of $6 billion as recently as 1983. Ways need to be found, consistent with the basic character of the Fund, to avoid such net repayments until the overall debt situation is much more stable.

The best way to encourage better borrowing-country policies and to improve their financial positions is to increase the level of credit that is available to them under new agreements with the Fund.[19] The first step in this direction is to use the Fund's current programs

18. Three-year rolling programs are now being prepared jointly for the poorer member countries borrowing under the Structural Adjustment Facility and Enhanced Structural Adjustment Facility. This model should be extended to the middle-income debtors and stretched over a considerably longer time horizon.

19. This is superior to the alternative of rescheduling of present loans, which would raise questions about the Fund's own creditworthiness and could impede the process of parliamentary ratification of its new programs in some countries (including the United States).

much more aggressively. Liquid resources now available total almost $50 billion. Under the "enlarged access" policy, adopted in 1981 and modified subsequently on several occasions, countries can borrow up to 90 percent of their quotas in a single year, and cumulatively up to 400 percent of their quotas. However, few new programs are providing annual tranches that fully utilize these ceilings. The Fund should thus begin to transfer considerably larger amounts to its borrowers, especially to the debtors now experiencing net negative transfers, if these nations are willing to commit themselves to effective policy reforms.

Such a policy change could lead rather quickly to larger programs for a number of countries, so there should also be an early increase in the quotas of all members. The present enlarged access should be increased back to the original limits of 150 percent of quota annually and 600 percent cumulatively, pending the quota increase, and either held there or dropped no further than the present limits when the new quotas are activated. These further increases in the availability of financing will enhance the incentives for borrowers to meet Fund conditions. So would a lengthening of the maturities of new Fund credits, which would reduce the chances of again generating negative net transfers prematurely.

The Fund was scheduled to consider a quota increase in 1988, but it deferred the issue for a year at the request of the United States, which wanted to avoid approaching the Congress before it had acted on the GCI for the World Bank. The issue is now scheduled for consideration in early 1989, and the new administration—after close consultation with the Congress—should seek a doubling in Fund quotas from their current level of about $100 billion. Along with the maintenance of "enlarged access," and an increase back to the earlier level of 150 percent of quota for annual drawings, at least until the new quotas are in place, this would enable the Fund to increase substantially its new loans to debtor countries (and others) with effective adjustment programs.

Such a quota increase would also have direct benefits for the United States. As described in Chapter 5, the United States could face a difficulty in financing its continuing current account deficits over the coming years, even if it adopts a fully credible adjustment program. Its financing needs will be even greater if it fails to do the latter. In either case, the United States may have to acquire large amounts of foreign currencies to share the exchange risk involved in such financing if private lenders are unwilling to buy enough dollar assets at acceptable prices and if foreign central banks insist on such sharing.

US holdings of foreign currencies are rather limited relative to its potential requirements for intervention, however, and the acceptance of new foreign currency liabilities (through the activation of the swap network or the issuance of foreign currency debt) would be extremely risky unless full market confidence had been restored. An IMF quota increase of 100 percent would augment the potential resources of the United States by about $25 billion, of which about $6 billion would be available immediately and without conditions. It should be recalled that the United States drew about $3 billion of DM and yen from the Fund as part of the dollar defense program launched in November 1978, and drew from the Fund on more than twenty other previous occasions.

A sizable quota increase and more extensive lending to the large debtor countries would help revive the global role of the Fund.[20] This would promote the interests of the United States by pluralizing the management of the international economic system in an organization that is demonstrably effective. Such a renewed role for the Fund, together with that of the Bank, should be a major objective of the foreign economic policy of the new administration.

The United States should seek the strengthened Fund's help in promoting the necessary adjustment in the current account imbalances of the major industrial countries and, especially, in maintaining new equilibrium exchange rates and supporting national policies once they have been achieved. When the United States announces the goal of eliminating its current account deficit, as recommended in Chapter 4, it should look to the Fund to work out the implications

20. Another possibility is renewed allocations of Special Drawing Rights (SDRs), as proposed by Williamson (1984), and the Institute of International Finance (1988). The SDR could be used increasingly as an "anchor" for a reformed monetary system, and as an additional source of support for Third World debtors. However, world reserves have risen sharply during the past three years—mainly as a result of the sizable intervention by foreign central banks to support the dollar in 1986–87. The monetary character of the SDR needs to be preserved if it is to play a central role in the system over the longer term, and all proposals for new allocation need to be judged carefully against that standard.

for the world economy as a whole and to recommend how the adjustment can best be allocated among countries in order to minimize any adverse effects. In particular, the Fund will need to protect the interests of the LDC debtors during the adjustment process. It will also have to steer the effort, outlined in Chapter 5, to channel the maximum counterpart of the American adjustment to the surplus countries.

As argued in Chapter 5, the United States has a major interest in reform of the international monetary system that helps to avoid another cycle of the huge currency and policy swings that have caused so much damage to the US economy, to its international financial position, and to the global trading system. Such reform, preferably in the direction of target zones and much more extensive policy coordination among the largest countries, will initially have to be negotiated and implemented by the G-7 (or an even smaller group of financial powers).[21] But such a reform can only become fully operational and legitimate if it is institutionalized in the IMF, the world body responsible for international monetary affairs. As current exchange rate arrangements evolve toward greater coordination, the Fund should play an increasingly central role. For a start, the Fund should publicize at least summary versions of its policy recommendations to countries under the present multilateral surveillance process, as proposed for the United States (through the Secretary of the Treasury) in the monetary policy chapter of the Omnibus Trade Act.

The IMF should thus figure significantly in the international economic strategy of the new administration. The United States itself will have to be willing to respond positively to Fund recommendations concerning its economy, as already suggested in the Omnibus Trade Act. As in the World Bank, Japan and a few other countries may need to be accorded larger voting shares, perhaps through special quota increases, to reflect more accurately the distribution of economic power and responsibility in the 1990s and beyond. Japan already has the second largest share of World Bank capital but remains only fifth in terms of IMF quotas—behind the

21. The possible tactical need to proceed first through a "G-2" between the United States and Japan, as Secretary Baker was forced to do by European footdragging in late 1986, is explored in Bergsten (1987a).

United Kingdom, Germany, and France, as well as the United States. This anomalous situation needs to be promptly corrected, and the United States may have to push the Europeans hard to get them to agree. Japan should be asked to increase substantially its financial support for the Bank and IDA, as well as for the Fund itself, as part of this leadership shift.

CONCLUSION

These proposals for strengthening the role of the international financial institutions can be pursued most effectively if the new administration takes the three sets of proposals—affecting the World Bank, the IDB, and the IMF—to the Congress together in a single package. Rather than divorcing the component parts from each other out of concern for congressional hostility, as has been the practice during the past few years, the administration should link the institutions together in a single piece of legislation. This will highlight both their numerous benefits for US interests and the modest budget outlays they require.

Omnibus IFI legislation in 1989 should include full payment of the US contribution to the GCI at the World Bank, which would require only $370 million in budget outlays; perhaps $9 billion of additional capital for the IDB, of which only $225 million would be paid in; and about $25 billion for the increased US quota at the IMF, with no outlays. Linking these funding proposals together would dramatize the benefits of the institutions for the United States and their cost-effectiveness. Such an arrangement would of course have to be worked out in close consultation with the Congress. Indeed, one reason for packaging the proposals together is that the case for each could be made simultaneously, and the Congress is always more attentive when the magnitude of a proposed program is greater.

New initiatives toward the IFIs would have major advantages for the international economic policy of the United States, both at home and abroad. Domestically, it would signal a strong commitment by the United States to full and active participation in international economic affairs. Internationally, it would indicate clearly that the United States intended to follow the multilateral route to the maximum extent possible, because it recognized that this route supported its national interests both in economic and foreign policy terms. With a unified domestic front and a credible international commitment, the United States would dispel many of the suspicions of its motives that have arisen during the past few years. As a result, it will become much more effective in pursuing its interests in the institutions themselves, and more generally.

Most importantly, the proposed program changes in the three IFIs could make a major contribution both to the resolution of the Third World debt crisis and to the correction of the US external deficit, and do so in a way that will contribute to better burden sharing among the allies. Substantial increases in IFI lending levels, faster disbursements, and a new World Bank debt guarantee program could generate a sharp reduction—or even elimination—of the negative financial transfer of the large debtor countries over the next four years. This would enable these countries to grow faster and to sharply reduce their trade surpluses or even run deficits again, contributing substantially to the global adjustment. A significant expansion of the roles of the IFIs can thus simultaneously help address the problems of each of the two major debtor regions of the world, the northern and southern continents of the Western Hemisphere.

8

Implementing the Strategy of Competitive Interdependence

THE POLICY PACKAGES AT HOME AND ABROAD

The United States should implement the domestic portion of the strategy proposed in this volume largely through three new legislative packages: one for reduction of the budget deficit, another for export expansion, and a third supporting the IFIs. Each would contribute significantly to the correction of the huge US external imbalance, and also achieve other priority goals of the United States. Each would need to be worked out through extensive consultation between the administration and Congress. The three packages would relate closely to each other and would together form a comprehensive response to some of the most urgent economic and foreign policy problems that will confront the new government. If they are faithfully implemented, it will be evident at home and abroad that the United States is doing everything within its power to strengthen its international economic and financial position—the "competitive" element of the proposed strategy.

The international portion of the strategy would involve a series of major negotiating efforts: to coordinate national economic policies in a way that will eliminate the international imbalances while sustaining global growth and stability; to achieve equilibrium levels for the dollar and the other key currencies, and then keep them there; to improve substantially the international monetary system; to ensure a successful Uruguay Round of multilateral trade talks; to expand sharply the Third World debt effort; to improve the international allocation of the costs and responsibilities of global economic management; and to expand substantially the programs and role of the IFIs. Each of these negotiations would build on initiatives that have been under way for some time, but each would push them considerably further as part of an integrated and comprehensive approach. This is the "interdependence" element of the proposed strategy.

Successful implementation of this program offers the best prospect for achieving the economic goals of the new administration. By cutting the trade deficit through macroeconomic policy changes at home and abroad, and by seeking to achieve and maintain a fully competitive exchange rate for the dollar, the strategy would support continued US growth. By countering the threat of an uncontrolled fall of the dollar, it would avert the main threat to continuing prosperity and prevent a surge of inflation. By renewing the process of trade liberalization and strengthening international policy cooperation, it would arrest the erosion of the global system on which so much of American (and world) prosperity and stability depend. By enhancing the capabilities of the IFIs, it would reduce the threat posed by Third World debt. By encouraging Japan and a few other countries to increase their contributions to international economic management, it would improve international burden sharing and reduce the risk of an unraveling of international security arrangements and economic cooperation. All these efforts would restore American leadership within the pluralistic power structure that will characterize global economic affairs for the foreseeable future.

Japan and the Asian NICs will probably need periodic injections of fiscal stimulus, and continuing structural reforms, to keep their domestic demand growing enough to reduce their surpluses to sustainable levels. Europe will have to correct its internal imbalances—in which Germany's surplus mirrors deficits almost everywhere else—and launch similar stimulus and structural efforts to sustain growth and reduce unemployment. These countries will have to accept substantial further appreciation of their currencies and sharp reductions in their surpluses.

But it is up to the United States to initiate the most crucial part of the global adjustment by taking decisive steps to bring its budget deficit under control. The rebound of the dollar in 1988 must be reversed, and additional depreciation will be required. Only the new administration can provide the impetus to conclude a successful Uruguay Round. It is largely up to the United States to revitalize the IFIs by supporting renewed expansion and innovation in their programs—especially an acceleration of lending and a new guarantee program at the World Bank, the IMF's next quota increase, and a capital increase for the IDB. It is the American economy that is at risk, in the first instance, and America's continuing preeminence in the world economy dictates that it now take the lead in restoring global stability.

The other key countries, especially Japan and Germany, must respond cooperatively to these American initiatives. They must keep their domestic demand growing rapidly for some time. They must cooperate to achieve and then maintain a set of equilibrium exchange rates, preferably through the adoption of target zones. Especially in the case of Japan, they must sharply increase their contributions to the financial resources available to debtor countries. They should support policy innovations such as the use of World Bank guarantees to help handle Third World debt.

Some of the surplus countries need to take substantial steps to liberalize trade. Japan must continue working to eradicate its barriers, in both agriculture and industry. Europe must reform its farm policies and roll back the state subsidies that prop up many of its industries. The NICs must allow their demonstrated export prowess to be reflected in their policies toward imports. Much of this liberalization can be achieved in the Uruguay Round, but some of it should be done unilaterally, and sooner.

A large international deal could thus be struck by the new administration.[1] Fortunately, each component is very much in the interest of the countries involved. However, some components (particularly those relating to trade and budgets) could face consid-

1. Even those who are skeptical of the merits of international policy coordination concur that "occasionally there is a clear international deal to be made. That was true in 1978; it appears to be true in 1987" (Fischer 1987, 45). Since no deal was actually made in 1987–88, it has become even more feasible (and necessary) in 1989.

erable domestic political opposition. Hence more can probably be accomplished in the context of an explicit international bargain, with the United States taking the lead.[2]

Each part of the proposed international deal builds on efforts that have been under way for some time. Policy coordination and a new exchange rate system have been under active discussion in the G-5/G-7 for three years. The Uruguay Round was formally launched in late 1986. A quota increase at the IMF was delayed for a year only at the insistence of the United States. The United States itself has already begun to experience export-led growth, and Japan has begun to rely heavily upon domestic demand-led growth. The Gramm-Rudman-Hollings legislation provides the budget timetable endorsed here. The components of the program will thus come as no surprise to the rest of the world, which should enhance the prospects for their early acceptance.

The importance of the program would be dramatized if its most significant measures, particularly in the macroeconomic sphere, were announced at a special international summit meeting in early 1989 or at the regular summit now scheduled for July in France. The new President should attempt to work out the budget package with the congressional leadership as early as possible, agreeing both on the magnitude of the deficit cuts and the major program changes that would be adopted to achieve the bulk of them. With this domestic achievement in hand, he should then approach his counterparts abroad, especially in the three surplus areas, seeking their agreement on complementary economic policies, currency management, and monetary system reform. It would also be useful to reaffirm the countries' commitment to the success of the Uruguay Round and to work out the new strategy to address Third World debt through the IFIs.

If all (or even most) of these negotiations were successful, a joint announcement of the results at a summit would boost global confidence dramatically.[3] The markets would be euphoric. The new

---

2. See Putnam and Henning (forthcoming) for an analysis of how international trade-offs made such a deal possible at the Bonn Summit in 1978.

3. The deterioration of the "economic summits" into media events with a heavy focus on political issues in the early 1980s was a natural corollary of the rejection by the first Reagan administration of international policy coordination. The new administration will have to decide whether it wants to try to use the process seriously, continue it on

administration would be off to the strongest possible start. International cooperation would take one of its largest steps forward since the creation of the postwar economic system at Bretton Woods in 1944.

ORGANIZING FOR THE EFFORT

The creation, development, international negotiation, and domestic implementation of the strategy proposed in this volume will be a herculean task for the new administration, particularly given the rapid timetable required for some of its major components. Success will be assured only if the new administration places the highest priority on these issues, works closely with the Congress from the outset, makes a major effort to convince the country of the wisdom of its strategy, and clearly designates one top official to lead and coordinate the effort. The President will have to devote a considerable amount of personal attention to the program, but he must empower a talented lieutenant who can hit the ground running to manage it on a day-to-day basis.

Organizational charts offer little help in such matters; the international economic "czar" could in principle be located in several different places in the administration. The Secretary of the Treasury has by far the best institutional position from which to lead this effort, however. He is designated by law to determine US international monetary policy, make decisions on intervention in the exchange markets, and represent the United States in all of the IFIs. Ministers of Finance hold the key economic policy positions in most other governments, so communication channels and negotiating partners are readily available to the Secretary. At home, the Secretary possesses the strongest institutional position vis-à-vis the Congress (partly due to his major role in key domestic issues such as tax policy and debt financing) and the best international economics staff in the government. The second Reagan administration was able to coordinate

---

a nonsubstantive basis, or drop the entire idea. The focus of the strategy proposed here, with its emphasis on substantially upgrading the priority accorded to international economic policy, suggests a renewed effort to employ the summits to help coordinate policies effectively (though without suggesting that they will be able to accomplish that task effectively on all occasions).

economic policy effectively with former Treasury Secretary Baker serving as Chairman of the Economic Policy Council, and the next administration should employ a similar approach.[4]

To be sure, the Treasury cannot undertake all of the domestic and international negotiations involved in such a program. A strong United States Trade Representative is needed, for example, to coordinate the components of trade policy and conduct most trade negotiations. The Chairman of the Federal Reserve Board plays a unique role in dollar management, and his leadership of monetary policy is of course critical. Valuable assistance can come from a number of other agencies including the Eximbank and Commerce (on export promotion), the State Department, the Council of Economic Advisers, and the Office of Management and Budget.

It would also be highly desirable for the Congress to organize itself better to handle international economic issues. Too many committees have jurisdiction over different issues. This was graphically revealed when 21 separate committees and 199 members of Congress participated in the legislative conference on the Omnibus Trade Act of 1988. One alternative would be the creation of a Joint Committee on International Economic Policy which, unlike the Joint Committee on Taxation or the Joint Economic Committee, would have legislative powers.

It is highly doubtful that the operating committees would agree to give up their jurisdictions, however. Hence the most practical solution, again building on recent experience, would be for the leadership in each chamber to ask the chairmen of the Senate Finance and House Ways and Means Committees to take responsibility for pulling together the congressional components of the international economic program. The two committees already have primary responsibility for core elements of any such effort, notably trade and tax policies, but also major expenditure matters (including the large entitlement programs). They played this coordinating role to a

---

4. President Reagan's earlier proposal to consolidate all trade functions under the Department of Commerce and abolish the United States Trade Representative was a mistake, and was quickly forgotten once the Secretary of the Treasury and Economic Policy Council asserted effective control over international economic policy as a whole. The main organizational problem of US international economic policy has been a failure to coordinate its monetary and trade aspects, which can only be achieved under strong leadership from Treasury.

considerable extent during the work on the Omnibus Trade Act. If their chairmen could make commitments for the Congress in consultations with the administration, the prospects for a cohesive and effective international economic strategy would be significantly improved.

CONCLUSION

An early and effective launch of a strategy of competitive interdependence by the new administration and Congress could set the stage for a prosperous new decade, perhaps the most successful and stable since the 1960s. In most of the industrial world there has been sustained growth for a number of years, inflation has been kept under control, profit margins restored, and productivity reinvigorated. In many of the developing countries there has been a shift toward more market-oriented policies, and there is even movement in this direction in the communist world.

Many of the benefits of this progress will not be reaped, however, unless the massive domestic and international imbalances—America's twin deficits, Japan's huge surplus and opaque markets, the overhang of Third World debt, the high unemployment and payments disequilibrium within Europe—are corrected. By remedying these imbalances, the strategy proposed here would remove the current threat of financial instability and provide a basis for continued, or even more rapid, economic growth and social progress around the world.

A failure to address the imbalances successfully could bring both financial disruption and economic downturn. A dollar collapse and a hard landing for the American economy could occur at any time. Double digit inflation could return. There could be severe and prolonged recession. Protectionist pressures and Third World debt could again assume crisis proportions, jeopardizing global stability. The stakes are enormous. The strategy proposed in this book thus commends itself to the new administration and Congress, and to their counterparts abroad, for rapid adoption in 1989 and the early 1990s.

Annex:
The Projection Models

Our estimates of future US trade and current account deficits under alternative policies and the proposed allocation of the foreign adjustment are based on two quantitative models.[1] The first is a modified version of the quarterly forecasting model of the US current account developed at the Federal Reserve Board by William Helkie and Peter Hooper.[2] William R. Cline has retained the core equations of this model while sharply reducing its size (for example, by substituting simpler sub-models for agricultural exports and oil imports). In addition, he adjusts the model to take account of its overprediction of export and import prices by 1987. Cline's modified model bridges the original model and current reality by assuming that half of this price gap is never closed but that the remaining half is eliminated over one year.

The Helkie–Hooper model, as changed by Cline (HHC), predicts aggregate US nonoil imports, oil imports, nonagricultural exports, and agricultural exports. Export prices are determined by the US wholesale price index with export weights, and by a variable for foreign prices (based on foreign consumer prices divided by exchange

Prepared by William R. Cline.

1. Full details of the models and estimated results are in William R. Cline, *United States External Adjustment and the World Economy* (Washington: Institute for International Economics, forthcoming).

2. See William L. Helkie and Peter Hooper, "An Empirical Analysis of the External Deficit, 1980–86," in Ralph C. Bryant, Gerald Holtham, and Peter Hooper, eds., *External Deficits and the Dollar: The Pit and the Pendulum* (Washington: Brookings Institution, 1988), 10–56.

rates against the dollar). US export prices rise by about 1 percent when the US export-weighted wholesale price rises by 1 percent (an elasticity of unity), and by 0.2 percent when foreign prices rise by 1 percent. There is thus some feedback from exchange rates to US export prices; as the dollar depreciates, part of the benefit to US firms takes the form of higher dollar prices, instead of being completely "passed through" to foreign buyers in the form of lower foreign currency prices.

Export volume (nonagricultural) in the HHC model depends on foreign income (with an elasticity of 2.2, which means that a 1 percent rise in GNP abroad causes a 2.2 percent increase in US exports); the size of the US capital stock relative to the foreign stock (as a measure of trend capacity); and the price of US exports relative to foreign consumer prices divided by foreign exchange rates, with price lags stretching over two years. Dollar export value equals quantity multiplied by price.

Prices of nonoil imports depend on foreign consumer prices, foreign exchange rates against the dollar (with lags over seven quarters), and an index of commodity prices. The elasticity of import prices with respect to foreign prices is almost unity, as is the elasticity with respect to the exchange rate, so the pass-through of foreign price and exchange rate movements over time is nearly total. The volume of nonoil imports depends on capacity utilization in foreign industrial countries, US income (with a total two-year elasticity of approximately 2), relative capital stock, and the ratio of import prices to the US GDP deflator (with lags over 7 quarters). The price elasticity is −1.15. Since it is close to unity, this elasticity means that nominal import levels remain relatively unchanged in response to exchange rate changes.

The HHC model also encompasses services, transfers, and the current account. Capital services play an important role. They are separated into earnings on direct investment, private portfolio holdings, and government obligations. Rates of return depend on interest rates, and the exchange rate has an important valuation effect on direct investment: depreciation of the dollar contributes to higher earnings on assets held abroad by American firms by virtue of a markup in their dollar value. In general, the capital services segment of the model shows US comparative advantage in international financial intermediation, as rates of return on US assets abroad tend to exceed those on US liabilities to foreigners. The model cumulates the current account so that net foreign liabilities build over time as the US remains in deficit, in turn causing the capital services account to deteriorate.

The second model, named External Adjustment with Growth (EAG), describes the foreign counterparts to the US accounts, although it focuses on trade and has only a simple current account component. The model divides the world into 17 countries and regions (the seven largest industrial countries individually, "Other Industrial Countries," OPEC, Taiwan, "Korea-Singapore-Hong Kong," Argentina, Brazil, Mexico, "Other Latin America," Africa, and "Rest of World"). All of world trade is incorporated in one or another of the cells of this 17 by 17 matrix. Trade is defined as exports from one partner to another; imports are merely the partner's exports to the country in question.

The EAG model separates oil trade implicitly. By identifying OPEC individually it isolates much of oil trade. The model further breaks down the exports of Mexico and the United Kingdom into oil and nonoil.

There is a trade equation for each cell in the trade matrix (for example, US exports to Germany). It relates the real volume of trade to income in the importing area, the direct prices of the exporter relative to prices in the importing area, and the cross-price competition of the exporter in question against all other exporters participating in the market of the importing area in question. Quarterly data for the 1973–87 period, drawn from the IMF's *Direction of Trade Statistics*, were used to estimate the trade equations. Prices are the IMF's unit value export price (which are uniform for a given exporting country or area in its trade with all of the other countries or areas). The direct price term for the importing area is the wholesale price index divided by the exchange rate against the dollar.

The estimation procedure sets upper and lower bounds on the acceptable elasticities (3.0 and 0.3, respectively, in absolute value). It applies nonlinear programming to minimize the sum of the squared residuals in obtaining the estimates, subject to these constraints.

Nominal dollar trade values are obtained by applying export price indices to the model estimates of trade quantities. After the model was simulated to obtain backcasts of the 1975–87 period, a recalibration was done so that the forecasting model places the 1987 estimates of trade flows at halfway between their actual values and those predicted by the unadjusted model. In the forecasts, nominal trade prices rise at the assumed rate of US inflation, augmented by any specified appreciation of a given country's currency against the dollar. The forecasts include versions in which uniform elasticities are applied to all countries, which enables us to examine the extent to which individual country results are influenced by unique elasticities as opposed to trade structure.

The forward simulations of both the HHC and EAG models first establish a baseline by specifying country growth rates and by freezing the real exchange rates at their levels in the fourth quarter of 1987. This approach implicitly treats the dollar's rebound in 1988 as transitory. In order to test the results of alternative policy scenarios, growth rates in different countries (including the United States) are varied and exchange rate changes are imposed in 1989 to achieve specified current account targets. For this book, the current account projections for the United States, including the effects of different growth rates and exchange rates, are drawn from the results of the HHC model. The proposed allocation of the adjustment—which countries should stimulate domestic demand and appreciate their currencies, and by how much—was based on results from the EAG model.

REFERENCES

Baker, James A. 1987. Remarks before a conference sponsored by the Institute for International Economics. Washington, 14 September.

Balassa, Bela, Gerardo M. Bueno, Pedro-Pablo Kuczynski, and Mario Henrique Simonsen. 1986. *Toward Renewed Economic Growth in Latin America.* Washington: Institute for International Economics.

Balassa, Bela, and Marcus Noland. 1988. *Japan in the World Economy.* Washington: Institute for International Economics.

Balassa, Bela, and John Williamson. 1987. *Adjusting to Success: Balance of Payments Policy in the East Asian NICs.* POLICY ANALYSES IN INTERNATIONAL ECONOMICS 17. Washington: Institute for International Economics, June.

Bank for International Settlements. 1988. *58th Annual Report, 1st April 1987–31st March 1988.* Basle, 13 June.

Baucus, Max. 1988. Statement to the Congressional Economic Leadership Institute Conference on Japan. Washington, 29 September.

Bergsten, C. Fred. 1975. *The Dilemmas of the Dollar.* New York: New York University Press for the Council on Foreign Relations.

———. 1983. "What Kind of Industrial Policy for the United States?" Testimony before the Subcommittee on Economic Stabilization, House Banking, Finance, and Urban Affairs Committee. Washington, 9 June.

———. 1984. "The Case for Leaning with the Wind." *Financial Times,* 24 October.

———. 1986. "America's Unilateralism." In *Conditions for Partnership in International Economic Management.* The Triangle Papers: 32. New York, Paris, Tokyo: The Trilateral Commission.

———. 1987a. "Economic Imbalances and World Politics." *Foreign Affairs,* 65, No. 4 (Spring).

———. 1987b. "The New Era in Economic Relations Between the United States and the Republic of China." Speech to the 11th Joint US–ROC Business Conference, New Orleans, LA, 21 November.

———. 1988. "Taming the Beast." *The Economist,* 2 July, 15–18.

Bergsten, C. Fred, Georges Berthoin, and Kinhide Mushakoji. 1976. *The Reform of International Institutions.* The Triangle Papers: 11. New York, Paris, Tokyo: The Trilateral Commission.

Bergsten, C. Fred, and William R. Cline. 1987. *The United States–Japan Economic Problem.* POLICY ANALYSES IN INTERNATIONAL ECONOMICS 13, revised. Washington: Institute for International Economics, January.

Bergsten, C. Fred, Kimberly Ann Elliott, Jeffrey J. Schott, and Wendy E. Takacs. 1987. *Auction Quotas and United States Trade Policy.* POLICY ANALYSES IN INTERNATIONAL ECONOMICS 19. Washington: Institute for International Economics, September.

Bergsten, C. Fred, Thomas Horst, and Theodore H. Moran. 1978. *American Multinationals and American Interests*. Washington: The Brookings Institution.

Bergsten, C. Fred, and Shafiqul Islam. *The United States as a Debtor Nation*. Washington: Institute for International Economics, forthcoming.

Bergsten, C. Fred, and John Williamson. 1983. "Exchange Rates and Trade Policy." In *Trade Policy in the 1980s,* edited by William R. Cline. Washington: Institute for International Economics.

Bonker, Don. 1988. *America's Trade Crisis: The Making of the U.S. Trade Deficit*. Boston: Houghton Mifflin.

Bosworth, Barry, and Robert Z. Lawrence. "America's Global Role: From Dominance to Interdependence." In *Restructuring American Foreign Policy,* edited by John Steinbruner. Washington: The Brookings Institution, forthcoming.

Bryant, Ralph C. 1988. "The U.S. External Deficit: An Update." Brookings Discussion Papers in International Economics No. 63. Washington: The Brookings Institution, January.

Bryant, Ralph C., Gerald Holtham, and Peter Hooper, eds. 1988. *External Deficits and the Dollar: The Pit and the Pendulum*. Washington: The Brookings Institution.

Choate, Pat, and Juyne Linger. 1988. "Tailored Trade: Dealing with the World as It Is." *Harvard Business Review,* 66, No. 1 (January–February): 86–93.

Cline, William R. 1980. "The Magnitude and Conditions of Lending by the International Monetary Fund." Hearings before the Subcommittee on International Trade, Investment, and Monetary Policy, House Committee on Banking, Housing, and Urban Affairs. Washington, 6 February.

———. 1987a. *Mobilizing Bank Lending to Debtor Countries*. POLICY ANALYSES IN INTERNATIONAL ECONOMICS 18. Washington: Institute for International Economics, June.

———. 1987b. *The Future of World Trade in Textiles and Apparel*. Washington: Institute for International Economics.

———. *United States External Adjustment and the World Economy*. Washington: Institute for International Economics, forthcoming.

Cockfield, Sir Arthur Francis. 1988. "Europe 1992: The Completion of the Internal Market." Address presented at the Institute for International Economics. Washington, 24 May.

Commission of the European Communities. 1988. *Research on the "Cost of Non-Europe": Basic Findings*. Vol. 1, Basic Studies, Executive Summaries. Brussels: Office for Official Publications of the European Communities.

Congressional Budget Office. 1987. "Revenue Estimates for Auctioning Existing Import Quotas." Memorandum to Chairman William Gray, House Budget Committee. Washington, 28 February.

———. 1988. *The Economic and Budget Outlook: An Update*. Report to the

Senate and House Committees on the Budget as Required by Public Law 93–344. Washington, August.

Council of Economic Advisers. 1988. *Economic Report of the President*. Washington, February.

DeRosa, Dean A., and William W. Nye. 1980. "Appendix 16A: 'Additionality' in the Activities of the Export-Import Bank of the United States." *The International Economic Policy of the United States: Selected Papers of C. Fred Bergsten, 1977–79,* edited by C. Fred Bergsten. Lexington, MA: Lexington Books.

Destler, I. M. 1986. *American Trade Politics: System Under Stress.* Washington: Institute for International Economics; New York: the Twentieth Century Fund.

Destler, I. M., Haruhiro Fukui, and Hideo Sato. 1979. *The Textile Wrangle: Conflict in Japanese–American Relations, 1969–1971.* Ithaca, NY: Cornell University Press.

Destler, I. M., and C. Randall Henning. *Exchange Rate Policy Making in the United States.* Washington: Institute for International Economics, forthcoming.

Destler, I. M., and John S. Odell. 1987. *Anti-Protection: Changing Forces in United States Trade Politics.* POLICY ANALYSES IN INTERNATIONAL ECONOMICS 21. Washington: Institute for International Economics, September.

Dornbusch, Rudiger. 1976. "Expectations and Exchange Rate Dynamics." *Journal of Political Economy,* 84, No. 6 (December).

Dornbusch, Rudiger, James Poterba, and Lawrence Summers. 1988. *The Case for Manufacturing in America's Future.* With a Foreword by Colby H. Chandler. Eastman Kodak, Co., Rochester, NY.

Eichengreen, Barry. "Hegemonic Stability Theories of the International Monetary System." In *Can Nations Agree? Essays in International Cooperation.* Washington: The Brookings Institution, forthcoming. Appeared in preliminary form as NBER Working Paper No. 2193, March 1987.

Faux, Jeff. 1988. "America's Economic Future." *World Policy Journal* (Summer): 367–414.

Feenstra, Robert C. 1988. "Auctioning U.S. Import Quotas and Foreign Response." University of California at Davis, July, processed.

Feldstein, Martin. 1988. "Thinking About International Economic Coordination." *Journal of Economic Perspectives,* 2, No. 2 (Spring): 3–13.

Fischer, Stanley. 1987. "International Macroeconomic Policy Coordination." National Bureau of Economic Research Working Paper No. 2244. Cambridge, MA, May.

Friedman, Benjamin. 1988. *Day of Reckoning: The Consequences of American Economic Policy Under Reagan and After.* New York: Random House.

Funabashi, Yoichi. 1988. *Managing the Dollar: From the Plaza to the Louvre.* Washington: Institute for International Economics.

Gault, Nigel. 1987. "What Would Eliminate the Current Account Deficit?" In Data Resources, Inc., *Review of the U.S. Economy*. (December): 11–25.

Geiger, Theodore. 1988. *The Future of the International System: The United States and the World Political Economy*. Boston: Unwin Hyman.

Gilpin, Robert. 1981. *War and Change in World Politics*. Cambridge, England: Cambridge University Press.

———. 1987. *The Political Economy of International Relations*. Princeton, NJ: Princeton University Press.

Goldberg, Paul M., and Charles P. Kindleberger. 1970. "Toward a GATT for Investment: A Proposal for Supervision of the International Corporation." *Law and Policy in International Business*, 2 (Summer): 295–325.

Graham, Edward M., and Paul R. Krugman. *Foreign Direct Investment in the United States*. Washington: Institute for International Economics, forthcoming.

Greenspan, Alan. 1988. Statement before the Senate Committee on Banking, Housing, and Urban Affairs. Washington, 13 July.

Hale, David D. 1988. "America in the Age of Pax Consortia or Why There Doesn't Have to be a Recession in 1989 or Even a Great Depression in 1990." Kemper Financial Services, Inc. May, processed.

Hathaway, Dale. 1987. *Agriculture and the GATT*. POLICY ANALYSES IN INTERNATIONAL ECONOMICS 20. Washington: Institute for International Economics, September.

Honma, Masayoshi, and Yujiro Hayami. 1986. "Structure of Agricultural Protection in Industrial Countries." *Journal of International Economics*, 20, No. 1/2 (February): 115–130.

Hooper, Peter, and Barbara Lowrey. 1979. "Impact of the Dollar Depreciation on the U.S. Price Level: An Analytical Survey of Empirical Estimates." Staff Study 103, Board of Governors of the Federal Reserve System, April.

Horlick, Gary N., Geoffrey D. Oliver, and Debra P. Steger. 1988. "Dispute Resolution Mechanisms." In *The Canada–United States Free Trade Agreement: The Global Impact*, edited by Jeffrey J. Schott and Murray G. Smith. Washington: Institute for International Economics and The Institute for Research on Public Policy.

Hufbauer, Gary Clyde, Diane T. Berliner, and Kimberly Ann Elliott. 1986. *Trade Protection in the United States: 31 Case Studies*. Washington: Institute for International Economics.

Hufbauer, Gary Clyde, and Howard F. Rosen. 1986. *Trade Policy for Troubled Industries*. POLICY ANALYSES IN INTERNATIONAL ECONOMICS 15. Washington: Institute for International Economics, March.

Hufbauer, Gary Clyde, and Jeffrey J. Schott. 1985a. *Trading for Growth: The Next Round of Trade Negotiations*. POLICY ANALYSES IN INTERNATIONAL ECONOMICS 11. Washington: Institute for International Economics, September.

Hufbauer, Gary Clyde and Jeffrey J. Schott, assisted by Kimberly Ann Elliott. 1985b. *Economic Sanctions Reconsidered: History and Current Policy*. Washington: Institute for International Economics.

Institute of International Finance, Inc. 1988. "A Proposal in Support of an Allocation of SDRs." Washington, 18 March, processed.

International Monetary Fund. 1988. *World Economic Outlook: Revised Projections of the Staff of the International Monetary Fund.* Washington, October.

Islam, Shafiqul. 1988. "America's Foreign Debt: Fear, Fantasy, Fiction & Facts." Paper presented at a Congressional Research Service Workshop. Washington, 1 April.

Kennedy, Paul. 1987. *The Rise and Fall of the Great Powers: Economic Change and Military Conflict from 1500 to 2000.* New York: Random House.

Keohane, Robert O. 1984. *After Hegemony: Cooperation and Discord in the World Political Economy.* Princeton, NJ: Princeton University Press.

Kindleberger, Charles P. 1973. *The World in Depression, 1929–39.* Berkeley and Los Angeles: University of California Press.

———. 1981. "Dominance and Leadership in the International Economy: Exploitation, Public Goods, and Free Rides." *International Studies Quarterly,* 25, No. 2 (June): 242–254.

Kissinger, Henry, and Cyrus Vance. 1988. "Bipartisan Objectives for Foreign Policy." *Foreign Affairs,* 66, No. 5 (Summer): 899–921.

Krugman, Paul R. 1986. "Introduction: New Thinking about Trade Policy." In *Strategic Trade Policy and the New International Economics,* edited by Paul R. Krugman. Cambridge, MA: MIT Press.

Lawrence, Robert Z. 1984. *Can America Compete?* Washington: The Brookings Institution.

———. 1987. "Imports in Japan: Closed Markets or Minds?" *Brookings Papers on Economic Activity* 2, 517–555.

———. "Threats to U.S. Livings Standards: The International Dimension." In *American Living Standards: Threats and Challenges,* edited by Robert Z. Lawrence and Robert E. Litan. Washington: The Brookings Institution, forthcoming.

Lawrence, Robert Z., and Robert E. Litan. 1986. *Saving Free Trade.* Washington: The Brookings Institution.

Lessard, Donald R., and John Williamson. 1985. *Financial Intermediation Beyond the Debt Crisis.* POLICY ANALYSES IN INTERNATIONAL ECONOMICS 12. Washington: Institute for International Economics, September.

———. 1987. *Capital Flight and Third World Debt.* Washington: Institute for International Economics.

Marris, Stephen. 1983. "Crisis Ahead for the Dollar." *Fortune,* 26 December.

———. 1984. *Managing the World Economy: Will We Ever Learn?* Princeton Essays in International Finance, No. 155. Princeton University.

———. 1985. *Deficits and the Dollar: The World Economy at Risk.* POLICY

POLICY ANALYSES IN INTERNATIONAL ECONOMICS 14. Washington: Institute for International Economics, December.

———. 1987. *Deficits and the Dollar: The World Economy at Risk.* POLICY ANALYSES IN INTERNATIONAL ECONOMICS 14, revised. Washington: Institute for International Economics, August.

———. *Europe, the Dollar, and 1992.* Washington: Institute for International Economics, forthcoming.

Matthews, R.C.O., C.H. Feinstein, and J.C. Odling-Smee. 1982. *British Economic Growth 1856–1973.* Stanford, CA: Stanford University Press.

McKinnon, Ronald I. 1984. *An International Standard for Monetary Stabilization.* POLICY ANALYSES IN INTERNATIONAL ECONOMICS 8. Washington: Institute for International Economics, March.

McPherson, M. Peter. 1988. "The European Community's Internal Market Program: An American Perspective." Remarks to the Institute for International Economics. Washington, 4 August.

Michaely, Michael. 1971. *The Responsiveness of Demand Policies to Balance of Payments: Postwar Patterns.* New York: Columbia University Press for the National Bureau of Economic Research.

Minarik, Joseph J., and Rudolph G. Penner. 1988. "Fiscal Choices." In *Challenge to Leadership: Economic and Social Issues for the Next Decade,* edited by Isabel V. Sawhill. Washington: The Urban Institute.

Morgan Guaranty Trust Company. 1988. "U.S. Social Security Surpluses: Pitfall or Opportunity?" *World Financial Markets,* No. 3 (1 July): 1.

Mulford, David. 1988. "International Economic Cooperation Since the Louvre Agreement." A presentation at the Institute for International Economics. Washington, 19 July.

Nau, Henry. 1984–85. "Where Reaganomics Works." *Foreign Policy,* No. 57 (Winter): 14–37.

Nye, Joseph S., Jr. 1988. "Understanding U.S. Strength." *Foreign Policy,* No. 72 (Fall): 105–129.

Office of Management and Budget. 1987. *Special Analyses: Budget of the United States Government Fiscal Year 1988.* Washington: Government Printing Office.

Office of Technology Assessment, US Congress. 1988. *Paying the Bill: Manufacturing and America's Trade Deficit.* Washington, June.

Organization for Economic Cooperation and Development. 1988. *Economic Outlook,* No. 43 (June).

Paarlberg, Robert L. 1988. *Fixing Farm Trade: Policy Options for the United States.* The Council on Foreign Relations Series on International Trade, edited by C. Michael Aho. Cambridge, MA: Ballinger.

Pelkmans, Jacques. 1988. "Is Protection Due to Financial Instability? A Sceptical View." In *The Political Economy of International Co-operation,* edited by Paolo Guerrieri and Pier Carlo Padoan. New York: Croom Helm.

Pelkmans, Jacques, and Alan Winters. 1988. *Europe's Domestic Market.* Chatham House Papers No. 43. London: Routledge.

Peterson, Peter G. 1988. "Deficit, Debt, and Demographics: Some International Aspects." In *The United States in the World Economy,* edited by Martin Feldstein. Chicago: The University of Chicago Press for the National Bureau of Economic Research.

Prestowitz, Clyde V., Jr. 1988. *Trading Places: How We Allowed Japan to Take the Lead.* New York: Basic Books.

Putnam, Robert D., and C. Randall Henning. "The Bonn Summit of 1978: A Case Study in Coordination." In *Can Nations Agree? Essays in International Cooperation.* Washington: The Brookings Institution, forthcoming. Appeared in preliminary form as Brookings Discussion Papers in International Economics No. 53, October 1986.

Reforming World Agricultural Trade: A Policy Statement by Twenty-Nine Professionals from Seventeen Countries. 1988. SPECIAL REPORT 7. Washington: Institute for International Economics, May.

Resolving the Global Economic Crisis: After Wall Street. A Statement by Thirty-Three Economists from Thirteen Countries. 1987. SPECIAL REPORT 6. Washington: Institute for International Economics, December.

Robinson, James D., III. 1988. "LDC Debt and Trade." Testimony before the Subcommittee on International Finance and Monetary Policy of the Senate Committee on Banking, Housing, and Urban Affairs. Washington, 2 August.

Rodriguez, Rita M., ed. 1987. *The Export-Import Bank at Fifty.* Lexington, MA: Heath & Co.

Sachs, Jeffrey D. 1985. "The Dollar and the Policy Mix: 1985." *Brookings Papers on Economic Activity* 1, 117–198.

Sampson, Gary P. 1987. "Pseudo-economics of the MFA—A Proposal for Reform." *The World Economy,* 10, No. 4 (December): 45–68.

Sampson, Gary, and Wendy Takacs. 1988. "Returning Textile Trade to the Normal Workings of GATT: A Practical Proposal for Reform." Institute for International Economic Studies Seminar Paper No. 404. Stockholm, January.

Schott, Jeffrey J. 1988. *United States–Canada Free Trade: An Evaluation of the Agreement.* POLICY ANALYSES IN INTERNATIONAL ECONOMICS 24. Washington: Institute for International Economics, April.

Schultze, Charles L. 1983. "Industrial Policy: A Dissent." *Brookings Review* (Fall).

Shultz, George P. 1981. "Risk, Uncertainty, and Foreign Economic Policy." The David Davies Memorial Lecture. London, 27 October.

———. 1985. "National Policies and Global Prosperity." Address before the Woodrow Wilson School of Public and International Affairs. Princeton, NJ: Princeton University, 11 April.

Solomon, Anthony M. 1987. "A Declining Dollar is One Piece in the Puzzle." *Business Week* (13 April): 20.

Solomon, Robert. 1987. Testimony before the Subcommittee on International Economic Policy of the US Senate Foreign Relations Committee. Washington, 20 March.

Stockman, David A. 1986. *The Triumph of Politics: How the Reagan Revolution Failed.* New York: Harper & Row.

Treverton, Gregory F. 1978. *The Dollar Drain and American Forces in Germany: Managing the Political Economics of Alliance.* Athens, OH: Ohio University Press.

Ueyama, Yasuhiko. 1988. "Japanese Insurance Companies: Our Strategy for Investing in America." *The International Economy* (July/August): 64–65.

US Congress. Joint Economic Committee. 1987. *The Economy at Midyear: A Legacy of Debt.* Washington, 5 August.

US House of Representatives. 1986. "Mandatory negotiations and action regarding foreign countries having excessive and unwarranted trade surpluses with the United States" (Gephardt Amendment). H.R. 4800, Washington, 9 May.

US International Trade Commission. 1985. *Review of the Effectiveness of Trade Dispute Settlement Under the GATT and the Tokyo Round Agreements.* USITC Publication 1793. Washington, December.

Vernon, Raymond. 1988. "Foreign-Owned Enterprise in the United States: Threat or Opportunity?" Cambridge, MA: Harvard University, 1 July.

Volcker, Paul A. 1988. Remarks to the Executive Committee Meeting, National Governors' Association, Winter Meeting. Washington, 21 February.

WEFA Group. 1988. US Macro Model: Medium-Term Forecast. Bala Cynwyd, PA.

Williamson, John. 1984. *A New SDR Allocation?* POLICY ANALYSES IN INTERNATIONAL ECONOMICS 7. Washington: Institute for International Economics, March.

———. 1985. *The Exchange Rate System.* POLICY ANALYSES IN INTERNATIONAL ECONOMICS 5, revised. Washington: Institute for International Economics, June.

———. 1988a. "The Dollar and the Trade Deficit: What More Needs to Be Done?" Paper presented at a Congressional Research Service Workshop. Washington, 1 April.

———. 1988b. *Voluntary Approaches to Debt Relief.* POLICY ANALYSES IN INTERNATIONAL ECONOMICS 25. Washington: Institute for International Economics, September.

Williamson, John, and Marcus Miller. 1987. *Targets and Indicators: A Blueprint for the International Coordination of Economic Policy.* POLICY ANALYSES IN

INTERNATIONAL ECONOMICS 22. Washington: Institute for International Economics, September.

World Bank. 1986 and 1987. *World Development Report.* Oxford: Oxford University Press for the World Bank.

———. 1988. *World Debt Tables: External Debt of Developing Countries, 1987–88 Edition.* Vol. 1, Analysis and Summary Tables. Washington, January.

Index

Other Publications from the Institute

POLICY ANALYSES IN INTERNATIONAL ECONOMICS SERIES

1 **The Lending Policies of the International Monetary Fund**
John Williamson/August 1982

2 **"Reciprocity": A New Approach to World Trade Policy?**
William R. Cline/September 1982

3 **Trade Policy in the 1980s**
C. Fred Bergsten and William R. Cline/November 1982

4 **International Debt and the Stability of the World Economy**
William R. Cline/September 1983

5 **The Exchange Rate System, Second Edition**
John Williamson/September 1983, rev. June 1985

6 **Economic Sanctions in Support of Foreign Policy Goals**
Gary Clyde Hufbauer and Jeffrey J. Schott/October 1983

7 **A New SDR Allocation?**
John Williamson/March 1984

8 **An International Standard for Monetary Stabilization**
Ronald I. McKinnon/March 1984

9 **The Yen/Dollar Agreement: Liberalizing Japanese Capital Markets**
Jeffrey A. Frankel/December 1984

10 **Bank Lending to Developing Countries: The Policy Alternatives**
C. Fred Bergsten, William R. Cline, and John Williamson/April 1985

11 **Trading for Growth: The Next Round of Trade Negotiations**
Gary Clyde Hufbauer and Jeffrey J. Schott/September 1985

12 **Financial Intermediation Beyond the Debt Crisis**
Donald R. Lessard and John Williamson/September 1985

13 **The United States–Japan Economic Problem**
C. Fred Bergsten and William R. Cline/October 1985, rev. January 1987

14 **Deficits and the Dollar: The World Economy at Risk**
Stephen Marris/December 1985, rev. November 1987

15 **Trade Policy for Troubled Industries**
Gary Clyde Hufbauer and Howard F. Rosen/March 1986

16 **The United States and Canada: The Quest for Free Trade**
Paul Wonnacott, with an Appendix by *John Williamson*/March 1987

17 **Adjusting to Success: Balance of Payments Policy in the East Asian NICs**
Bela Balassa and John Williamson/June 1987

18 **Mobilizing Bank Lending to Debtor Countries**
William R. Cline/June 1987

19 **Auction Quotas and United States Trade Policy**
C. Fred Bergsten, Kimberly Ann Elliott, Jeffrey J. Schott, and Wendy E. Takacs/September 1987

20 **Agriculture and the GATT: Rewriting the Rules**
Dale E. Hathaway/September 1987

21 **Anti-Protection: Changing Forces in United States Trade Politics**
I. M. Destler and John S. Odell/September 1987

22 **Targets and Indicators: A Blueprint for the International Coordination of Economic Policy**
John Williamson and Marcus H. Miller/September 1987

23 **Capital Flight: The Problem and Policy Responses**
Donald R. Lessard and John Williamson/December 1987

24 **United States–Canada Free Trade: An Evaluation of the Agreement**
Jeffrey J. Schott/April 1988

25 **Voluntary Approaches to Debt Relief**
John Williamson/September 1988

BOOKS

IMF Conditionality
John Williamson, editor/1983

Trade Policy in the 1980s
William R. Cline, editor/1983

Subsidies in International Trade
Gary Clyde Hufbauer and Joanna Shelton Erb/1984

International Debt: Systemic Risk and Policy Response
William R. Cline/1984

Economic Sanctions Reconsidered: History and Current Policy
Gary Clyde Hufbauer and Jeffrey J. Schott, assisted by Kimberly Ann Elliott/1985

Trade Protection in the United States: 31 Case Studies
Gary Clyde Hufbauer, Diane T. Berliner, and Kimberly Ann Elliott/1986

Toward Renewed Economic Growth in Latin America
Bela Balassa, Gerardo M. Bueno, Pedro-Pablo Kuczynski, and Mario Henrique Simonsen/1986

American Trade Politics: System Under Stress
I. M. Destler/1986

The Future of World Trade in Textiles and Apparel
William R. Cline/1987

Capital Flight and Third World Debt
Donald R. Lessard and John Williamson, editors/1987

The Canada–United States Free Trade Agreement: The Global Impact
Jeffrey J. Schott and Murray G. Smith, editors/1988

Managing the Dollar: From the Plaza to the Louvre
Yoichi Funabashi/1988

Reforming World Agricultural Trade
Twenty-nine Professionals from Seventeen Countries/1988

World Agricultural Trade: Building a Consensus
William M. Miner and Dale E. Hathaway, editors/1988

World Agricultural Trade: Building a Consensus
William M. Miner and Dale E. Hathaway, editors/1988

Japan in the World Economy
Bela Balassa and Marcus Noland/1988

America in the World Economy: A Strategy for the 1990s
C. Fred Bergsten/1988

SPECIAL REPORTS

1 **Promoting World Recovery: A Statement on Global Economic Strategy**
by Twenty-six Economists from Fourteen Countries/December 1982

2 **Prospects for Adjustment in Argentina, Brazil, and Mexico: Responding to the Debt Crisis**
John Williamson, editor/June 1983

3 **Inflation and Indexation: Argentina, Brazil, and Israel**
John Williamson, editor/March 1985

4 **Global Economic Imbalances**
C. Fred Bergsten, editor/March 1986

5 **African Debt and Financing**
Carol Lancaster and John Williamson, editors/May 1986

6 **Resolving the Global Economic Crisis: After Wall Street**
Thirty-three Economists from Thirteen Countries/December 1987

7 World Economic Problems
Kimberly Ann Elliott and John Williamson, editors/April 1988

FORTHCOMING

The United States as a Debtor Country
C. Fred Bergsten and Shafiqul Islam

Domestic Adjustment and International Trade
Gary Clyde Hufbauer and Howard F. Rosen, editors

United States External Adjustment and the World Economy
William R. Cline and Stephen Marris

Energy Policy for the 1990s: A Global Perspective
Philip K. Verleger, Jr.

The Outlook for World Commodity Prices
Philip K. Verleger, Jr.

Economic Relations Between the United States and Korea: Conflict or Cooperation?
Thomas O. Bayard and Soo-Gil Young, editors

Exchange Rate Policy Making in the United States
I. M. Destler and C. Randall Henning

Equilibrium Exchange Rates: An Update
John Williamson

Foreign Direct Investment in the United States
Edward M. Graham and Paul R. Krugman

The Politics of International Monetary Cooperation
C. Fred Bergsten, I. M. Destler, C. Randall Henning, and John Williamson

The International Monetary Fund: The Record and the Prospects
C. David Finch

Reciprocity and Retaliation: An Evaluation of Aggressive Trade Policies
Thomas O. Bayard

More Free Trade Areas?
Jeffrey J. Schott

Oil Crisis Intervention: A Blueprint for International Cooperation
Philip K. Verleger, Jr.

Pacific Area Trade: Threat or Opportunity for the United States?
Bela Balassa and Marcus Noland

Third World Debt: A Reappraisal
William R. Cline